Abolition and the Transformation of Atlantic Commerce in Southern Sierra Leone, 1790s to 1860s

ABOLITION AND THE TRANSFORMATION OF ATLANTIC COMMERCE IN SOUTHERN SIERRA LEONE, 1790s TO 1860s

PHILIP MISEVICH

AFRICA WORLD PRESS

TRENTON | LONDON | CAPE TOWN | NAIROBI | ADDIS ABABA | ASMARA | IBADAN | NEW DELHI

AFRICA WORLD PRESS
541 West Ingham Avenue | Suite B
Trenton, New Jersey 08638

Cover design: Ashraful Haque
Book design: Lemles Tadesse

Cataloging-in-Publication Data may be obtained from the Library of Congress.

ISBNs: 978-1-56902-640-3 HB
       978-1-56902-641-0 PB

To Kelly, with Love and Admiration

TABLE OF CONTENTS

Acknowledgments

This project began to take shape more than a decade ago while I was in graduate school at Emory University. In the years that have passed between then and now, the book and its author have changed in many ways, though the better parts of both are firmly rooted in Atlanta. The mentorships and friendships that flourished while I was there have withstood the test of time. I owe my greatest debt to David Eltis, whose unrivaled knowledge of the slave trade, slavery, and the Atlantic World shaped this book in countless ways. David remains one of the humblest scholars I have ever met, despite his prolific academic career. His steady feedback has helped me better understand and express what this book is about and pushed me not to forget the "big picture." I am equally indebted to Kristin Mann, whose guidance has meant so much to me. Kristin's deep understanding of African history in general, and nineteenth-century Lagos in particular, has framed how I think about slavery and abolition in Sierra Leone's past. Edna G. Bay, Clifton Crais, and Pamela Scully have also influenced this book in meaningful ways.

Many other colleagues have strengthened this book through either their direct feedback or ongoing encouragement. Weekly meetings to discuss the *Voyages* database with Marcy Alexander, Alex Borucki, Daniel Domingues da Silva, David Eltis, Jane Hooper, Nafees Khan, Greg O'Malley, Nick Radburn, Rebecca Shumway, Allen Tullos, and Jelmer Vos have reminded me why public scholarship on slavery and the slave trade is so important and of the value of reaching broad audiences. Walter Hawthorne has been supportive of my career for many years, for which I am grateful and as a result of which I have significantly benefitted. He and Allen Howard carefully read and extensively commented on this project in its early stages. Additional support has come from Arthur Abraham, Richard Anderson, Manuel Barcia, Steve Behrendt, George Brooks, Sylviane Diouf, Seymour Drescher, Suzan Eltis, Stanley Engerman, Jorge Felipe, Henry Louis Gates Jr., Oscar Grandio, Trina Hogg, Adam Jones, Katrina Keefer, Benjamin Lawrance, Sean Kelley, Martin Klein, Paul Lachance, Henry Lovejoy, Leonardo Marques, Joseph Miller, Philip Morgan, Bruce Mouser, Ugo Nwokeji, Adenike Ogunkoya, Olatunji Ojo, Paul Richards, David Richardson, Padraic Scanlan, Suzanne Schwarz, Silke Strickrodt, Joseph Yannielli, and Michael Zeuske. I count myself lucky to have trained as a historian at a time when Sierra Leone was open to visitors. I traveled there for the first time in the summer of 2004 and have been hooked ever since. Joe Opala helped introduce me to that country and continues to find new stories about it that excite me. Abu Koroma and Albert Moore guided me through the Public Archives in Freetown. Many other Sierra Leoneans opened their doors to me and provided good company and food, including especially Taziff Koroma, who was a close friend and colleague. Sadly, Taziff passed away before this book was finished, though I trust he knew the impact he had on me. Marcus Rediker has been generous with his time and an enthusiastic advocate of my work. Our time together in Sierra Leone breathed new life into my scholarship and introduced me to the world of documentary filmmaking. Konrad Tuchscherer, who joined us on that trip, has been a steady source of inspiration. Two decades ago, Konrad first exposed me to the wonders of African history; today we are colleagues in the same department and remain the closest of friends.

Various institutions and agencies offered much needed time and support while I completed this book. Emory, Denison, and St. John's Universities provided stimulating intellectual environments and demanding critics. The Bill and Carol Fox Center for Humanistic Inquiry hosted me as a Fellow for an entire year during which I was surrounded by engaging housemates. Granville, Ohio, and Jamaica, Queens, are as different as two towns can be, yet I made comfortable homes in both places and remain deeply attached to my former and current colleagues. I received funding at critical stages of the completion of this book from Fulbright-Hays, the National Endowment for the Humanities, and the Franklin Research Center at Duke University. The Lapidus Center for the Historical Analysis of Transatlantic Slavery selected me as an in-residence fellow during the 2016-17 academic year. The Schomburg Center for Research in Black Culture, of which the Lapidus Center is a part, is one of the most dynamic places in the world to study Africa and the Diaspora. It was my good fortune to spend so much time there developing and revising this project. Large parts of chapter two were previously published in a volume I co-edited in 2016 with Kristin Mann, entitled *The Rise and Demise of Slavery and the Slave Trade in the Atlantic World*. I appreciate that Rochester University Press allowed me to republish that work here.

I could not be happier with the well-oiled team at Africa World Press, which guided this book across the finish line. I am thankful to the two anonymous reviewers for their insightful feedback and criticisms, which saved me from more than a few errors and conceptual shortcomings. Kassahun Checole and Girma Demeke were beyond helpful during every step of the publication process. They were encouraging and patient, for which I am thankful. Philip Schwartzberg of Meridian Mapping made the wonderful maps that appear in the book. Paul Lovejoy, to whom I introduced myself through an embarrassing email gaffe nearly twenty years ago, has been steadfast in his support of my research. This book is much better than it would otherwise be because of his editorial oversight.

As the scope of this book grew over time, so too did my nuclear and extended families and it is to them that I have accumulated my deepest debts and wish to express my profoundest appreciation. My parents and siblings have always been proud of what I do, which is important to me. Their presence lifts my spirits. My wife and son transformed and were no doubt transformed by this book over many years. Nate has exposed me to a kind of joy I could never have imagined possible. My life with Kelly reminds me that there is so much more to life than work, no matter how much I love what I do. Anyone who has met them knows why I am as happy as I am.

INTRODUCTION

This book explores the relationship between the slave trade, agricultural production, and colonialism in Africa. For three centuries, the slave trade integrated the societies of Africa, Europe, and the Americas and first enticed the West to establish sustained communities along the continent's littoral. Yet just as merchants opened centers for slave embarkation in southern Sierra Leone – the Sherbro and Gallinas areas, on the border of modern day Sierra Leone and Liberia – around 1800, a complex series of events led Britain on a campaign to abolish the Atlantic slave trade and assume control over Freetown, its first West African colony and the hub of the suppression movement on the continent.[1] Over the first six decades of the nineteenth century, the inhabitants of southern Sierra Leone were thus caught between two contrasting ideological, political, and commercial forces that collided along their shore, and which were to have profound effects on their lives.

By the 1860s, the British anti-slave trade campaign had triumphed, but this did not end the enslavement of Africans on the continent. While slaves no longer had to endure the traumas of the Middle Passage, changes in the economies of the Atlantic World meant that slaves increasingly faced plantation-like conditions in Africa itself, where they were held in larger numbers.[2] At the root of this transformation was Europe's growing demand for West African "legitimate commerce," primarily vegetable oils, which Europeans used to manufacture soap and lubricate industrial machinery. It was in the context of competition for such commodities that Britain, France, Portugal, and to a lesser extent other Western nations began expanding beyond the littoral their control over African land.[3] On the frontier of Britain's first West African colony, southern Sierra Leone was swept up in the colonization movement before most other parts of the continent: from their early-nineteenth century base in Freetown, the British annexed parts of Sherbro in 1861 and extended their authority into the interior in the decades that followed.

Between the 1460s, when Europeans first arrived off the Sierra Leone coast, and 1861, when they colonized parts of the Sherbro, the inhabitants of southern Sierra Leone were increasingly affected by changes in the Atlantic World. At the same time, their actions helped to shape Africa's dynamic relationship with Europe. During these four centuries, the Sherbro and Gallinas evolved from sites on the fringes of major foreign and domestic commercial networks to centers for the production and trade of Atlantic commerce, exporting more slaves in the post-1807 era than any area west of the Bight of Benin and supplying thousands of tons of rice to sustain the slave trade and Freetown's settlers.[4] In the first half of the nineteenth century, southern Sierra Leone was thus central to the evolution of the slave trade, the Atlantic World, and British colonialism in Africa. The abolition campaign drove each of these processes and drastically reshaped African societies.

This book examines the lives of peoples and communities that were drawn into the Atlantic slave trade in the era of abolition. It explores one region's integration into commercial and ideological systems that crossed the Atlantic. Rooted in an exploration of the enslavement and trade of human beings, the story inevitably invokes feelings of sadness, sorrow and, to most citizens of the modern era, anger and disbelief. But as enslaved people always knew, and scholars of the slave trade have often demonstrated, such sentiments tell only part of the story. Even in the face of the extreme pressures that Europeans placed on African communities, Africa and its inhabitants played a vital role in shaping the contours of Atlantic history.[5] Moreover, in the case of southern Sierra Leone, the trade in slaves was one (albeit extremely important) part of a diverse exchange of goods between Africans and Europeans, which on the African end also included ivory, timber, gold, and perhaps most importantly, provisions. While we should never forget that millions of individuals suffered from the growth of the slave trade, some Africans, including many southern Sierra Leoneans, exploited opportunities that the Atlantic encounter opened to enrich themselves and their communities and provide security for their families.

Transformations in Atlantic commerce are central to this analysis. As James Searing noted in his study of the Lower Senegal, scholars of the slave trade have primarily focused on the volume of slaves and other commodities that left the continent.[6] The emphasis on quantitative assessment has often implicitly assumed that the trade had a lesser impact on regions that exported fewer numbers of captives. Yet even for parts of the coast from which the volume of the slave trade was comparatively small, its effect on local communities could be substantial. As in the Senegambia, southern Sierra Leone's slave trade was supported by and contributed to an explosive growth in the production and exchange of foodstuffs, which Europeans and Africans needed to feed slaves while they were held on the coast and in transit across the ocean. This book thus uses external trade as a window onto commercial change in Africa itself, exploring the relationship between abolition, foreign and domestic slaving, and local agricultural production and trade. It examines the impact that new markets for slaves and produce had on the regions that supplied those commodities. Finally, the study seeks to understand how the establishment and growth of Freetown transformed Sierra Leone's slave trade, and to assess the impact of the colony's antislavery agenda on slaves and slave owners who lived on the colony's primarily Mende- and Sherbro- speaking southeastern frontier.

Slavery, Abolition, and Colonialism: The Making of Southern Sierra Leone in the Nineteenth Century

The British campaign against the slave trade fundamentally changed Sierra Leone's relationship with the Atlantic World. As the slave trade entered its final phase in the nineteenth century, the British transformed the Sierra Leone estuary into its main base against illegal slaving activity. From there British naval officers sailed along the coast in search of vessels they suspected were breaking international treaties that banned participation in the transatlantic slave trade, capturing vessels engaged in illicit activity. The combined pressures from British naval patrols and colonial settlers in Freetown brought major changes to the organization of the slave trade along the Sierra Leone coast. To avoid detection from naval cruisers, slave dealers moved their operations into the swampy creeks that crisscrossed southern Sierra Leone, which British vessels struggled to patrol. Britain's nineteenth-century assault on the slave trade therefore pushed the Sherbro and Gallinas more directly into the export trade, turning southern Sierra Leone into a major center for slave embarkation after 1807. The growing slave trade bound these emerging ports tightly to the Cuban sugar industry and infused the ports with Cuban merchants and cultural influences.[7] Over the first sixty years of the nineteenth century, a diaspora of foreign slave dealers settled on the Sherbro and Gallinas coast and brought with them new trade goods that they circulated throughout southern Sierra Leone.

Changes in the coastal organization of slave exports transformed the relationship between southern Sierra Leone and its hinterland. While the pre-1807 transatlantic trade drew slaves from a catchment area that stretched relatively deep into the interior of Upper Guinea, a number of factors, including in particular a drop in slave prices in the nineteenth century, caused the slaving frontier to draw nearer to the coast and concentrated to Mende- and Sherbro-speaking regions the areas from which slaves originated. As the volume of the Gallinas and Sherbro slave trade increased in the 1820s, the traffic continued to feed

4

primarily on peoples within about sixty miles of the coast. The first half of the nineteenth century thus witnessed southern Sierra Leone's slaving ports place increasing pressures on the peoples who lived in their immediate hinterland.

In addition to causing major changes to the external slave trade, the abolition period also witnessed the opening of large new markets for the agricultural goods that Africans in southern Sierra Leone produced. Spiking populations along the coast drove this process. Both the slave trade and colonialism pushed people toward the Sierra Leone littoral at a scale previously unmatched. Freetown's population reached an estimated 15,000 by the early 1820s. Though they were not quite as large as the British colony, slave factories often held thousands of captives in barracoons awaiting shipment. From the point captives were first enslaved until they reached the New World in the holds of transatlantic vessels, they required daily meals. Few scholars have appreciated the magnitude of the provisions trade needed to feed so many individuals, regardless of how insufficient slave diets were.[8] Throughout Sierra Leone, rice was the food of choice; given the poor soils of Freetown and the Gallinas, the crop was imported primarily from the fertile lands of the Sherbro. By the 1820s, Sherbro planters and merchants supplied more than one thousand tons of rice each year to satisfy these external markets alone. For southern Sierra Leone, the slave trade and the growth of Freetown stimulated agricultural production and forged new relationships between communities along the coast and in the interior.

As Atlantic slave exports slowed and ultimately ceased in the 1850s, the dispersal of slaves from southern Sierra Leone underwent a massive transformation. With the onset of the Industrial Revolution in Europe, African slave owners put their laborers to work on plantations where they produced vegetable oils needed to support western industrial development. New slave markets north of Sierra Leone, particularly in Portuguese Guinea (modern-day Guinea Bissau), helped drive this shift, consuming enslaved laborers in large numbers to develop expanding groundnut plantations. Muslim merchants helped meet the new demand for enslaved Africans by penetrating southern Sierra Leone's slave markets and pioneering new slaving routes that brought captives north via canoe. Originally avoiding Freetown to ensure that abolitionist-minded British officials would not interfere with their activities, emboldened slave traders eventually found a market for slaves within the colony, where Africans who had recently been liberated from slave vessels sought children as domestic laborers and wives. This analysis of changes in the domestic slave trade illustrates that internal African Diasporas were as vital as their transatlantic counterparts in developing the nineteenth century global economy.

Although slaves were the ultimate victims of the transformations described above, they were hardly passive figures. Slave actions and agency shaped in meaningful ways Britain's abolition discourse and agenda in Africa. They understood and cleverly used to their own advantage Europe's growing moral uncertainty about participation in the Atlantic slave trade. European promises of "freedom," which emanated loudly from Freetown into the African interior, led captives to flee from their owners in the hinterland and seek British protection in the colony. Over the nineteenth century, this small but steady migration of fugitive slaves transformed the colonial landscape. For a variety of reasons, not all captives could flee from their owners. Others used the threat of flight to negotiate improved conditions for themselves and their families, resisting the harsher labor conditions that changes in nineteenth century Atlantic World commerce created. In one dramatic case, a group of enslaved Africans who worked on Bunce Island, in the Sierra Leone estuary, rose up in revolt against the exploitative conditions they faced, citing Britain's abolition campaign as a source of inspiration. As this implies, the abolition era was one in which slaves, owners, and colonial officials undertook complex negotiations over their rights and responsibilities toward each other. In an era when the Atlantic slave trade was under assault, slaves sought new opportunities to improve their own lives and limit the excesses of the slave system.[9]

Historiographical Contexts

This book addresses several themes that have been at the heart of scholarship on Africa, the slave trade, the Atlantic World, and Sierra Leone over the past six decades. It assesses local, regional, and transatlantic factors that contributed to the growth and decline of the slave trade and investigates the organization of the trade along the coast and in the African interior. The project explores the relationship between the slave trade and agricultural production and examines how communities reorganized the domestic slave trade as they transitioned from Atlantic slaving to the cultivation of peanuts and palm products. Finally, by exploring transformations in Atlantic commerce on the frontier of Britain's first West African colony, the study reassesses the relationship between Atlantic ports and their hinterlands and seeks to reframe the debate about the link between slavery and colonialism.

Over the past six decades, scholars have developed a vastly improved understanding of the magnitude of the Atlantic slave trade and its effects on specific regions and ports in Europe, Africa, and the Americas. The online launch of *Voyages: The Trans-Atlantic Slave Trade Database* (www.slavevoyages.org), which includes details on the trading activities of more than 35,000 unique slave voyages, represents the most recent attempt to document this largest coerced migration in human history. In addition to transforming our understanding of the volume and structure of the slave trade, the *Voyages* project provides unparalleled information about the age and gender of captives who were embarked on transatlantic slavers. One central point that has emerged clearly from this major digital initiative is that the operation of the transatlantic trade varied widely from one African region to another. As a result, historians of Africa have been tasked with exploring and explaining local factors that account for regional differences in the structure and composition of slave exports.[10]

Despite significant scholarly work on this issue, many questions about the relationship between the slave trade and the economic, social, and political changes it generated in Africa remain unanswered or poorly understood. This book seeks to investigate several areas of inquiry that will ultimately provide a new picture of the process by which Africa was integrated into the Atlantic World and raises questions about the impact that integration had on Africans who lived in southern Sierra Leone. Why, for example, did the Sherbro and Gallinas rise to prominence as slave ports in the nineteenth century? How did the growth of these slave ports affect the origins of captives who were caught up in the transatlantic trade? And what impact did the slave trade and its abolition have on the communities where it took hold? These questions are central not only to African and Atlantic World history but to the global processes of abolition and imperialism.

The impact of the slave trade on Africa has been hotly debated since as far back as the era of abolition itself. Following the lead of some abolitionists, many modern scholars have argued that the slave trade was the root cause of African political and economic underdevelopment. According to these individuals, the trade stripped the continent of its most productive laborers, increased inequality and social oppression within societies and brought major disruptions to African demographic stability. The trade also fostered political centralization (or fragmentation), which increased warfare and enslavement. The structure of the trade, they continue, was inherently unequal: in return for human cargo, African merchants received poorly manufactured goods and destructive and addictive luxury items such as tobacco and alcohol.[11]

A contrasting school of thought contends that the slave trade formed just one part of what were very complex and dynamic local and regional African economies, in which Atlantic imports and exports were as a whole comparatively insignificant. While such scholars show an appreciation for the atrocious conditions that slaves themselves were forced to endure, they argue that African and European merchants traded as equal partners or that the terms of trade often favored Africans. Moreover, several researchers have suggested that while the slave trade may have preyed on and victimized some societies, it strengthened and unified others. At a continental level, therefore, the transatlantic trade brought positive developments along with negative ones. Put another way, the operation of the slave trade illustrates African "agency" in the development of the Atlantic World; it did not cause the continent's underdevelopment.[12]

The point, however, should surely not be to highlight the "winners and losers" of an abstract and singular Atlantic slave trade,[13] but rather to examine how particular regions and communities met the challenges that participation in networks of Atlantic exchange posed, and consider how they exploited its opportunities. Such an approach undermines the stark contrasts that scholars too often draw in their assessments of the impact of the slave trade on Africa and raises fruitful questions about how Africans engaged with transatlantic trade. Among the Balanta of Guinea Bissau, for example, Walter Hawthorne has demonstrated that trade with Europeans provided the region with access to cheaper supplies of iron, which they used to manufacture tools that improved rice cultivation and weapons that enhanced their capacity to wage war. Atlantic commerce was for the Balanta a double-edged sword: it supported an agricultural revolution while at the same time facilitating the group's ability to conduct slave raids and produce captives for sale to European merchants.[14]

This book focuses primarily on the social and commercial effects of southern Sierra Leone's integration into the Atlantic World. It supports the idea that the slave trade created new opportunities for the production and sale of agricultural commodities even as it drained the region of thousands of inhabitants. But, unlike elsewhere in Africa, southern Sierra Leone's commercial transformation occurred on the frontier of Freetown, where a major new market for provisions opened that African farmers in the Sherbro helped supply, placing the provisions trade at the center of both the Atlantic slave trade and British abolitionist and imperial activities. Given the overlapping nature of the trade in human and non-human commodities, it is worth considering how these two industries interacted: who traded provisions? How did the organization of the provisions trade compare with that of the slave trade? In what ways did the provisions trade fit within broader British notions of legitimate commerce, considering rice produced in the Sherbro facilitated the export of slaves from southern Sierra Leone?

That final question in particular opens an avenue to address another issue that has dominated Africanist scholarship for several decades, namely the impact of Africa's mid-century transition from supplying slaves to the Americas to trading primarily in agricultural commodities. Historians have often examined and debated the effects of this commercial transition on African societies. Some have argued that the suppression of Atlantic slaving and the growth of the trade in vegetable oils caused a "crisis of adaptation" among African ruling elites. Whereas the collection and marketing of human cargo was dominated by a small group of wealthy individuals, the new commerce opened possibilities for poorer farmers – and even slaves, in some cases – to enrich themselves thorough trade. Others have countered that the same elites who dominated the slave trade maintained control over the exchange of vegetable products. For these scholars, the commercial transition underscores the flexibility of African political structures, which enabled leaders to use abolition as an opportunity to enhance their legitimacy and wealth.[15]

Studies of the commercial transition in Africa have primarily privileged political change and offered analyses at local levels. This book takes a much broader regional view of commercial change in Sierra Leone, shining light on a large area between the Gallinas and Portuguese Guinea. This region witnessed the commercialization of two different vegetable commodities: peanuts dominated the area north of Freetown and palm products featured south of the colony. The production of these goods developed unevenly, beginning with groundnuts in the 1830s and later including palm oil and kernels in the 1850s and 60s. For Africans in Sierra Leone, the mid-nineteenth century was a time of multiple ongoing commercial transitions, rather than a single undifferentiated process through which Africans turned away from the slave trade and toward commercial agricultural production. This approach illustrates how the uneven growth of legitimate commerce in Sierra Leone affected the organization of the domestic slave trade across the wider Upper Guinea Coast. It reveals that the peanut boom created a massive new market for coerced labor in the Nunez and Pongo Rivers and in Portuguese Guinea. In response to the new demand for enslaved labor in peanut-producing areas, Muslim merchants from north of Freetown migrated into southern Sierra Leone and tapped into its slave markets, from which they developed a new lateral slaving route that brought captives north by a mixture of sea and land travel. At times, this south-to-north route included stops in Freetown itself, where the growing process of urbanization created demands for women and children as domestic laborers. This picture complicates the story of the commercial transition in African history. It reveals that Africans did not merely put slaves to work locally once the Atlantic trade ended. Instead, slave dealers exploited changes in regional labor markets, adapting internal slaving routes to fit local needs.

This book also brings together analyses of various internal and external Atlantic World pressures on Sierra Leone society to provide a new perspective on the relationship between abolition, slavery, and colonialism. Studies of colonial policy toward domestic African slavery have long emphasized Europe's hesitance to confront the institution in the nineteenth century, and for good reason: Whereas British officials actively suppressed the transatlantic traffic, the delicate nature of slavery itself – and the relatively limited number of Europeans in Africa for much of the century – prevented a similar approach to internal slaveholding. The way Europe confronted domestic slavery underscores, to many scholars, one major contradiction of Europe's "civilizing mission": on the one hand, colonists spread rhetoric about "freedom" and free labor without the means to enforce their ambitious agenda; on the other, those same officials encouraged the large-scale cultivation of commodities that slave labor proved central to producing. Colonists attempted to resolve this contradiction in a number of ways. In some cases, they simply ignored the existence of slavery altogether or distinguished domestic slavery from the harsher plantation-based institution that prevailed in the Americas. In the Gold Coast, for example, British officials limited the size of their colonial holdings, which minimized the areas in which slavery was considered illegal. In Lagos, the British employed a model that they had previously developed in India, abolishing the legal status of slavery while doing little to advertise slaves' new rights.[16] In each of these cases, official policy rested in part on what Kristin Mann has called a "smoke and mirrors" act, in which officials were forced to balance humanitarian principles with colonial realities.[17]

This book approaches the issue from the perspective of slaves and slave owners who lived outside of the British-controlled Freetown colony rather than through the eyes of metropolitan officials and colonists within the settlement. I highlight the six decades between the 1790s and 1850s as ones of particular uncertainty for colonial officials who were charged with developing policies addressing domestic slavery. Lack of a clear colonial vision enabled slaves to take initiatives that had significant consequences for Britain's abolitionist agenda. At every turn, slaves exploited the British campaign against the slave trade in an attempt to improve their conditions on the continent. In some cases, they achieved this by fleeing into the colony, where British officials granted them freedom. In others, slaves used the mere threat of flight to negotiate better treatment from their owners in the interior. Slaves' initiatives complicated the simplistic distinctions that British officials made between foreign and domestic slavery – a distinction that was central to British anti-slavery policies – and forced British officials to continuously reflect on and define the boundaries of their colonial possessions in Sierra Leone. While the magnitude of the "fugitive slave" problem in this period was relatively small, its impact on British policymaking was thus considerable. By the 1850s, the issue had become tied to broader African and European concerns about the citizenship and general legal status of Liberated Africans who lived in Freetown. The resulting uncertainty led Britain to annex large parts of coastal territory adjacent to the colony. This complicated picture lays bare the many ironies and unintended consequences of Britain's abolition and colonization initiatives: British colonialism in Sierra Leone increased slave trading and slavery on the frontier of Freetown; and slave agency drove the British to undertaken more aggressive colonial expansion.

Emphasis on slave agency, Liberated African initiatives, and colonial uncertainty situates this work in the lengthy – if uneven – historiography of Sierra Leone. While many Africanist historians in the 1960s collected and assessed oral traditions to uncover the precolonial African past, several who were skeptical of oral sources – or, at least, more comfortable with written evidence – saw promise in the rich corpus of historical documents that Europeans generated in Upper Guinea. The works they produced tended to approach Freetown as either isolated from developments in the Sierra Leone interior or as a site from which European influence and initiatives radiated outward. Christopher Fyfe's *A History of Sierra Leone*, for example, now more than sixty years old, remains the most thorough analysis of the British colony, though it largely focuses on Freetown itself and the settlement's Krio population in particular, as does work by several prominent Sierra Leonean scholars. Others have contributed long-term regional syntheses, detailing historical change in Upper Guinea over many centuries, during which Freetown's influence was either nonexistent or represented a temporary blip on the historical radar – one site amongst many that generated change. [18]

Adam Jones's research deserves special attention. Over several decades, Jones has carefully gathered written and oral data on the precolonial Gallinas area. *From Slaves to Palm Kernels,* Jones' careful analysis of political and commercial change in southern Sierra Leone, illustrates, among other things, the complex ways by which the region experienced and adapted to integration into local, regional, and transatlantic commercial networks. My work is deeply indebted to Jones' many contributions to Sierra Leone history. But while Europeans play important roles in his analysis – as slave traders, merchants, and eventually colonizers – Jones' story is situated in the context of prevailing questions in the Africanist literature of the 1960s and 70s. His work prioritizes internal African initiatives that shaped change in the Gallinas. *Abolition and the Transformation of Atlantic Commerce* assesses change in southern Sierra Leone primarily through the lens of the slave trade and its abolition.

Following the destructive civil war in the 1990s and early 2000s that tragically took so many Sierra Leonean lives, historians began in the first decade of the twenty-first century to physically and analytically revisit the country, arming themselves with new interpretive trends and insights that had developed while the country was closed down to foreign academics and pushing Sierra Leone scholarship in exciting new directions. Suzanne Schwarz has brought to life the dynamics of Freetown under Sierra Leone Company rule, emphasizing the religious, commercial, and cultural forces that inspired Britons to settle in the region and the disconnect between metropolitan ideas and colonial realities in implementing British abolitionist agendas in a foreign setting. Her work has also revealed the potential for life stories of Liberated Africans to shed new and rich detail on their movements and activities within Freetown upon their emancipation. Other scholars have used the documentation of Liberated Africans to consider questions about the identity of recaptives in the nineteenth century. Richard Anderson, Katrina Keefer, and Gibril Cole have mined unique sources around the Atlantic World to illustrate where Liberated Africans came from and how their backgrounds shaped life in early colonial Freetown. Bronwen Everill's comparative study of Sierra Leone and Liberia provides a broader framework in which to consider abolitionist projects, illustrating similarities and important differences in the local dynamics that shaped the histories of these two neighboring settlements. Padraic Scanlan's book, *Freedom's Debtors*, traces the evolution of British colonial administrations in Freetown and their antislavery policies, making a powerful case that the colony was on the cutting-edge of antislavery history. His work challenges the assumption that Britain's abolitionist project was rooted in selfless humanitarianism, emphasizing instead the profits that colonial officials and naval officers earned through their involvement in the abolition campaign. Over just a single decade, Sierra Leone has therefore been placed at the center of major debates over imperialism, abolitionism, capitalism, slavery, and the slave trade.[19]

Abolition and the Transformation of Atlantic Commerce builds on and challenges this literature by offering a new context for understanding nineteenth-century change in West Africa. Freetown looms large in this story, not as a colonial core from which imperialism marched inevitably forward or a project shaped by financial incentives but rather as a site from which Europeans and Africans debated basic questions about slavery, freedom, and colonialism. It offers a view of Freetown from the settlement's frontier, from which antislavery and colonialism appear incoherent and often messy. That perspective not only illustrates how British concerns with the interior consistently required them to rethink their antislavery agenda in Africa but also how the slave trade itself adapted to and was transformed by British antislavery pressures.

At its broadest level, this study contributes to the explosive growth of literature on the Atlantic World. It joins the now large group scholars who argue that slave trade studies should begin in the African interior, beyond the ports where slaves were embarked on transatlantic vessels.[20] *Abolition and the Transformation of Atlantic Commerce* is one of a relatively small number of studies to link transformations on the African coast with the effects they had deeper inland. It provides a fresh interpretation of the origins and development of colonialism in Sierra Leone, situating the phenomenon in the broader context of European debates over the suppression of the slave trade and Britain's ambitious abolition campaign.

Sources and Methods

Research for this project was carried out on three continents: North America, Africa, and Europe. In Sierra Leone, I collected and assessed large bodies of archival and oral data. Outside of Africa, I analyzed an extensive corpus of documentary materials. Each of these sources and settings posed challenges and opportunities. In Sierra Leone, the majority of my research was based on materials held in the Sierra Leone National Archives (SLNA), on the campus of Fourah Bay College. The records in the SLNA are well preserved and arranged, thanks to the unparalleled efforts of Christopher Fyfe and Albert Moore, who together have overseen the preservation of materials in the archives over the past seven decades. A more recent Endangered Archives grant has enabled Paul E. Lovejoy and the team with which he has worked to support additional preservation efforts, including the digitization of vast collections of nineteenth-century materials. The archive's relative accessibility enabled me to assess almost all of the pre-1860s documents that were available. Most importantly, the collection includes holdings from the Liberated African Department, not the least important of which are the Registers of Liberated Africans, on which chapter two is based.[21]

Attempting to identify the ethnolinguistic origins of names from the Registers of Liberated Africans drew me into the exhilarating world of Sierra Leone fieldwork. I spent much of my time in Freetown working with knowledgeable informants sifting through thousands of nineteenth-century African names. However, on several occasions I left the hustle and bustle of African urban life to discuss my project with people living in communities in southern Sierra Leone. This included lengthy excursions to Bo, Shenge, Bonthe (on Sherbro Island), and Pujehun, where I was exposed to the complex ways by which individuals, households, and larger communities represent and remember their past. Oral testimonies helped me interpret through local cultural lenses documents that Europeans wrote about Africa and Africans.[22] In that sense, fieldwork played an invaluable part in shaping my study, even if I cite few interviews.

The National Archives (TNA), in Kew Gardens, holds an unrivaled amount of written materials on Sierra Leone. The sheer size of TNA's Sierra Leone collection made tackling it quite a daunting challenge. It includes early records of the Company of Royal Adventurers of England Trading to Africa and its successors, which are arranged under the T70 series. TNA also holds the full collection of Sierra Leone colonial correspondence, housed under the CO267 series, which comprises 702 volumes and spans the full period of British colonial occupation.[23] My work has also benefitted from the FO84 series, which includes official British correspondence on the slave trade and its suppression.

Finally, I made extensive use of missionary collections. The American Missionary Association, which established a station in the Sherbro in the 1840s and carefully recorded developments in southern Sierra Leone, have proven central to this project. Other missionary archives provide detailed information on British and American activities at local levels. That relatively few colonial and missionary officials lived in Sierra Leone in the first half of the nineteenth century – a time when Britain had a limited idea of its future in Africa – enabled Africans to more frequently have their voices heard and preserved in archival records during this period. This study is a major beneficiary of that reality.

The Structure and Organization of the Book
The book is organized into five chapters: the first is chronologically arranged while the others engage overlapping themes. Chapter one explores the growing relationship between southern Sierra Leone and the Atlantic World. In this chapter, I assess changing patterns of Atlantic commerce and their effects on the broad Upper Guinea region. Chapter two explores how the

growth of the Gallinas and Sherbro as slave ports affected the origins of Africans pulled into the transatlantic slave trade. Whereas the pre-1807 trade from Sierra Leone tended to draw slaves from a catchment area more than one hundred miles beyond the littoral, the captives embarked in nineteenth-century southern Sierra Leone came primarily from regions in the Sherbro- and Mende-speaking interior, within about sixty miles of the coast.

The next two chapters turn to aspects of agricultural production and trade in the era of abolition. Chapter three explores the competing demands among settlers in Freetown and Gallinas for rice produced in the Sherbro. The chapter examines how the provisions trade to Freetown was organized, and concludes that it shared many similarities with that of the slave trade. Chapter four considers the ways in which new demands for agricultural commodities produced across Upper Guinea affected the internal slave trade between the 1830s and 1860s.

The final chapter addresses the impact that Freetown's antislavery agenda had on slaves who lived on its southeastern frontier. Although British colonial officials did not act directly to suppress slavery in the hinterland, beginning in the 1790s, small numbers of enslaved people fled to the settlement to claim freedom for themselves. Through such actions, slaves forced questions and concerns about domestic slavery onto Britain's colonial agenda, requiring colonial officials to intervene in political affairs beyond the confines of their settlement. Slaves in the process earned leverage to negotiate new rights and better treatment from their owners. In the long run, the fugitive slave issue contributed to Britain's decision to annex part of the Sherbro in 1861.

Notes

1   The literature on the antislavery campaign is vast. For several important contributions, see Christopher Lloyd, *The Navy and the Slave Trade: The Suppression of the African Slave Trade in the Nineteenth Century* (London: Longmans, Green, 1949); Mary Wills, "The Royal Navy and the Suppression

of the Atlantic Slave Trade, c. 1807-1867: Anti-Slavery, Empire, and Identity" (PhD diss., University of Hull, 2012); Howard Temperley, *British Antislavery, 1833-1870* (London: Longman, 1972); Eric Williams, *Capitalism and Slavery* (Chapel Hill: University of North Carolina Press, 1944); David Brion Davis, *The Problem of Slavery in the Age of Revolution, 1770-1823* (Ithaca: Cornell University Press, 1975); ibid, *The Problem of Slavery in the Age of Emancipation* (New York: Knopf, 2014); Thomas Bender, ed., *The Antislavery Debate: Capitalism and Abolitionism as a Problem in Historical Interpretation* (Berkeley: University of California Press, 1992); David Eltis, *Economic Growth and the Ending of the Transatlantic Slave Trade* (New York: Oxford University Press, 1987); David Eltis, Stanley L. Engerman, Seymour Drescher, and David Richardson, eds., *The Cambridge World History of Slavery: Volume 4, AD 1804-AD 2016* (New York: Cambridge University Press, 2017); Christopher Leslie Brown, *Moral Capital: Foundations of British Abolitionism* (Chapel Hill: Published for the Omohundro Institute of Early American History and Culture, 2006); Seymour Drescher, *Abolition: A History of Slavery and Antislavery* (New York: Cambridge University Press, 2009); ibid, "The Shocking Birth of British Abolitionism," *Slavery & Abolition* 33 (2012): 571-93; Robin Blackburn, *The American Crucible: Slavery, Emancipation and Human Rights* (New York: Verso, 2011); Manisha Sinha, *The Slave's Cause: A History of Abolition* (New Haven: Yale University Press, 2016). A few recent examples rooted in Africa include Bronwen Everill, *Abolition and Empire in Sierra Leone and Liberia* (New York: Palgrave Macmillan, 2013); Padraic X. Scanlan, *Freedom's Debtors: British Antislavery in Sierra Leone in the Age of Revolution* (New Haven: Yale University Press, 2017); A.F. Afigbo, *The Abolition of the Slave Trade in Southeastern Nigeria, 1885-1950* (Rochester, NY: University of Rochester Press, 2006); and Kristin Mann, *Slavery and the Birth of an African City: Lagos, 1760-1900* (Bloomington: Indiana University Press, 2007), esp. ch. 3.

2   Walter Rodney first made this point in the 1960s. See his "African Slavery and Other Forms of Social Oppression on the Upper Guinea Coast in the Context of the Atlantic Slave-Trade," *Journal of African History* 7, no. 3 (1966): 431-43. Paul E. Lovejoy, *Transformations in Slavery: A History of Slavery in Africa*, 3rd ed. (Cambridge: Cambridge University Press, 2011), more directly tackles the issue. See also Paul E. Lovejoy and Jan S. Hogendorn, *Slow Death for Slavery: The Course of Abolition in Northern Nigeria, 1897-1936* (New York: Cambridge University Press, 1993); and Mohammed Bashir Salau, *Plantation Slavery in the Sokoto Caliphate: A Historical and Comparative Study* (Rochester: University of Rochester Press, 2018).

3   See, for example, Michael Crowder, *Colonial West Africa* (London: F. Cass, 1978), ch. 2; and Martin Lynn, *Commerce and Economic Change in West Africa: The Palm Oil Trade in the Nineteenth Century* (Cambridge: Cambridge University Press, 1997), ch. 8. On the increasing militarization of British co-

lonial policy in Sierra Leone in the early-nineteenth century, see Scanlan, *Freedom's Debtors*, esp. 18-25.

4   Estimates of the slave trade come from David Eltis et al., *Voyages: The Trans-Atlantic Slave Trade Database* (hereafter *Voyages*), online at http://www.slavevoyages.org.

5   John K. Thornton, *Africa and Africans in the Making of the Atlantic World, 1400-1800*, 2nd ed. (Cambridge: Cambridge University Press, 1998). Patrick Manning usefully divides the literature on the slave trade into works that emphasize external forces in developing African history and those that stress internal factors. The point, of course, should be to examine how internal and external forces interacted with each other. See Patrick Manning, "Contours of Slavery and Social Change in Africa," *American Historical Review* 88 (1983): 835-57.

6   James F. Searing, *West African Slavery and Atlantic Commerce: The Senegal River Valley, 1700-1860* (Cambridge: Cambridge University Press, 1993), x.

7   Several recent works on nineteenth-century Cuba have underscored the island's dynamic plantation system and slaves' resistance to it. Ada Ferrer, *Freedom's Mirror: Cuba and Haiti in the Age of Revolution* (New York: Cambridge University Press, 2014); Camillia Cowling, *Conceiving Freedom: Women of Color, Gender, and the Abolition of Slavery in Havana and Rio de Janeiro* (Chapel Hill: University of North Carolina Press, 2013); Sarah L. Franklin, *Women and Slavery in Nineteenth-Century Colonial Cuba* (Rochester: University of Rochester Press, 2012); Aisha K. Finch, *Rethinking Slave Rebellion in Cuba: La Escalera and the Insurgencies of 1841-1844* (Chapel Hill: University of North Carolina Press, 2015); Manuel Barcia, *Seeds of Insurrection: Domination and Resistance on Western Cuban Plantations, 1808-1848* (Baton Rouge: Louisiana State University Press, 2008); ibid, *The Great African Slave Revolt of 1825: Cuba and the Fight for Freedom in Matanzas* (Baton Rouge: Louisiana State University Press, 2012). The standard work on the nineteenth-century Cuban political economy remains Franklin W. Knight, *Slave Society in Cuba during the Nineteenth Century* (Madison: University of Wisconsin Press, 1970).

8   Important exceptions include Jane Hooper, *Feeding Globalization: Madagascar and the Provisioning Trade, 1600-1800* (Athens, OH: Ohio University Press, 2017); several chapters in Robin Law, Suzanne Schwarz, and Silke Strickrodt, eds., *Commercial Agriculture, the Slave Trade and Slavery in Atlantic Africa* (London: James Currey, 2013); and, for early Freetown under Company rule, Suzanne Schwarz, "Commerce, Civilization, and Christianity: The Development of the Sierra Leone Company," in *Liverpool and Transatlantic Slavery*, ed. David Richardson, Suzanne Schwarz, and Anthony Tibbles (Liverpool: Liverpool University Press, 2007). On Africa's contribution to the Columbian Exchange more generally, see Judith A. Carney and Richard Nicholas Rosomoff, *In the Shadow of Slavery: Africa's*

Botanical Legacy in the Atlantic World (Berkeley: University of California Press, 2009).

9 The idea that slaves and owners negotiated with each other over rights and responsibilities comes from work on slavery in the United States. In particular, see Eugene D. Genovese, *Roll, Jordan, Roll: The World the Slaves Made* (New York: Vintage, 1976).

10 Serious scholarly estimates of the volume of the slave trade began with Philip D. Curtin, *The Atlantic Slave Trade: A Census* (Madison: University of Wisconsin Press, 1969). Since then, a number of scholars have updated Curtin's findings, though it is worth noting that Curtin's estimates remain well within the margin of error he first proposed. The most important of these works include Paul E. Lovejoy, "The Volume of the Atlantic Slave Trade: A Synthesis," *Journal of African History* 23, no. 4 (1982): 473-501; David Eltis et al., *The Trans-Atlantic Slave Trade: A Database on CD-ROM* (Cambridge: Cambridge University Press, 1999); and the updated online version, http://www.slavevoyages.org; David Eltis and David Richardson, eds., *Extending the Frontiers: Essays on the New Transatlantic Slave Trade Database* (New Haven: Yale University Press, 2008); ibid, *Atlas of the Transatlantic Slave Trade* (New Haven: Yale University Press, 2010); Alex Borucki, David Eltis, and David Wheat, "Atlantic History and the Slave Trade to Spanish America," *American Historical Review* 120, no. 2 (2015): 433-61. The implications of regional differences in the sex ratios of captives have been explored in David Eltis and Stanley L. Engerman, "Was the Slave Trade Dominated by Men?," *Journal of Interdisciplinary History* 23 (1992): 237-57; ibid, "Fluctuations in Sex and Age Ratios in the Transatlantic Slave Trade, 1663-1864," *Economic History Review* 46 (1993): 308-23; G. Ugo Nwokeji, *The Slave Trade and Culture in the Bight of Biafra: An African Society in the Atlantic World* (New York: Cambridge University Press, 2010), ch. 6. On children in the slave trade, see selected chapters in Gwyn Campbell, Suzanne Miers, and Joseph C. Miller, eds., *Children in Slavery Through the Ages* (Athens, OH: Ohio University Press, 2009); Colleen Vasconcellos, *Slavery, Childhood, and Abolition in Jamaica, 1788-1838* (Athens, GA: University of Georgia Press, 2015); and Benjamin N. Lawrance, *Amistad's Orphans: An Atlantic Story of Children, Slavery, and Smuggling* (New Haven: Yale University Press, 2015). Many local and regional studies of Africa in the era of the slave trade grapple with important questions about the trade's causes and consequences. See Joseph C. Miller, *Way of Death: Merchant Capital and the Angolan Slave Trade, 1730-1830* (Madison: University of Wisconsin Press, 1988); Robert W. Harms, *River of Wealth, River of Sorrow: The Central Zaire Basin in the Era of the Slave and Ivory Trade, 1500-1891* (New Haven: Yale University Press, 1981); Linda M. Heywood and John K. Thornton, *Central Africans, Atlantic Creoles, and the Foundation of the Americas, 1585-1660* (New York: Cambridge University Press, 2007); Roquinaldo Ferreira, *Cross-Cultural Ex-*

change in the Atlantic World: Angola and Brazil during the Era of the Slave Trade (New York: Cambridge University Press, 2012); Mariana P. Candido, *An African Slaving Port and the Atlantic World: Benguela and Its Hinterland* (New York: Cambridge University Press, 2013); Robin Law, *The Slave Coast of West Africa, 1550-1750: The Impact of the Atlantic Slave Trade on an African Society* (Oxford: Clarendon Press, 1991); ibid, *Ouidah: The Social History of a West African Slaving "Port," 1727-1892* (Athens, OH: Ohio University Press, 2004); Silke Strickrodt, *Afro-European Trade in the Atlantic World: The Western Slave Coast, c. 1550-c. 1885* (Suffolk: James Currey, 2015); Mann, *Slavery and the Birth*; David Northrup, *Trade without Rulers: Pre-Colonial Economic Development in South-Eastern Nigeria* (Oxford: Clarendon Press, 1978); Bayo Holsey, *Routes of Remembrance: Refashioning the Slave Trade in Ghana* (Chicago: University of Chicago Press, 2008); Rebecca Shumway, *The Fante and the Transatlantic Slave Trade* (Rochester: University of Rochester Press, 2011); Walter Rodney, *A History of the Upper Guinea Coast, 1545-1800* (Oxford: Clarendon Press, 1970); Philip D. Curtin, *Economic Change in Precolonial Africa: Senegambia in the Era of the Slave Trade* (Madison: University of Wisconsin Press, 1975); Richard Roberts, *Warriors, Merchants, and Slaves: The State, and the Economy in the Middle Niger Valley, 1700-1914* (Stanford: Stanford University Press, 1987); Searing, *West African Slavery;* Boubacar Barry, *Senegambia and the Atlantic Slave Trade* (Cambridge: Cambridge University Press, 1998); Martin A. Klein, *Slavery and Colonial Rule in French West Africa* (Cambridge: Cambridge University Press, 1998); Walter Hawthorne, *Planting Rice and Harvesting Slaves: Transformations along the Guinea Bissau Coast, 1400-1900* (Portsmouth, NH: Heinemann, 2003); ibid, *From Africa to Brazil: Culture, Identity, and an Atlantic Slave Trade, 1600-1830* (New York: Cambridge University Press, 2010); Toby Green, *The Rise of the Trans-Atlantic Slave Trade in Western Africa, 1300-1589* (New York: Cambridge University Press, 2012); Daniel B. Domingues da Silva, *The Atlantic Slave Trade from West Central Africa, 1780-1867* (New York: Cambridge University Press, 2017).

11 The literature on this topic is vast. For an early summary, see Paul E. Lovejoy, "The Impact of the Atlantic Slave Trade on Africa: A Review of the Literature," *Journal of African History* 30 (1989): 365-94. For studies that emphasize the negative consequences of the slave trade on Africa, see Rodney, "African Slavery"; J. E. Inikori, ed., *Forced Migration: The Impact of the Export Slave Trade on African Societies* (New York: Africana Pub. Co., 1982); Patrick Manning, *Slavery and African Life: Occidental, Oriental and African Slave Trades* (Cambridge: Cambridge University Press, 1990); Lovejoy, *Transformations*; Walter Rodney, *How Europe Underdeveloped Africa* (Washington D.C.: Howard University Press, 1981). Local and regional studies include Barry, *Senegambia;* Edward A. Alpers, *Ivory and Slaves: Changing Pattern of International Trade in East Central Africa to the Later Nineteenth Century* (Berkeley: University of California Press, 1975); Rodney, *A*

History. On alcohol in Africa, see Emmanuel Akyeampong, *Drink, Power, and Cultural Change: A Social History of Alcohol in Ghana, c. 1800 to Recent Times* (Portsmouth, NH: Heinemann, 1996); Jose C. Curto, *Enslaving Spirits: The Portuguese-Brazilian Alcohol Trade at Luanda and Its Hinterland, c. 1550-1830* (Leiden: Brill, 2004). On the demographic effects of the slave trade, see John Thornton, "The Slave Trade in Eighteenth Century Angola: Effects on Demographic Structures," *Canadian Journal of African Studies* 14 (1980): 417-27; G. Ugo Nwokeji, "The Atlantic Slave Trade and Population Density: A Historical Demography of the Biafran Hinterland," *Canadian Journal of African Studies* 34, no. 3 (2000): 616-55; and Patrick Manning, "The Enslavement of Africans: A Demographic Model," *Canadian Journal of African Studies* 15, no. 3 (1981): 499-526. For a moving assessment of the human consequences of slave mortality in the Americas, see David Richardson, "Consuming Goods, Consuming People: Reflections on the Transatlantic Slave Trade," in *The Rise and Demise of Slavery and the Slave Trade in the Atlantic World*, ed. Philip Misevich and Kristin Mann (Rochester: Rochester University Press, 2017), 31-63.

12   The most forcefully and coherently argued of these views is Thornton, *Africa and Africans*. For an economic treatment that stresses the relative insignificance of the Atlantic trade to African economies, see David Eltis and Lawrence C. Jennings, "Trade between Western Africa and the Atlantic World in the Pre-Colonial Era," *American Historical Review* 93 (1988): 936-59. See also J.D. Fage, "Slaves and Society in Western Africa, c. 1445-c. 1700," *Journal of African History* 21 (1980): 289-310; ibid, "African Societies and the Atlantic Slave Trade," *Past and Present* 125 (1989): 97-115; and Curtin, *Economic Change*. While I recognize the problem with historians "giving" agency to historical subjects, the concept of African agency still prevails in studies of the slave trade. For a useful essay that problematizes the concept of agency, see Walter Johnson, "On Agency," *Journal of Social History* 37, no. 1 (2003): 113-24.

13   The expression comes from the introduction to Joseph E. Inikori and Stanley L. Engerman, eds., *The Atlantic Slave Trade: Effects on Economies, Societies, and Peoples in Africa, the Americas, and Europe* (Durham: Duke University Press, 1992).

14   Hawthorne, *Planting Rice*.

15   The debate over the effects of the commercial transition began with K. Onwuka Dike's *Trade and Politics in the Niger Delta, 1830-1885* (Oxford: Clarendon Press, 1956). For a useful review of the literature, see Robin Law, "The Historiography of the Commercial Transition in Nineteenth Century West Africa," in *African Historiography: Essays in Honour of Jacob Ade Ajayi*, ed. Toyin Falola (Harlow: Longman, 1993), 91-115. Works that argue that the transition transformed African political and social structures include A.G. Hopkins, "Economic Imperialism in West Africa: Lagos, 1880-92," *Economic History Review* 21 (1968): 580-606, where

the expression "crisis of adaption" first appeared; Martin A. Klein, *Islam and Imperialism in Senegal: Sine-Saloum, 1847-1914* (Edinburgh: Edinburgh University Press, 1968); ibid, "Social and Economic Factors in the Muslim Revolution in Senegambia," *Journal of African History* 13 (1972): 419-41. The most forceful alternative argument, which stresses continuity during the commercial transition, comes from Ralph A. Austen, "The Abolition of the Overseas Slave Trade: A Distorted Theme in West African History," *Journal of the Historical Society of Nigeria* 5, no. 2 (1970): 257-74. In a more localized setting, the continuity interpretation receives support in Adam Jones, *From Slaves to Palm Kernels: A History of the Galinhas Country (West Africa), 1730-1890* (Wiesbaden: F. Steiner, 1983), 86-88. More generally, see Robin Law, ed., *From Slave Trade to 'Legitimate' Commerce: The Commercial Transition in Nineteenth Century West Africa* (Cambridge: Cambridge University Press, 1995).

16   The standard work on colonial policies toward slavery is Suzanne Miers and Richard Roberts, eds., *The End of Slavery in Africa* (Madison: University of Wisconsin Press, 1988). More recently, see Suzanne Miers and Martin Klein, eds., *Slavery and Colonial Rule in Africa* (London: Frank Cass, 1999). Much of the research on the relationship between colonialism and slavery has been focused on the Gold Coast. See Raymond E. Dumett and Marion Johnson, "Britain and the Suppression of Slavery in the Gold Coast Colony, Ashanti, and the Northern Territories," in Miers and Roberts, *The End of Slavery,* 71-116; Raymond E. Dumett, "Pressure Groups, Bureaucracy and the Decision Making Process: The Case of Slavery Abolition and Colonial Expansion in the Gold Coast, 1874," *Journal of Imperial and Commonwealth History* 9 (1981): 193-215; Gerald M. McSheffrey, "Slavery, Indentured Servitude, Legitimate Trade, and the Impact of Abolition on the Gold Coast, 1874-1901: A Reappraisal," *Journal of African History* 24 (1983): 349-68; Trevor R. Getz, *Slavery and Reform in West Africa: Toward Emancipation in Nineteenth-Century Senegal and Gold Coast* (Athens, OH: Ohio University Press, 2004); and Kwabena Opare-Akurang, "The Administration of the Abolition Laws, African Responses and Post-Proclamation Slavery in the Gold Coast, 1874-1940," in Miers and Klein, *Slavery and Colonial Rule,* 149-66. For French West Africa, see Klein, *Slavery and Colonial Rule.* For a case study focusing on British African colonies outside of the Gold Coast, see Ismail Rashid, "'Do Dady nor Lef me Make dem Carry me': Slave Resistance and Emancipation in Sierra Leone, 1894-1928," in Miers and Klein, *Slavery and Colonial Rule,* 208-31.

17   Mann, *Slavery and the Birth,* 13.

18   Representative works that focus on Freetown in general or the Krio in particular include Christopher Fyfe, *A History of Sierra Leone* (Oxford: Oxford University Press, 1962); Akintola Wyse, *The Krio of Sierra Leone: An Interpretive History* (London: Hurst, in Association with the International African Institute, 1989); and Barbara E. Harrell-Bond, Allen M. Howard,

and David E. Skinner, *Community Leadership and the Transformation of Freetown (1801-1976)* (The Hague: Milton Publishers, 1978). For regional studies, see Rodney, *A History*; George E. Brooks, *Landlords and Strangers: Ecology, Society, and Trade in Western Africa, 1000-1630* (Boulder: Westview Press, 1993); ibid, *Eurafricans in Western Africa: Commerce, Social Status, Gender, and Religious Observance from the Sixteenth to the Eighteenth Century* (Athens, OH: University of Ohio Press, 2003); ibid, *Western Africa and Cabo Verde, 1790s to 1830s: Symbiosis of Slave and Legitimate Trades* (Bloomington: AuthorHouse, 2010).

19   Suzanne Schwarz, "Reconstructing the Life Histories of Liberated Africans: Sierra Leone in the Early Nineteenth Century," *History in Africa* 39 (2012): 175-207; ibid, "Extending the African Names Database: New Evidence from Sierra Leone," *African Economic History* 38 (2010): 137-63; and ibid, "Commerce." Gibril R. Cole, *The Krio of West Africa: Islam, Culture, Creolization, and Colonialism in the Nineteenth Century* (Athens, OH: University of Ohio Press, 2013); Richard Anderson, "Recaptives: Community and Identity in Colonial Sierra Leone, 1808-1863" (PhD diss., Yale University, 2015); Scanlan, *Freedom's Debtors*; Katrina H. B. Keefer, "Scarification and Identity in the Liberated Africans Department Register, 1814-1815," *Canadian Journal of African Studies* 47, no. 3 (2013): 537-53; Ibid, "Group Identity, Scarification, and Poro among Liberated Africans in Sierra Leone, 1808-1819," *Journal of West African History* 3, no. 1 (2017): 1-25. See also Joseph J. Bangura, *The Temne of Sierra Leone; African Agency in the Making of a British Colony* (New York: Cambridge University Press, 2017); Bruce L. Mouser, *American Colony on the Rio Pongo: The War of 1812, The Slave Trade, and the Proposed Settlement of African Americans, 1810-1830* (Trenton, NJ: Africa World Press, 2013); Paul E. Lovejoy and Suzanne Schwarz, eds., *Slavery, Abolition and the Transition to Colonialism in Sierra Leone* (Trenton: Africa World Press, 2015). Scholarship on the *Amistad* affair and its aftermath has also recently been rooted in the history of slavery and abolition in the Sierra Leone interior. See Marcus Rediker, *The Amistad Rebellion: An Atlantic Odyssey of Slavery and Freedom*, Updated Edition (New York: Penguin Books, 2013); Joseph Yannielli, "'Mo Tappan': Transnational Abolitionism and the Making of a Mende-American Town," *Journal of the Civil War Era* 8 (2018): 190-214; and ibid, "George Thompson among the Africans: Empathy, Authority, and Insanity in the Age of Abolition," *Journal of American History* 96 (2010): 979-1000.

20   The effect of the slave trade on the African littoral is still imperfectly understood, but the coast has received more attention than the African interior. For recent studies, see Rediker, *The Amistad Rebellion*; Mann, *Slavery and the Birth*; Law, *Ouidah*; Robin Law and Silke Strickrodt, eds., *Ports of the Slave Trade (Bights of Benin and Biafra): Papers from a Conference of the Centre of Commonwealth Studies, University of Stirling, June 1998* (Stirling: Centre for Commonwealth Studies, 1999). For a study that traces the en-

slavement of Africans from the interior to the coast, see Stephanie E. Smallwood, *Saltwater Slavery: A Middle Passage from Africa to American Diaspora* (Cambridge: Harvard University Press, 2007). The Nigerian Hinterland Project aims to root the study of the slave trade in the African hinterland. Its aims are described online at http://www.yorku.ca/ nhp/areas/nhp.htm.

21 On the Registers of Liberated Africans, see Daniel Domingues da Silva, David Eltis, Philip Misevich, and Olatunji Ojo, "The Diaspora of Africans Liberated from Slave Ships in the Nineteenth Century," *Journal of African History* 55, no. 3 (2014): 347-69; Richard Anderson, Alex Borucki, Daniel Domingues da Silva, David Eltis, Paul Lachance, Philip Misevich, and Olatunji Ojo, "Using African Names to Identify the Origins of Captives in the Transatlantic Slave Trade: Crowd-Sourcing and the Registers of Liberated Africans, 1808-1862," *History in Africa* 40 (2013): 165-91; ibid, "Extending"; Henry B. Lovejoy, "The Registers of Liberated Africans of the Havana Slave Trade Commission: Implementation and Policy, 1824-1841," *Slavery & Abolition* 37, no. 1 (2016): 23-44. Henry Lovejoy has created a comprehensive digital project for the exploration of Liberated Africans, accessible at www.liberatedafricans.org.

22 For the difficulties assessing oral data in decentralized regions, see Jones, *From Slaves to Palm Kernels*, preface; ibid, "White Roots: Written and Oral Testimony on the 'First' Mr. Rogers," *History in Africa* 10 (1983): 151-62. Walter Hawthorne has written a spirited defense of the use of oral traditions in his *Planting Rice*. Several noteworthy works that deal with precolonial Sierra Leone have also addressed questions about oral data. See Mariane C. Ferme's, *The Underneath of Things: Violence, History, and the Everyday in Sierra Leone* (Berkeley: University of California Press, 2001); and Rosalind Shaw, *Memories of the Slave Trade: Ritual and the Historical Imagination in Sierra Leone* (Chicago: University of Chicago Press, 2002).

23 Although this series includes some records of precolonial West Africa in its early volumes, the vast majority of the collection is focused on the period after 1807.

Chapter 1. Southern Sierra Leone and the Atlantic World from the Fifteenth through the mid-Nineteenth Centuries

Southern Sierra Leone is a small part of a large African region that scholars generally identify as Upper Guinea. Africans who settled throughout this area, which stretches between modern-day Senegal in the north and the Ivory Coast in the southeast, had their lives shaped by centuries of migrations from the interior to the coast, including especially by peoples from the Mali Empire.[1] Though African communities across Upper Guinea had noteworthy differences, the prolonged diaspora of merchants and travelers who originated in Mali provided the area with a degree of political, social, and cultural unity. In the fifteenth century, the region also began a complex process of interaction with European merchants on the Atlantic littoral. Europeans visited Upper Guinea primarily for agricultural commodities, whose value, at least in strict economic terms, surpassed that of enslaved people. However, the explosive growth in the production of American plantation staple crops over the eighteenth century generated unrivaled demand for coerced labor in the New World. In response to this drastic change in the Atlantic economy, slave merchants in Europe, Africa, and the Americas forged new relationships and intensified older ones to facilitate the flow of enslaved men, women, and children from Upper Guinea. Between the mid-eighteenth and mid-nineteenth centuries, the slave trade thus came to dominate Atlantic commerce throughout Upper Guinea with drastic consequences for Sierra Leone in general and southern Sierra Leone in particular.

In the nearly four centuries between the rise of the slave trade from Upper Guinea and its suppression, southern Sierra Leone was transformed from a relative commercial backwater into the most active center for slave embarkation west of the Bight of Benin. For much of this period, the region's participation in Atlantic commerce proceeded organically, growing out of longstanding ties between British, African, and Anglo-African merchants and bound closely with the evolution of trade in African agricultural commodities. However, the abolition of the British slave trade and the establishment of Freetown revolutionized southern Sierra Leone's commercial landscape and transformed the organization of the transatlantic slave trade from Sierra Leone. Once based on the use of large islands and coastal bulking centers, slave merchants increasingly exploited southern Sierra Leone's swampy coastal terrain to circumvent Britain's campaign to suppress the traffic. New merchants, coming primarily from Cuba and drawing on Cuban capital and commercial networks, expanded the region's slave supplies, which became central to the boom in the Cuban sugar industry. That this occurred on Freetown's doorstep proved particularly embarrassing to colonial officials engaged in the campaign to suppress the transatlantic slave trade.

Southern Sierra Leone in a Regional Perspective
Geographical and Historical Landscapes
Southern Sierra Leone shares many characteristics with Upper Guinea, of which it is a part. With the exception of the "mountains" around the Sierra Leone estuary, the entire Upper Guinea Coast is relatively flat. Geological activity submerged the land, allowing the Atlantic Ocean to flood it periodically and turn river waters brackish for many miles inland. The result, as George E. Brooks has noted, is "an irregular succession of drowned river estuaries and marshy lowlands interspersed with innumerable

low-lying islands and islets, many barely rising above the surface of the sea."[2] Beyond the coastal lowlands, Upper Guinea's interior opens into broader plains, extending between thirty and eighty miles wide, before rising in several areas to plateaus and more mountainous country. These basic geographic and hydrological features shaped the histories of communities across Upper Guinea.

The region's numerous waterways were central to the lives of its inhabitants in the precolonial period. Between The Gambia and Cape Mount, more than two-dozen rivers debouch separately into the Atlantic, flowing generally in a westerly or southwesterly direction. Europeans used these waterways to distinguish particular parts of Upper Guinea from each other. From their base in Senegal, for example, the French spoke of the "Rivers of the South" in reference to Guinea Bissau, whereas the British in Freetown designated a similar area the "Northern Rivers." For centuries, inhabitants of these lands used rivers and streams as highways, on which merchants carried commodities and ideas about foreign peoples and practices. Militaries with more destructive ambitions also exploited the same passageways in large dugout canoes in search of human and non-human plunder.[3]

As with other parts of Upper Guinea, southern Sierra Leone's coherence is based on its geographical, cultural, and historical features. In the Sherbro estuary, four rivers – the Bagroo (Gbangbar), Jong (Taia), Bum (Sewa), and Kittam (Waanji) – combine to create an outlet to the sea.[4] Further east, the Kerefe and Mano Rivers form the respective western and eastern boundaries of the Gallinas country, through which the larger Moa River also cuts. During the rainy season, which begins around May and can last as long as seven months, the Kerefe River floods, allowing travelers to reach the Kittam by canoe and, through interlocking creeks and streams, travel as far as Freetown. Historically, these waterways have integrated the region, enabling settlements to communicate and trade with each other.[5]

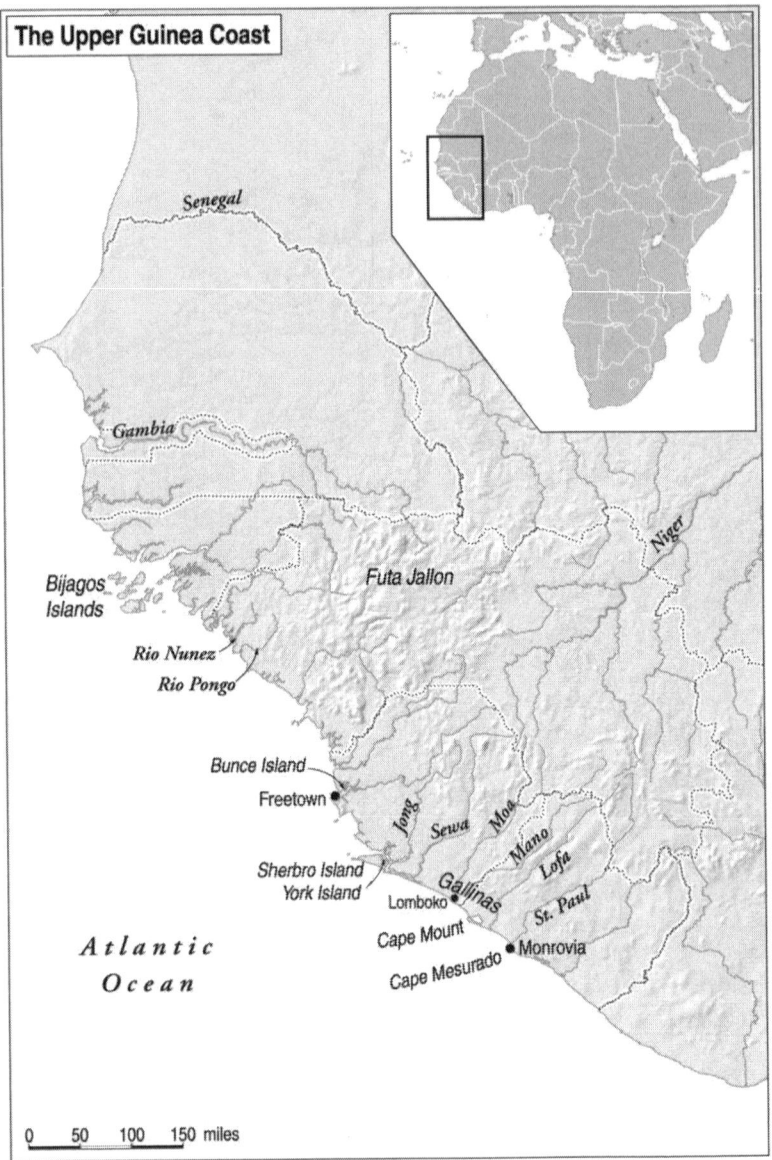

Map 1.1, The Upper Guinea Coast

Southern Sierra Leone's geographic and commercial integration helps frame the loose boundaries of this study. It includes the territory between the Sherbro estuary and the Mano River – the eastern boundary of the Gallinas. In some cases the study moves as far northwest as Portuguese Guinea and as far southeast as Cape Mount, following the flows of peoples and goods. Since the relationship between the coastal area and the interior with which it communicated changed over time, it is difficult to pinpoint precise geographic limits but in general the Sherbro- and Mende-speaking parts of the interior, reaching at times as far as one hundred miles from the Atlantic coast, lie at the heart of the story.

The history of southern Sierra Leone and the broader Upper Guinea region developed in the context of dynamic and longstanding relationships between the states and societies of the Western Sudan, in the interior, and those of the coast. This relationship was based on mutually beneficial trade through which coastal areas supplied salt and fish and in exchange received gold, cattle byproducts, and other commodities that were available further inland. The littoral's inhospitable environment attracted primarily those populations victimized by warfare and displacement, meaning that coastal societies were generally far less powerful than peoples living inland. As Walter Rodney concluded, "the peopling of the Upper Guinea Coast was a result of continuous dislocation of population from the interior to the coast," a process, he noted, that was "largely precipitated by political events in the Sudanese states."[6]

Before the mid-fifteenth century, waves of migration between the Western Sudan and the Upper Guinea Coast established the broad ethnolinguistic patterns that Europeans encountered in later periods. A brief overview of the region's language families illustrates this point. The two major language families that dominated Sierra Leone then, as now, were the West Atlantic and Mande groups. Historical linguists have further subdivided the former, including in it a smaller configuration of "Mel" languages, which include Temne, Bullom, Krim and Gola. While scholars debate the chronology of the spread of Mel languages, they concur that speakers of those languages were the first to settle along the Upper Guinea coast. In Sierra Leone, Bullom languages dominated the littoral as far north as the Scarcies River and south to around the Gallinas.[7]

More dramatic shifts in the population occurred in a period between the thirteenth and sixteenth centuries, a result of commercial and political changes in the interior. Driven away by peoples from the powerful Mali Empire, waves of people speaking Susu migrated toward the coast in large numbers, where they settled around the Futa Jallon highlands, in modern Guinea, and integrated through marriage with Africans who spoke Yalunka. Under pressure from the Susu newcomers, Africans speaking various other languages, including Temne, moved further west, toward the Sierra Leone peninsula. Over time, Temne speakers drove a wedge between Bullom communities. Bullom living north of the Sierra Leone estuary kept that name while those to its south came over time to be called Sherbro.[8] A growing commercial sophistication along the coast inspired additional migration from the interior, the dynamics of which are preserved and remembered in oral traditions that have been passed down over generations. In an often-repeated story, for example, Kono- and Vai-speakers claim to have migrated together toward the coast from the interior in search of salt. When they reached the agriculturally rich savanna, Kono speakers decided to settle while Vai speakers moved on until they reached the coast between the Gallinas and Cape Mount, where today they remain heavily concentrated.[9] For the most part these large migrations predated Sierra Leone's contact with Europeans. By the time the Portuguese arrived along the coast in the 1460s, the region's ethnolinguistic makeup was relatively well established.[10]

Around Sierra Leone, the Mende were the major exception to this pattern of ethnolinguistic continuity. They began to show up in documentary records only in the early eighteenth century. Their sudden appearance followed a time of great turbulence in the history of Upper Guinea: the famed Mani Invasions. Details about this mysterious event remain hazy. Beginning in the 1540s, the Karou Kingdom conquered the Quoja, a rival polity located around Cape Mount. Despite their victory, the Karou adopted Vai, the language of the local population. Over the next fifteen years the Karou intermarried with women from the defeated Quoja Kingdom. Social and cultural exchanges between the kingdoms created a fluid population, from which the Mani rulers drew to further enhance the size and strength of their army. P.E.H. Hair has convincingly argued that the Mani group consisted of a core of Vai-speaking military leaders who recruited Bullom soldiers during their campaign.[11]

From its base at Cape Mount, the Mani army divided itself into three parts: one traveled north by war canoe along the coast; the two others followed in parallel lines inland. The army conquered large territories around the Sherbro region and further north, along the coast. In the process, the Mani army transformed the region's political landscape, establishing a number of "kingdoms" along the coast between Port Loko and Sherbro Island. However, these polities seem to have had a limited effect on social and cultural patterns over time: very little evidence remained of the Mani incursion after the invasions; the political leaders who were appointed to oversee the Mani-controlled territories appear to have assimilated quickly into the local societies where they were established.[12]

The Mani Invasions are related to the emergence of Mende peoples, though scholars disagree over the precise nature of that relationship. Arthur Abraham, the leading scholar of Sierra Leone history, has identified two competing arguments over the issue: one proposes a "fusion theory" to explain the emergence and expansion of Mende speakers; the other argues for the independent emergence of Mende peoples. In the former case, the Mende appear as products of interaction and disruption that warfare during Mani incursions generated. As invading Mani armies mixed with the indigenous communities they conquered, they created a new linguistic and cultural group that provided the foundation on which Mende society was built. Alternatively, P.E.H. Hair and later Abraham himself suggest that the Mende derived from a group once called "Hondo," which appears in written records as far back as the seventeenth century.[13] While there is insufficient evidence to fully support either view, the significant point for this chapter is to highlight an issue on which the competing theories agree: by the mid-eighteenth century, when slave exports from Upper Guinea increased in earnest, the contours of Sierra Leone's ethnolinguistic communities were well documented and appear to have been relatively stable.

Commercial and Social Organization
For most of southern Sierra Leone before the mid-fifteenth century, the gathering and production of food dominated local economies. Fishing supplied most of the protein that Sherbro and Mende communities consumed. Hunting was important, too. Where the environment allowed it, Africans raised poultry and goats – indeed the Gallinas derives its name from the Portuguese word for chicken – but the prevalence of the deadly tsetse fly limited the introduction of cattle into the heavily wooded lands south of Freetown. Communities produced agriculture beyond subsistence levels but hardly at large commercial scales, limiting the development of extensive regional trade networks.[14]

Rice was the staple crop throughout the Sherbro and Gallinas and their hinterlands. Although "wet" or paddy rice cultivation became prominent in the twentieth century, contemporary accounts suggest that before then, "dry" (rain-fed) varieties prevailed.[15] Maize and millet rounded out African diets but they were not nearly as desirable as rice. During periods of drought and famine, hungry communities resorted to eating palm cabbage, consuming the fronds of oil palms to stave off starvation. With the opening of Atlantic trade, Africans in southern Sierra Leone added cassava to their diets, which for many people, particularly those who were poor and enslaved, became their primary staple.[16] Communities mixed these starches with palm oil to create a stew or sauce that they seasoned with peppers and other spices obtained elsewhere along the coast.

Little is known of the social organization of southern Sierra Leone communities before the eighteenth century, but as elsewhere along the African littoral in the precolonial period, production was probably organized within households and according to gender and generational norms and hierarchies. Given the high ratio of land to labor, men, women, and children each proved invaluable in performing tasks related to the cultivation of food. In his early-sixteenth century account of Sierra Leone, for example, Valentim Fernandes noted, "the men have as many wives as they can. And the more wives they have the richer they are, for the women labour, sow and reap, and do all the work. And the men rest."[17] Fernandes's observation, however steeped in hyperbole, points to the well-known idea that African communities based their wealth on the number of dependents they controlled.[18] In addition to wives, powerful men sought to attract other followers, including immigrants, slaves (in Sherbro, *wono*; in Mende, *nduwe*), and individuals held in various states of coercion. Although the topic has been a contentious one, scholars generally agree that slavery did exist in most parts of Upper Guinea prior to the arrival of Europeans, though its significance in local economies was uneven and the institution did not resemble the chattel variety that dominated the Americas.[19]

Precolonial Mende and Sherbro societies were also arranged by complex and at times misunderstood political and social structures. Neither group was integrated into a single large centralized state. Moreover, as several scholars have noted, statements about descent and residency patterns in southern Sierra Leone seemed to simplify historical realities. Anthropologists, for example, have characterized Mende and Vai societies as patrilineal in descent and virilocal in residence. Sherbro societies, on the other hand, were contrasted as matrilineal. Yet such sweeping generalizations about lineage organization represent ideals and do not account for the complex dynamics of African social relations and should therefore be received with caution. As Adam Jones astutely observed, the very process of recording a 'family tree' creates a genealogical model which tends to distort reality, forcing it into a patrilineal or matrilineal mould. Mende and Vai people, like ethnographers, often invent labels to describe the roles of different individuals and social groups, without paying much attention to the variety of interchange which exists in practice or to the complex set of obligations owed by any individual.[20]

The fundamental unit of southern Sierra Leone society was the household (Mende, *mawe*). The sizes of households varied depending on leaders' wealth and other factors. They could be as small as one family that controlled a few dependent relatives or large enough to accommodate several generations of families and many extended kin. The eldest male resident generally wielded authority over the household, though as with generalizations about descent, this represented more of an ideal than a rule. Households (*mawesei*) were grouped together into larger compounds (*kuwui*), which included wider kin networks, all of whom theoretically claimed descent from the settlement's founders. An elder man or women, in combination with other "big men" and "big women," oversaw each compound's affairs, making decisions about land usage and other political and legal issues. Compounds could be further integrated to form towns, which consisted of larger settlements and the farms and villages they controlled. By the early-nineteenth century, large Mende and Sherbro towns could include as many as fifteen *kuwuisia* and three thousand inhabitants, though generally they were much smaller.[21]

The demands of rice production dictated the routines by which communities in southern Sierra Leone households lived. Individual households organized seasonal labor demands. The first phase of rice production began around December, when men selected farm sites. In recent times, farmers have preferred locations on which mature brush has already grown; given the historical abundance of land in the region, this was probably equally true centuries ago. Workers first "brushed" the fields, a dangerous and labor-intensive process that entailed felling large trees with axes and removing the remaining growth from the plot. Laborers left the remaining debris out to bake in the sun and eventually burned it, which increased the fertility of the soil. Just before the rains arrived, farmers planted the rice crop. Throughout the rainy season, members of the household were involved in weeding the crops and keeping birds away from the germinating grains. Harvesting rounded out the season; it began around September and lasted several months. Southern Sierra Leone's secondary crops overlapped with that of rice production. Communities planted maize along with rice but harvested it a month or two earlier. They left cassava – a far more durable crop – in the ground until hungry communities needed it.[22] As a whole, agricultural labor in southern Sierra Leone placed demands on local populations throughout the year, leaving a short break between the end of the rice harvest and the commencement of the brushing period.

The labor involved in the clearing and cultivation of southern Sierra Leone rice farms was distinctly gendered. At the risk of some simplification, men performed the most strenuous physical tasks while women maintained the farms on a day-to-day basis.[23] Demand for men's labor typically peaked during the heavy brushing period, when they worked together to cut and burn the land in preparation for planting. At times, the labor required for this task was greater than a single household could supply. Elder men in such cases might turn to the *Poro* – a secret society into which all men from Sierra Leone were initiated in coming-of-age ceremonies – to make claims on younger laborers and assist each other in the cutting of farms. Once men cleared the fields, women and children assumed control over the cultivation process. From the time the rains began until a month or two after they let up, women planted, weeded, harvested, processed, and, in the case of surpluses, marketed the rice crop. Children and elderly men and women rid the fields of birds.[24]

While local agricultural production dominated southern Sierra Leone's economy, its inhabitants were by no means isolated from Upper Guinea's wider commercial world before the mid-fifteenth century. The region as a whole formed part of two major trade networks that evolved centuries before Europeans arrived along the coast. One network connected coastal Sierra Leone to the hinterland of Western Sudan, driven by interior demand for salt and fish. The other moved goods between the north and the south, fueled by trade in kola nuts, which grew south of Freetown and were in high demand among merchants further north. Less is known about the salt trade in southern Sierra Leone than in the area north of Freetown, but the two regions obtained salt in similar ways. Africans collected salty seawater in shallow ponds during periods of high tide and left the water to evaporate in the hot sun. Once it evaporated, the seawater left a thin layer of crusted salt that hardened together with mud. Coastal salt producers subsequently strained the solution and left the salty water to dry in large containers. It is unlikely that salt manufactured in southern Sierra Leone was traded as far inland as that which originated in the Senegambia, yet the Kono/Vai migration story recounted above suggests that supplies of salt – or at the very least knowledge of areas where the mineral was produced – could reach a considerable distance beyond the coast.[25]

The kola trade, by contrast, was the engine that drove West African coastal commerce throughout much of the precolonial era. The Sierra Leone region as a whole was probably the most prominent supplier of kola during this period. The word kola itself is of Temne origin; inhabitants throughout West Africa adopted the word over time, revealing kola's enduring value. Collected from trees that grow as high as sixty-five feet, Africans prized kola nuts for their medicinal properties. The caffeine in the nut serves as a stimulant, helping to alleviate thirst and hunger – pressing concerns for merchants who traveled over long distances in search of economic opportunities. Kola also served social and cultural purposes. It played a central role in marriage ceremonies and other significant events. Between the Sierra Leone estuary and Cape Mount, merchants collected and shipped north toward Senegambia large supplies of kola. As early as the twelfth century, and surely well before then, significant quantities of kola were reaching the Sahel, just south of the Sahara Desert.[26] When Portuguese navigators arrived along the coast of Sierra Leone in the 1460s, they encountered a region on the fringes of most major commercial routes in West Africa. Even in the case of important commodities such as kola, the merchants who carried on this commerce were generally outsiders who entered the region to collect and transport goods to more distant lands. The growth of transatlantic trade in the centuries after European contact transformed this pattern, increasing southern Sierra Leone's significance in regional and international affairs and breathing new interest in the economic potential of the African littoral. Transatlantic trade also added value to indigenous commodities such as camwood and ivory, on which Africans came to place new value. Finally, the growth of commerce between Africans and Europeans had important social consequences. It opened new avenues for women and men to accumulate wealth and ultimately provided the foundation for the explosive growth of the Atlantic slave trade from the Upper Guinea Coast in the mid-eighteenth century.

Africans, Europeans, and the Growth of Atlantic Commerce

Southern Sierra Leone's integration into the commercial systems of the Atlantic World developed unevenly between the mid-fifteenth and nineteenth centuries. During this period, Europeans from at least four different nations actively engaged in the region's coastal commerce. Fierce rivalries ensured that no single state dominated the European end of the trade for too long. In the 1460s, Portuguese and Luso-African – the children born to African women whom Portuguese men fathered – merchants enjoyed a monopoly on trade throughout most of Africa. A century later they encountered stiff competition from Dutch, French, and English voyagers. The nature of coastal trading itself changed during this period. From a minor business that exploited Africa's preexisting commercial networks, trade between

Europeans and Africans eventually put heavy demands on new kinds of products, including in particular camwood. Slaves featured in trade between Africans and Europeans in this period but in general produce drove the commercial system in Sierra Leone.[27]

Sierra Leone was drawn into Atlantic trade as part of the expansion of Portuguese influence along the coast in the mid-fifteenth century. The Portuguese colonization of the Cape Verde Islands represented a major turning point in this history. Although Lisbon-based officials attempted to restrict non-sanctioned trade between Portuguese settlers in Cape Verde and Africans on the mainland, clandestine commerce was widespread by as early as the last quarter of the fifteenth century. Cotton fiber, tobacco, and *aguardente* – brandy made with sugar cane – were the lynchpins of the trade; the Portuguese exchanged them for woven cloths (*panos*). Over time, enslaved Africans were forcibly carried to and settled on the Cape Verde Islands, where they duplicated mainland production patterns, driving down the price of woven cloth. Salt, though unrecorded, was surely another major export to the continent.[28]

The intricacies of Cape Verde's trade with the mainland are clear from the few European written accounts that describe it. Summarizing what was known of the coastwise commerce in the early-seventeenth century, Dierick Ruiters, a Dutch merchant, explained that

> the trade we call 'coastal' is mostly undertaken, in small ships, pinnances and launches, by Portuguese who live on Santiago Island. First they load these with salt, which they conveniently obtain for nothing on the islands of Maio and Sal and they sail to Serra-Lioa with the salt and trade it for gold, ivory and kola. Then from Sierra-Lioa they sail again to Joala and Porto d'Ale [the Petit Côte], where they trade a portion of the kola for cotton cloths. They also sometimes trade ivory obtained in Serra-Lioa for Cape Verde cloths...from there they sail again east to Cacheo where they trade the rest of their kola and their remaining goods for slaves.[29]

As European manufactures began circulating in greater quantities they came to complement or in some cases replace salt in this coastal commerce.[30]

This trade network, which George E. Brooks has called the "Guinea of Cabo Verde" commercial system, continued to link the archipelago with parts of Upper Guinea over the sixteenth century but the extent to which it involved southern Sierra Leone is unclear. More than likely, the Sherbro and Gallinas represented the outer fringes of direct Portuguese and Luso-African influence. Direct trade with Sierra Leone seems to have been focused on the rivers north of the peninsula. The well-documented voyage of the caravel *Santiago*, for example, which departed from Lisbon in 1526, sailed only as far as the Kolente (Great Scarcies) River, where it spent three months loading rice, ivory, and slaves before it moved to Cacheu, further north.[31]

The picture that emerges of the early Atlantic trade with Sierra Leone is one of relative continuity with Upper Guinea's preexisting commercial systems. Cape Verdean and Portuguese merchants supplied many of the same commodities that already circulated within Africa and added only luxury items such as tobacco and alcohol. Kola was a central part of Upper Guinea trade both before and after the Portuguese colonized the archipelago. Atlantic trade probably increased the value of ivory and slaves, but supplies of those goods were limited and therefore trade in them probably had little impact on local societies.

From its weak foundation in the Cape Verde commercial nexus, southern Sierra Leone's role in Atlantic commerce evolved slowly over subsequent centuries. European merchants preferred traveling to more lucrative African trading regions further south and east and viewed Sierra Leone primarily as a stopping point for wood, water, and provisions. But even this limited role allowed Europeans to become more knowledgeable about southern Sierra Leone's commercial prospects and led to bursts of exchange. Whereas Portuguese traders identified the Gallinas as commercially insignificant in the early sixteenth century, dec-

41

ades later they engaged in petty trade there for ivory, pepper, and gold. Sherbro was even more heavily involved with Europeans at this time. Indeed, by the first quarter of the seventeenth century, the Sherbro coast was important enough to merit the establishment of Dutch trading posts on the Boom Kittam and in Cape Mount.[32]

It was only once the British commenced trading in southern Sierra Leone that the region began sustained exchanges with merchants of the Atlantic World. While British engagement with the Sierra Leone coast went back to the ravaging exploits of the Hawkins family in the mid-sixteenth century,[33] British merchants began their activity in earnest there nearly a century later. In 1618, the British founded the "Gynney and Binney" Company and followed that with the Company of Royal Adventurers Trading into Africa (1663) and the Royal African Company (1672).[34] Still more interested in gold and slaves, neither of which was available in large quantities in southern Sierra Leone, the chartered Companies nonetheless enabled the British to wrestle control of the limited Sierra Leone trade from European competitors. By the 1660s, British agents had established factories at York Island, in the Sherbro, and at Bunce Island, in the Sierra Leone estuary. From these settlements they operated an extensive coasting trade, employing nearly two-dozen small craft to collect produce for direct shipment to England.[35] Factors did at times purchase slaves, but in very small numbers.

British merchants traveling to southern Sierra Leone in the seventeenth century remained interested in camwood and to a lesser extent ivory. The latter commodity had long been a staple of Afro-European commerce. The Portuguese merchant Francisco de Lemos Coelho described a regular trade in ivory between Sierra Leone and Cape Verde operating as early as the 1550s. In his well-known account of West Africa from the late 1600s, Jean Barbot noted that Sierra Leone's ivory was "better than in any other place in Guinea" because of its exceptionally white color. While British merchants complained that their Portuguese rivals had spoiled the ivory trade around the Sierra Leone estuary, this was apparently less of a problem in the Sherbro, where Barbot claimed that more than four tons could be supplied in two month's time at a reasonable price.[36]

Camwood was the staple of British trade in southern Sierra Leone into the eighteenth century; it was far more valuable than ivory. A hard timber used to make red dye, Europeans prized camwood from Sherbro for its brightness and durability. In one of the more detailed statements about the quality of the dye it produced, Barbot commented that, "the Cam-wood is a much better sort of red wood for dyers use, than the Brazil, and accounted the best in all Guinea. It will serve seven times over, and the last time is still effectual."[37] Its value held the eye of foreign merchants. In the 1620s, Wood and Company, a London firm, held a European monopoly on the Sherbro trade, although they struggled to enforce it given that they lacked support from local rulers. The magnitude of this trade is unknown, but qualitative evidence suggests that Company merchants increased their supply over time. In 1648, one vessel was able to load just twenty-two and a half tons of camwood in the Sherbro. Six decades later, a Royal African Company agent supplied 78 tons to a single English merchant. Yet the shipment occurred just prior to a collapse in the Sherbro camwood trade: by 1718, the same factor obtained just twenty-two tons of camwood during an entire season and in the early 1720s, the supply of the timber was said to be "quite exhausted."[38]

What did African merchants and rulers obtain in exchange for this high-quality redwood? Whereas early trade with Cape Verde-based merchants was rooted in the supply of salt and cloth, the camwood trade was far more complex, demonstrating the evolution of Afro-European trade over two centuries. By the eighteenth century (and likely well before), Sherbro merchants had obtained a deep and sophisticated knowledge of European commodities. They easily distinguished chintz from silks and rum from brandy. Without access to the goods that were in highest demand, British factors were doomed to failure. Underscoring this point and illustrating African control over trade with Europeans, John Ball, a merchant on York Island, explained that "the best goods for trade are large brass kettles from 5-20, there's no trading without them. The Small kettles they have, only breed a Disturbance, the Natives threatening to throw them in our people's Faces."[39]

In addition to reflecting the growing sophistication of Afro-British commerce, the camwood trade also reveals the complex relationship between the southern Sierra Leone littoral and its hinterland, where the timber grew. Camwood was particularly abundant up the Boom River, which was navigable for mid-sized vessels up to the town of Baga, some sixty miles inland. Smaller sloops could travel as far as two hundred miles up the river, though few apparently did. The collection and internal shipment of the timber was closely tied to Sierra Leone's rainfall patterns. During the rainy season, strong downstream currents prevented merchants from traveling upstream. Merchants generally made the trip inland near the end of the dry season, between April and May, when the depth of the Boom was reduced in some areas to less than ten feet. During these months, camwood was noted to be plentiful and cheap. Once inland, Africans collected and shipped the wood downstream around the end of the rainy season, when higher water levels enabled canoes to quickly descend back down toward the coast.[40]

The seasonal pattern of the camwood trade fit neatly into the routines of agricultural production in southern Sierra Leone. Limited evidence suggests that African men were charged with cutting and shipping the timber. Men felled the trees in the dry season before they turned their attention to brushing rice farms. Once the wood arrived on the coast, male labor was also more readily available, since by then tasks associated with rice cultivation had passed to women and children. However, this simplified description was in reality probably far more complex; the tasks required for the production of wood and rice did at times clash. When they did, Africans unsurprisingly gave rice the higher priority. In 1726, an African headman on the Rokelle River accounted for the poor supply of camwood by explaining that his men were busy on their farms and that they would return to cutting wood after they prepared the fields.[41]

The impact of the camwood trade on southern Sierra Leone communities is difficult to assess. As a starting point it is worth noting that Africans controlled each step in the production process. John Clark, the York Island factor, noted that "country people" cut the wood, de-barked it, and brought it down to the Sherbro factory. Expansion of the industry thus placed new demands on local labor, including the men who prepared and transported the wood and the women, slaves, and children who supported the industry in other ways. During the height of the timber season, Africans established makeshift towns on the banks of the Boom River, where local inhabitants cooked and performed other vital tasks. The magnitude of the operation was significant: in a later reference to the explosive growth of Freetown's timber trade in the 1820s, one merchant suggested that as many as two thousand families were directly and indirectly involved in the trade along the banks of the Rokelle River.[42] Such evidence suggests that considerable numbers of people were involved in the Sherbro-based industry in the seventeenth and early-eighteenth centuries.

In the two and a half centuries after Portuguese voyagers arrived along the Upper Guinea coast, southern Sierra Leone's engagement with the Atlantic World thus underwent many transformations. From a region on the outskirts of the Portuguese/Cape Verde commercial nexus, the Sherbro and to a lesser extent the Gallinas were increasingly drawn into Britain's transatlantic trading sphere. The growth of the camwood trade secured British influence along the coast. Although Portuguese and Dutch mariners knew of the high quality of Sherbro camwood, English traders never faced any significant competition in that trade. While the Sherbro and Gallinas still played a comparatively marginal role in the broader evolution of Afro-European commerce in this era, the establishment of a sustained trade in agricultural commodities between Britain and Sierra Leone set a lasting foundation for the region's long-term involvement in British transatlantic trading, which would later include large numbers of slaves.

One essential element of this foundation was the emergence of a permanent British and (shortly thereafter) Anglo-African merchant community along the southern Sierra Leone littoral. The origins of this community dated back to the establishment of Royal African Company settlements on York Island and elsewhere along the coast. From these small factories, Company employees became entangled in the social, cultural, and political developments of the region. Many factors married African women, further integrating themselves into local affairs. The wives improved the men's status in a number of ways: they served as cultural intermediaries, providing valuable knowledge of local trade practices; and they had children who over time became dominant commercial middlemen, controlling trade between European captains and southern Sierra Leone merchants.[43]

Between the 1660s and the mid-eighteenth century, at least five different Anglo-African families emerged as powerful brokers of trade in southern Sierra Leone: the Caulkers, Clevelands, Tuckers, Rogers, and Cumberbusses. The Caulkers were the most powerful of these families. Their involvement in Africa originated with the arrival in 1684 in the Sherbro of Thomas Corker. At some point during that decade, Corker married a woman identified in documentary sources as Ya Kumba, the "Dutchess of Sherbro." The couple's sons, Stephen and Robin, carefully cultivated ties with British- and other Afro-Atlantic communities. Several Corkers were included on Company payrolls by the early eighteenth century. By the middle of the century the Caulkers claimed land and widespread political authority along the Sherbro littoral – an illustration of the relationship between commercial and political prestige.[44]

Other British factors exploited similar paths toward achieving local power and influence, although some were more successful than others. Zachary Rogers married a woman identified as "the great woman." Together, he and his wife built a powerful commercial enterprise in southern Sierra Leone. By 1714, the

Rogers family was actively trading in the Gallinas goods they received directly from Company officials in England. In the following decade, merchants complained that Rogers had monopolized the camwood trade between the Gallinas and Cape Mount. Rogers's children further strengthened the family's position by marrying into the powerful Massaquoi family, establishing a new political power base around the Gallinas.

The Afro-British social networks that these lineages created and sustained proved essential for Sierra Leone's involvement in the Atlantic slave trade in the eighteenth and nineteenth centuries. Although the Upper Guinea coast had always provided small numbers of slaves to passing European vessels, it was only in the middle decades of the 1700s that the region became a comparatively significant supplier of slaves. In that period, Sierra Leone began to export more than one thousand captives per year. With strong ties to the British Atlantic World and to the communities in the African interior, southern Sierra Leone's coastal brokers became central players in the region's transition to the slave trade.

The Atlantic Slave Trade from Southern Sierra Leone

The foreign slave trade from southern Sierra Leone developed as part of broader socio-cultural and economic transformations that reshaped the nineteenth-century Atlantic World. Indeed, the emergence of Sherbro and Gallinas as major slaving centers was in many ways a direct – if unintended – consequence of the abolition of the British slave trade in 1807 and, to a lesser degree, the establishment of Freetown in the Sierra Leone estuary. Even before these two related developments, southern Sierra Leone merchants played indirect roles in facilitating slave exports and maintained close ties to slave dealers in other Upper Guinea ports. An assessment of the southern Sierra Leone slave trade must therefore begin with a consideration of the broader evolution of the Atlantic economy and the expansion of slaving throughout Sierra Leone.

The transatlantic slave trade peaked in the second half of the eighteenth century in response to demands among slave owners in the Americas for coerced labor. During this period, plantation economies in North and South America and the Caribbean produced staple commodities – sugar, rice, indigo, tobacco, and coffee – in almost unimaginable quantities. Few Atlantic-facing settlements were untouched by the slave system that developed in response to spiking demands for these crops. In Africa, slave supplies in the mid-eighteenth century increased across nearly every coastal region. From the nearly three-quarters of a million Africans who were forced onto slave vessels during the last quarter of the seventeenth century, the trade in the next hundred years increased over each 25-year period, reaching its horrifying height in the last quarter of the eighteenth century, when more than two million Africans were stuffed into the holds of slave ships – a rate of more than eighty thousand captives embarked each year. Over the duration of the transatlantic slave trade, some twelve and a half million captives were forced onboard vessels bound for the Americas.[45]

Sierra Leone's share of this total was comparatively small. With the exception of the neighboring Windward Coast, Sierra Leone supplied fewer slaves than any other West African region and accounted for perhaps three percent of all Africans who ended up on slave ships.[46] Through the seventeenth century, the region was capable of filling perhaps one or two small vessels per year, amounting to no more than a few hundred captives per annum. As Table 1.1 shows, slave departures increased slightly in the first quarter of the eighteenth century and more than doubled over the subsequent two-and-a-half decades. A major increase began in the 1750s and 60s, when exports climbed to between three and five thousand slaves per year, where they remained for roughly a century, until the British targeted and ultimately suppressed the slave trade from Sierra Leone. During this period the Sierra Leone slave trade increased not only in raw volume but also in comparative significance. At its height in the 1790s, Sierra

Leone supplied more than six percent of all African captives embarked on transatlantic slavers.

Table 1.1: Slave Exports from Africa and Sierra Leone, 1625-1866 (Rounded to the Nearest Hundred and with Sierra Leone's Share of Total in Parenthesis)

Years	Slaves Embarked in Africa	Slaves Embarked in Sierra Leone
1501-1525	13,400	0
1526-1550	50,800	0
1551-1575	61,000	1,200 (2.0%)
1576-1600	152,400	200 (.1%)
1601-1625	352,800	0
1626-1650	315,000	1,400 (.4%)
1651-1675	488,100	900 (.2%)
1676-1700	719,700	4,600 (.6%)
1701-1725	1,088,900	6,600 (.6%)
1726-1750	1,471,700	16,600 (1.1%)
1751-1775	1,925,300	84,000 (4.4%)
1776-1800	2,008,700	94,700 (4.7%)
1801-1825	1,877,000	89,300 (4.8%)
1826-1850	1,771,000	84,400 (4.8%)
1851-1866	225,600	4,800 (2.1%)
Totals	12,521,400	388,700 (3.1%)

Source: Eltis et al., *Voyages*, http://slavevoyages.org/estimates/TrZaetOV

Prior to the significant increase in slave exports in the 1750s, foreign merchants stopped in Sierra Leone primarily to replenish themselves, its large harbor providing relief for captains and crews who had spent weeks at sea. Since well before the explosive growth of the sugar industry, voyagers in search of agricultural commodities exploited the region's natural resources, anchoring in the Sierra Leone estuary to restock supplies of wood and water. Slave ship captains continued this pattern: they generally stopped briefly in the estuary to refresh themselves before continuing on toward the larger slave markets further south along the coast. At times, captains of these "coasting" voyages did purchase slaves in Sierra Leone, but they tended to do so in very small numbers. Before the 1750s, the Sierra Leone coast as a whole lacked the facilities to bulk and store large numbers of captives – facilities that generally proved crucial for the supply of large numbers of African slaves.

The voyage of the North American sloop *Rhode Island* provides an illustration of Sierra Leone's role in the coasting trade of the eighteenth century. Departing from New York late in 1748, the *Rhode Island* arrived in the Sierra Leone estuary in January of the following year. Upon its arrival, Peter James, the vessel's captain, paid the "King Tom Custom for wood and water," a fee that local rulers collected prior to commencing trade, which James settled with thirteen gallons of rum. Over the next two months, the New-York based captain cruised slowly down the coast, purchasing just twenty-two slaves between the Sierra Leone River and Cape Mount – a rate of just one slave for every three days of travel. The sloop eventually continued on to Cape Coast Castle, along the Gold Coast, where it loaded seventy slaves in a single day, completing the vessel's total charge of 120 captives. Filled with human cargo, the small sloop departed the African coast and arrived back in New York in the summer of 1749.[47]

An analysis of the *Rhode Island*'s trade-book, in which the captain recorded his day-to-day transactions, underscores the difficulties of purchasing slaves in regions like Sierra Leone, where no single African polity dominated trade, population density was low, and commercial activity was limited. In the trade-book James lists multiple African slave dealers with whom he exchanged goods. Yet the merchants supplied just one or two captives at a time. For Europeans whose priority was speed – sailors wanted more than anything to depart the coast and avoid staying in unfamiliar and deadly disease environments – Sierra Leone proved less than ideal as a slave-trading site. In one case, for example, James recorded the purchase of two male slaves in exchange for eighty gallons of rum, one barrel of beef, one barrel of tar, an assortment of cheese and butter, and twenty "bars" of tobacco and sugar – an assortment valued at 121 bars in total.[48] At Kittam, in the Sherbro, James' transactions appear even more complex. For a single enslaved girl, James paid the following, worth slightly more than 55 bars: two trading guns, two muskets, powder, two kettles, one piece blue baft, three iron bars, one piece blue calico, three beads (unit of measurement unknown), one dozen knives, three brass pans, one bar of tobacco, three hundred flints, and three gallons of rum.[49] Captains such as James were surely frustrated by the complex assortment of commodities required for the purchase of slaves and the extremely localized demands that Africans made for European goods, particularly considering the limited returns.

However, in the decade after the *Rhode Island* sailed, Sierra Leone's participation in the Atlantic slave trade underwent a significant expansion. As Table 1.1 demonstrates, the region experienced a fivefold increase in its supply of slaves between the 1750s and 1770s. The factors that contributed to this change are complex; they include local, regional, and global developments. From an Atlantic perspective, for reasons not yet well understood, the 1750s witnessed a general increase in the time it took for vessels to load slaves in major areas of embarkation south and east of Upper Guinea. The slow-down glutted African markets with European voyagers in search of captives. This had important effects, particularly for merchants who launched slave voyages from more marginal American and European ports. Those merchants generally used smaller vessels and arrived along the African coast with more limited purchasing power. Unable to compete with larger and better-stocked rivals, they turned instead to Africa's smaller slaving ports, which included Sierra Leone. This shift accounts for the increase in trade between Sierra Leone and North America in the third quarter of the eighteenth century and the relatively small vessels that captains commonly sailed into Sierra Leone.[50]

While increased competition provides one explanation for Sierra Leone's growing slave export trade, innovations in coastal supply methods provide another. Without a more systematic way to deliver captives, the region would not have been able to meet the spiking demand for African slaves. Merchants from private British commercial firms responded to the new pressures on Sierra Leone's slave exports by establishing a number of factories along the littoral, enabling traders to hold captives in larger numbers as dealers awaited the arrival of slave vessels. North of the peninsula, for example, Miles Barber founded in 1754 a settlement on Factory Island, on the Iles de Los. Within decades, Barber's enterprise included two large barracoons, a wharf to facilitate loading and unloading goods, a warehouse, longboats for trading up the adjacent rivers, and facilities to repair vessels in need.[51] In the Sierra Leone estuary, the London firm Grant, Oswald and Company purchased Bunce Island, once a Royal African Company stronghold but which had been mostly dormant after a prominent African merchant attacked it in 1728. Over the second half of the eighteenth century the British company revitalized the fort, turning it into the most prominent port for slave embarkation in all of Sierra Leone during the time they operated it.[52]

Islands became a central feature of the Sierra Leone slave trade in this period. As Bruce Mouser notes, they were geographically well suited to exploit commercial opportunities along the coast. The Iles de Los and Bunce Island each offered convenient access to internal sources of slaves and had natural resources that gave inhabitants a degree of self-sufficiency for at least part of the year.[53] Islands also provided a geo-political advantage, keeping Europeans isolated from entanglements on the mainland. To maintain that isolation, merchants secured the islands with forts, which they armed with canons. Such precautions could not generally protect against a full-scale European naval assault, but they did offer effective protection against attacks from African leaders, with whom British merchants did not always keep cordial relations.

Not surprisingly, the factors living on these islands were products of the British Atlantic World. As Table 1.2 illustrates,

Britain dominated the Sierra Leone slave trade for as long as that nation was legally engaged in the trade. Although they faced periodic competition from French and North American vessels, British merchants transported more than double the combined total of slaves that their two primary competitors did up to 1807. Yet this national assessment conceals a more complex picture. Within the United Kingdom, local specialization led voyages from some British ports to visit Sierra Leone more frequently than those traveling from others. The Iles de Los, for example, attracted voyages from Liverpool between the 1770s and 1790s; London merchants dominated the trade to Bunce Island.[54]

Table 1.2: Slave Exports from Sierra Leone by National Carrier, 1751-1866 (Rounded to Nearest Hundred)

	Spain/ Uruguay	Portugal/ Brazil	Great Britain	Netherlands	U.S.A.	France	Denmark	Totals
1751-1760	0	0	12,000	300	2,200	2,900	0	17,400
1761-1770	0	0	30,300	0	3,000	8,400	600	42,300
1771-1780	0	0	33,100	300	900	2,200	0	36,600
1781-1790	0	100	16,000	0	3,200	10,900	1,200	31,400
1791-1800	0	0	27,800	200	20,400	2,800	0	51,100
1801-1810	300	300	17,300	0	23,200	0	1,500	42,600
1811-1820	16,400	400	0	200	1,000	4,600	0	22,600
1821-1830	14,400	800	0	500	900	27,000	0	43,500
1831-1840	39,900	3,900	0	0	0	100	0	43,900
1841-1850	9,500	11,500	0	0	0	0	0	21,000
1851-1866	4,800	0	0	0	0	0	0	4,800
Totals	85,300	17,000	136,500	1,500	54,800	58,900	3,300	357,200

Source: *Voyages, http://slavevoyages.org/estimates/rtg4McrB*

Merchants at these two slaving ports also maintained complex relationships with the African mainland. They established along the coast a series of small outfactories, or "subfactories," which the merchants used to collect slaves and produce in small quantities and carry them back to the larger facilities. Longboats and canoes provided the essential means of transportation and communication between the settlements; they allowed traders to expand their business activities throughout the Upper Guinea coast. From Factory Island, Barber's commercial network reached as far as Cape Mount, where he owned a floating factory. He also operated a land-based settlement at Gallinas and kept up regular commerce with the Sherbro. Though it is less-well documented, traders at Bunce Island also kept up a regular intercourse with merchants settled in nearby rivers. The island settlements also received visitors, attracting African traders who had goods to offer. Over the second half of the eighteenth century, the Atlantic slave trade thus increasingly integrated the Sierra Leone littoral. A dispersed network of outfactories enabled merchants to travel and trade between ports as far north as the Rio Pongo and as far south as Cape Mount.[55] African slave dealers along coastal Sierra Leone also maintained independent commercial relationships with each other, a point that transatlantic traders took advantage of when it served to expedite loading times for their vessels. While most British voyagers preferred to deal with factors at Bunce Island or the Iles de Los, several captains traded directly with African and Afro-European merchants. In November of 1787, the British ship *Crescent* arrived in Sierra Leone after a month's passage from Bristol. William Roper, the vessel's captain, contracted with William Cleveland on the Banana Islands, delivering to Cleveland a mixed assortment of goods in exchange for a cargo of captives. Roper spent several months off the Banana Islands, in southern Sierra Leone, before he traveled up to the Iles de Los, where he purchased slaves and other goods from Mr. Bolland. He then sailed into the Rios Pongo and Nunez, where he met with a number of additional merchants. While in the Pongo, Roper continued to receive slaves that William Cleveland sent via canoe from the Banana Islands. At times, Cleveland's agent even delivered goods on Bolland's account, which suggests that these two men maintained an active working relationship. Their cooperation enabled Roper to load 268 slaves over a span of about four months.[56]

The eighteenth-century slave trade from Sierra Leone thus involved a complex network of peoples and ports. It linked coastal merchants north and south of the Sierra Leone peninsula and attracted slave dealers from the hinterland. Sherbro and Gallinas formed one part of this commercial nexus. The region was closely integrated with Bunce Island and the Iles de Los through its ability to supply produce and small numbers of captives. This north-south system was thoroughly Anglo-centric in its commercial orientation: vessels flying British and North American flags purchased slaves from British and Anglo-African dealers and shipped them to colonies in the British Americas.

In the late-eighteenth and early-nineteenth centuries, the British campaign to end the slave trade radically transformed the traffic in Sierra Leone. The success of the movement to end British participation in the slave trade, which led in 1807 to the passage of the Slave Trade Act, removed from the trade the nation that most actively engaged in slaving along the coast of Sierra Leone. Over subsequent decades, the British Government widened the scope of its campaign against the traffic. It signed treaties with rival European powers to limit the scope and scale of the transatlantic trade. To enforce its efforts, Britain dispatched naval vessels to West Africa, which patrolled the coast in search of slave vessels that were operating in breech of the treaties. Although the Atlantic slave trade continued on for some six decades after the Slave Trade Act, Britain's anti-slavery initiatives radically changed its organization and operation.

Sierra Leone was more directly affected by Britain's campaign to suppress the slave trade than any other region in Africa. Even before the passage of the Slave Trade Act, antislavery activity was heavily concentrated there. In the late-eighteenth century, Granville Sharp and other wealthy British humanitarians financed the founding of what ultimately became Freetown, an abolition-inspired settlement located on the south bank of the Sierra Leone estuary. The settlement was constantly short of funding. Recognizing its potential as a site from which to expand its abolition activity, the British government decided in 1808 to assume formal control over Freetown, making it Britain's first West African colony and one of the first colonial establishments in all of Africa.[57] Its significance was further enhanced over subsequent decades when the British used the colony as their primary base from which to confront the ongoing illicit traffic in African captives: in 1819, Freetown became the host of a Court of Mixed Commission, which was responsible for trying cases of vessels that naval officers had seized for operating illegally. The courts processed hundreds of cases and condemned many vessels. Often, condemned vessels had enslaved Africans onboard, whom the British resettled in Freetown. Over more than three decades, Freetown thus absorbed tens of thousands of Liberated Africans whom the antislavery squadron removed from the holds of transatlantic vessels.[58]

The combined pressures of Freetown's antislavery influence and Britain's naval campaign to suppress the transatlantic traffic had drastic effects on the organization of the Sierra Leone slave trade in the nineteenth century. The bulking centers that for a century had provided relatively safe sites from which to organize slave trading became major liabilities after 1807. The fortifications proved no match for heavily armed British cruisers. In the years following legislation against the British slave trade, Bunce Island and the Iles de Los were thus effectively shut down as slaving ports.[59] Given the dominance of British vessels in the Sierra Leone traffic, the abolition of that nation's slave trade stripped the region's slave dealers of their most frequent customers, even if British merchants and capital continued to circulate throughout Upper Guinea.[60] Slave dealers in the era of abolition thus confronted an Atlantic World in flux. On the African coast they were forced to adopt new and more clandestine approaches to the organization of the slave trade; in the Americas, the abolition campaign required Sierra Leone to forge new commercial relationships with traders and places outside of the Anglo-Atlantic World.[61]

Under these circumstances, southern Sierra Leone became a much more suitable place for the direct embarkation of captives.

The region's swampy creeks, shifting sandbars, and inland waterways made it relatively easy for merchants operating there to conceal captives from British naval cruisers.[62] Beginning in the 1810s, the center of gravity of the Sierra Leone trade thus moved from open offshore islands to inland creeks, which created new opportunities for Sherbro and Gallinas merchants to engage in the transatlantic traffic. Estimates of slave exports from Sierra Leone in the nineteenth century indicate that the security that shallow waterways in southern Sierra Leone provided against British naval cruisers made up for any disruption caused by this reorientation. While for a century beginning in the 1750s the volume of the Sierra Leone slave trade remained stable, Table 1.3 illustrates that southern Sierra Leone was central to maintaining the high volume of exports in the era of abolition. Up to 1810, southern Sierra Leone ports provided just a few hundred captives per year directly to foreign vessels. In the subsequent decade, the region's slave trade doubled. Exports reached their highpoint in the 1820s, when an estimated 3,600 captives per year were forced onto slavers anchored in southern Sierra Leone – a level the region nearly maintained in the following decade. The 1840s saw the southern Sierra Leone slave trade began its decline: exports dropped by nearly two-thirds over that decade. By the 1850s, the region was no longer a major player in the transatlantic slave trade.

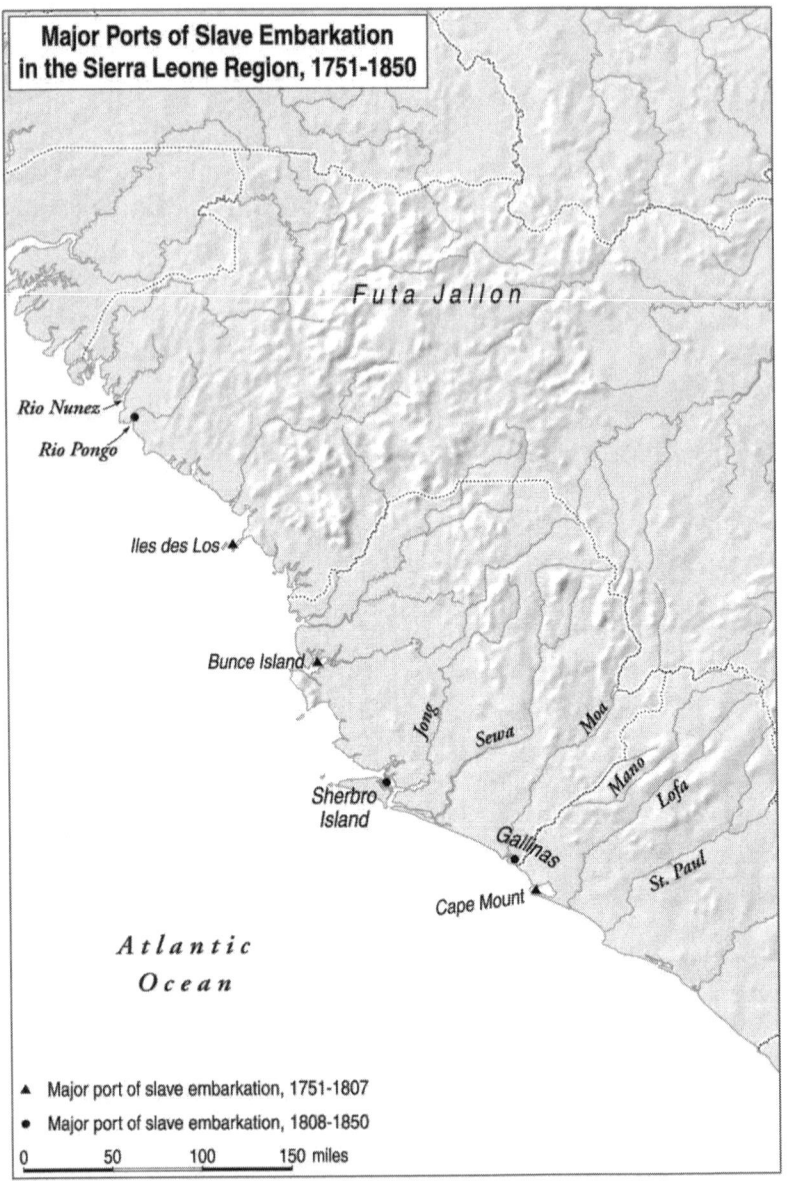

Major Ports of Slave Embarkation in the Sierra Leone Region, 1751-1850

Futa Jallon

Rio Nunez

Rio Pongo

Iles des Los

Bunce Island

Jong

Sewa

Moa

Mano

Lofa

Sherbro Island

Gallinas

St. Paul

Cape Mount

Atlantic Ocean

▲ Major port of slave embarkation, 1751-1807

● Major port of slave embarkation, 1808-1850

0   50   100   150 miles

Map 1.2, Major Ports of Slave Embarkation in the Sierra Leone Region, 1751-1850

The expansion of the southern Sierra Leone slave trade coincided with a significant restructuring of relationships between African slave ports and American slave societies. British abolition effectively shut down the traffic to British colonies in the Americas, leaving Brazil and Cuba to dominate the American end of the traffic. The trade to Brazil in the era of abolition was organized through the South Atlantic System: captains sailed vessels from Brazil to West Central Africa, loaded them with enslaved Africans, and returned directly to Brazil, where they disembarked the captives.[63] Cuba, on the other hand, became the destination for the vast majority of captives who were embarked at Gallinas and Sherbro. Roughly seven out of every ten captives taken from southern Sierra Leone ended up in Cuba.[64] This picture shifted slightly in the mid-1840s, when Cuban slave merchants faced legitimate competition from their Brazilian counterparts, but nevertheless Cuba continued to import more enslaved Africans from southern Sierra Leone throughout the period.

Table 1.3, Slave Exports from Southern Sierra Leone, 1750-1866 (Rounded to Nearest Hundred)

Years	Estimated Departures
1751-1760	3,100
1761-1770	3,700
1771-1780	1,900
1781-1790	1,100
1791-1800	2,500
1801-1810	3,600
1811-1820	9,700
1821-1830	37,000
1831-1840	36,100
1841-1850	13,900
1851-1866	4,800
Total	117,400

Source: David Eltis et al., *Voyages: The Trans-Atlantic Slave Trade Database*[65]

Additional evidence points to the growing influence of Cuban merchants in the southern Sierra Leone trade. Around 1820, British naval officers began documenting a shift in the origins of slave dealers operating in Sherbro and Gallinas. Whereas previous merchants had come from Britain or the United States, a small diaspora of Cuban-based traders came to control the southern Sierra Leone trade into the mid-1840s. According to Adam Jones, the Spanish had "a greater impact on Galinhas society than any other non-African nation." Even those dealers not originally from Cuba were deeply tied to Havana commercial firms. In the later half of the 1840s, a small infusion of Brazilian traders complicated this picture, but an aggressive British blockade ultimately forced both Cuban and Brazilian merchants to flee from the region.[66]

Pedro Blanco was the most notorious of the many slave dealers who spent time in the Gallinas. After visiting the area on a slaver several times in the early 1820s, Blanco settled there in 1828 as an agent of a Havana commercial firm. In the following decade, Blanco expanded his enterprise, employing his own agent at Cape Mount and also eventually at Sherbro, giving him a reach that extended far along the Upper Guinea Coast. Blanco was deeply entrenched in Cuban commercial affairs. He formed a partnership, "Blanco and Carballo," with a commercial house in Havana that had contacts throughout the Atlantic World. He also worked with the notorious House of Martinez, among the most noteworthy of the firms entangled in the slave business, which had an almost global reach. Blanco's wealth was such that merchants accepted his bills "with as much facility as a bill upon the Lords of the Treasury." By the time he departed from the Gallinas in the late-1830s, he had amassed a fortune estimated at nearly a million dollars – doubtless an exaggeration but one that reveals how merchants perceived him. Blanco's success, however, did not last; his once-booming firm went bankrupt in 1848.[67]

Blanco established himself as a dominant presence in the slave trade from southern Sierra Leone in the 1820s and 30s. In the Gallinas, he carved out a large commercial complex along the coast that included his own house, commercial facilities to conduct trade and stock supplies in bulk, and barracoons to hold more than a thousand captives. Lomboko, as the complex became known, looms large in the historical literature and representation of the slave trade. It was the site in 1839 through which the famous *Amistad* captives passed prior to being embarked on the mysterious transatlantic slaver, the *Teçora*, and forced across the Atlantic Ocean to Cuba. As a result, we know more about it than most other nineteenth-century slaving establishments in Africa. Unlike it appears in the famous Stephen Spielberg film, however, where a large castle - what viewers must assume represented Lomboko – is brought down by an onslaught of direct cannon-fire from naval vessels engaged in the suppression campaign, the Lomboko complex was built in a more traditional African style, its buildings made primarily of local materials and not intended for permanent occupation. Given the looming presence of British antislavery patrols and their willingness to launch direct attacks on slaving factories, this approach made good sense. Slave dealers such as Blanco understood that British officers were breathing down their necks and organized their commercial activities accordingly. It is for this reason that there are few extant remains of Blanco's activities – or Lomboko's factories – today.

Virtually every aspect of the organization of the slave trade from Lomboko emphasized deception, secrecy, and speed. In addition to concealing his operations in dense mangrove swamps, Blanco employed an army of Africans who kept lookout for slave vessels in search of captives and British patrols aiming to disrupt the traffic. African employees perched themselves high up on the area's imposing cotton trees, from which they gained sweeping views of the horizon. They developed signals to communicate with passing vessels: a bonfire to alert slavers to the presence of the patrols; a single light to indicate that the coast was clear. Operating at night became a priority. Once a slave vessel snuck into the Gallinas, swarms of canoes circulated between it and Blanco's factories, loading human and non-human commodities with seemingly equal ease. So perfected had their routine become that Blanco was thought capable of loading a full cargo of slaves in just a few hours. Such were the requirements of the slave trade in the era of abolition.[68]

Through men such as Blanco, the Cuban merchant community in southern Sierra Leone brought with it new assortments of foreign goods, which they distributed throughout the region in exchange for African captives. Doubloons – gold coins minted in Spain or the Spanish Americas – began to circulate, for example. More important to Africans was the variety of Cuban tobacco, generally rolled in cigars, spirits, and other luxury goods that abounded. Federico Alvarez, a Havana-based merchant who supplied those commodities, was an important part of the operation. Alvarez maintained close relationships with Blanco and Carballo; he regularly shipped goods to their agents in Africa. The traders' ties were exposed when in 1839 a British naval officer seized the schooner *Amalia*, which had been illegally engaged in slave trading, and which Alvarez had helped stock prior to its departure from Havana the previous year. Court proceedings against the vessel revealed the partnership between Alvarez and Blanco and Carballo.[69]

Under the direction of Spanish merchants and with the backing of Havana firms, the transatlantic slave trade from southern Sierra Leone continued into to the early 1850s. Early in that decade, British naval officers finally succeeded in ending the traffic from Sherbro and Gallinas. That it took more than four decades to do so reveals just how profitable the trade continued to be, even in the face of active Royal Navy pressure to suppress it. Indeed, given the ports' proximity to Freetown, Sherbro and Gallinas were probably the most heavily policed points of slave embarkation in the nineteenth century. Yet it took British patrollers three separate blockades and a number of direct assaults on the region's slave factories to dislodge slave dealers from their settlements.[70]

Conclusion

In the four centuries that followed the arrival of Europeans along the Upper Guinea Coast, southern Sierra Leone evolved from a relative commercial backwater to the largest center for slave embarkation west of the Bight of Benin. Perhaps ironically, that shift was a consequence of Britain's nineteenth-century campaign to suppress the transatlantic slave trade. Prior to the Slave Trade Act in 1807, merchants in the Sherbro and Gallinas supplied considerably more produce than they did African captives. In short, and with another hint of irony, Africans in southern Sierra Leone offered precisely what abolition-minded colonists later argued would save the continent from the scourge of slavery. Yet, as historians have come to realize in most parts of Africa, the supply of agricultural commodities such as camwood and ivory in no way prohibited the use and trade of slaves. Between the 1620s and the 1750s, Sierra Leone as a whole supplied both human and non-human goods, though the latter were always more important.

For the Gallinas and Sherbro, the decisive turn toward the slave trade began in the 1810s and 20s, when Cuban merchants began using the region's inhospitable environment to avoid detection from British cruisers. As a result, the southern Sierra Leone littoral was directly drawn into the Atlantic slave traffic, supplying thousands of men, women, and children each year to primarily Cuban sugar plantations. This development represented a commercial transition as well as a socio-cultural one. Over four decades, the region witnessed an infusion of Cuban people and goods as part of its violent integration into the Atlantic World.

Notes

1   On Medieval West Africa, see, most recently, Michael A. Gomez, *African Dominion: A New History of Empire in Early and Medieval West Africa* (Princeton: Princeton University Press, 2018).
2   Brooks, *Landlords and Strangers*, 21.
3   All studies on regions within Upper Guinea emphasize the significance of rivers but see in particular, Rodney, *A History*, 2. Not all of the rivers

were equally useful for transporting people and goods, but most were navigable by canoe for meaningful distances.

4   Following Davidson, I am using the Sherbro names for these rivers. The Mende names follow in parentheses. John Davidson, "Trade and Politics in the Sherbro Hinterland, 1849-1890," (PhD diss, University of Wisconsin, 1969), 2.

5   Jones, *From Slaves to Palm Kernels*, 4-5.

6   Rodney, *A History*, 4-5; C. Wondji, "The States and Cultures of the Upper Guinea Coast," in *General History of Africa: Africa from the Sixteenth Century to the Eighteenth Century*, ed. B.A. Ogot (London: Heinemann Press, 1992), 368-98. In his study on Senegambia, Boubcar Barry also describes the West African coast as a site of population dislocation in the period before and shortly after European contact. See Barry, *Senegambia*.

7   Upper Guinea received considerable attention from linguists in the 1960s. Joseph H. Greenberg, *The Languages of Africa*, 2nd ed. (Bloomington: Indiana University Press, 1966), first proposed the division between West Atlantic and Mande. See also David Dalby, "The Mel Languages: A Reclassification of Southern 'West-Atlantic,'" *African Language Studies* 6 (1965): 17; and Yves Person, "Ethnic Movements and Acculturation in Upper Guinea since the Fifteenth Century," *African Historical Studies* 4, no. 3 (1971): 669-89. For a more recent survey, see Arthur Abraham, *An Introduction to the Pre-Colonial History of the Mende of Sierra Leone* (Lewiston: Edwin Mellen Press, 2003), ch. 1.

8   Rodney, *A History*, 9-11; Brooks, *Landlords and Strangers*, 29-33. On Yalunka, see C. Magbaily Fyle, *The Solima Yalunka Kingdom: Pre-Colonial Politics, Economics and Society* (Freetown: Nyakon Publishers, 1979). On Temne history, see Kenneth C. Wylie, *The Political Kingdoms of the Temne: Temne Government in Sierra Leone, 1825-1910* (New York: Africana Pub. Co., 1977); and Bangura, *The Temne*.

9   Rodney, *A History*, 14. The high degree of intelligibility between Kono and Vai languages makes it likely that these groups did indeed migrate together. In the Vai language, the term Kono means "wait here," or "stay here," which gives some support to the broader migration story above, though it makes Vai individuals the primary actors in configuring Upper Guinea's ethnolinguistic patterns rather than Kono speakers. Personal communication with Konrad Tuchscherer, January 27, 2009.

10 P.E.H. Hair, "Ethnolinguistic Continuity on the Guinea Coast," *Journal of African History* 8 (1967): 247-68.

11 Walter Rodney, "A Reconsideration of the Mane Invasions of Sierra Leone," *Journal of African History* 8, no. 2 (1967): 219-46, provides one of the first careful assessments of the Mani Invasions. The most recent work on the topic is Abraham's *An Introduction*, 18-20; and David Dwyer, "The Mende Problem," in *Studies in African Comparative Linguistics with Special Focus on Bantu and Mande*, ed. Koen Bostoen and Jackmy Maniacky (Ter-

vuren: Royal Museum for Central Africa, 2005), 29-42. On the Vai, see Adam Jones, "Who were the Vai?," *Journal of African History* 22, no. 2 (1981): 159-78; and ibid, "The Kquoja Kingdom: A Forest State in Seventeenth Century West Africa," *Paideuma* 29 (1983): 23-43. Jones's research draws on Dapper's "Kquoja Account." See Olfert Dapper, *Naukeurige Beschrijvinge der Afrikaensche Gewesten* (Amsterdam: J. van Meurs, 1668). For a fascinating biography of Fatima Massaquoi, a prominent Vai princess born in early twentieth century, see Vivian Seton, Konrad Tuchscherer, and Arthur Abraham, eds., *The Autobiography of an African Princess: Fatima Massaquoi* (New York: Palgrave Macmillan, 2013).

12 Jones, *From Slaves to Palm Kernels*, 18-19.

13 P.E.H. Hair, "An Ethnolinguistic Inventory of the Lower Guinea Coast before 1700: Part I," *African Language Review* 7 (1968): 56. For the "fusion" argument, see Rodney, "A Reconsideration," 236-237; Person, "Ethnic Movements," 685. The division between these two camps comes from Abraham, *An Introduction*, 22-25.

14 Jones, *From Slaves to Palm Kernels*, 19-20.

15 T.J. Alldridge, one of two Traveling Commissioners in Sierra Leone who had extensive knowledge of the Sherbro region, suggested that Africans in southern Sierra Leone began to cultivate wet rice only in the late-nineteenth century and with help from American missionaries. See T.J. Alldridge, *A Transformed Colony: Sierra Leone as It Was and as It Is; Its Progress, Peoples, Native Customs and Undeveloped Wealth* (London: Seeley & Co., 1910), 347. This was apparently not the case further north in the Scarcies, where wet rice was cultivated from the mid-nineteenth century. See G.M. Roddan, "Cultivation of Swamp Rice in Sierra Leone," *Tropical Agriculture* 19 (1942): 84-86. In her book on rice farming in the region north of Freetown, Edda L. Fields-Black warns that a lack of documentation of wet-rice cultivation in European sources does not necessarily imply its absence – a point with which I concur. However, in the absence of more detailed linguistic research in the Sherbro region, I have leaned on accounts of contemporary observers. See Edda L. Fields-Black, *Deep Roots: Rice Farmers in West Africa and the African Diaspora* (Bloomington: Indiana University Press, 2008).

16 Davidson, "Trade and Politics," 18. On the consumption of palm cabbage, see George Thompson, *An Account of the Missionary Labors, Sufferings, Travels, and Observations, of George Thompson, in Western Africa, At the Mendi Mission* (Cleveland: D. Ide, 1852), 57. Alfred W. Crosby, *The Columbian Exchange: Biological and Cultural Consequences of 1492* (Westport: Greenwood Publication Co., 1972), sketches the broader context of cassava's establishment in Africa.

17 Th. Monod, A. Teixeira da Mota et. R. Mauny, eds., *Description de la Côte Occidentale d'Afrique (Sénégal du Cap de Monte, Archipels)* (Bissau, 1951), re-

printed in English in Christopher Fyfe, *Sierra Leone Inheritance* (London: Oxford University Press, 1964), 28.

18   Anthropologists and historians have long applied this "wealth-in-people" model to African societies. For an overview, with critical insights, see Jane I. Guyer and Samuel M. Eno Belinga, "Wealth in People as Wealth in Knowledge: Accumulation and Composition in Equatorial Africa," *Journal of African History* 36, no. 1 (1995): 91-120.

19   Walter Rodney's well-known article, "African Slavery," which argued against the existence of slavery in Africa before the growth of the Atlantic slave trade, focused on Upper Guinea. He later modified his stance in "The Guinea Coast," in *Cambridge History of Africa*, vol. 4, ed. Richard Gray (Cambridge: Cambridge University Press, 1975-1985), 223-324. Many scholars have since argued for the existence of slavery in the region. Examples for the Mende, Sherbro, and Vai include Jones, *From Slaves to Palm Kernels*, 19; Carol P. MacCormack, "Slaves, Slave Owners, and Slave Dealers: Sherbro Coast and Hinterland," in *Women and Slavery in Africa*, ed. Claire C. Robertson and Martin A. Klein (Portsmouth: Heinemann, 1997), 271-94; Svend E. Holsoe, "Slavery and Economic Response among the Vai (Liberia and Sierra Leone)," in *Slavery in Africa: Historical and Anthropological Perspectives*, ed. Suzanne Miers and Igor Kopytoff (Madison: University of Wisconsin Press, 1970), 287-303. For slavery in precolonial Africa more generally, see the introduction to Miers and Kopytoff, *Slavery in Africa*; Claude Meillassoux, *The Anthropology of Slavery: The Womb of Iron and Gold* (Chicago: University of Chicago Press, 1991); Lovejoy, *Transformations*; and Sean Stilwell, *Slavery and Slaving in African History* (New York: Cambridge University Press, 2014).

20   Jones, *From Slaves to Palm Kernels*, 11. The standard work on Sherbro ethnography is H.U. Hall, *The Sherbro of Sierra Leone* (Philadelphia: The University Press, University of Pennsylvania, 1938). Lynda R. Day, "Historical Patterns in a Stateless Society: Sherbro Land, 1750-1898" (MA thesis, University of Wisconsin, 1980), emphasizes the matrilineal nature of Sherbro society. For Mende ethnography, see Kenneth Little, *The Mende of Sierra Leone: A West African People in Transition* (London: Routledge & Kegan Paul Limited, 1951); and Sylvia Ardyn Boone, *Radiance from the Waters: Ideals of Feminine Beauty in Mende Art* (New Haven: Yale University Press, 1990). For the Vai, see Svend E. Holsoe, "The Cassava-Leaf People: An Ethnohistorical Study of the Vai People, with Particular Emphasis on the Tewo Chiefdom" (PhD diss, Boston University, 1967).

21   Little, *The Mende*, 96-98; Davidson, "Trade and Politics," 8-9.

22   Kenneth Little, "The Mende Farming Household," *The Sociological Review* 40, no. 4 (1948): 37-56. For Sherbro, see Davidson, "Trade and Politics," 18-20.

23 Carol MacCormack, "Control of Land, Labor and Capital in Rural Southern Sierra Leone," in *Women and Work in Africa*, ed. Edna G. Bay (Boulder: Westview Press, 1982), 35-53.

24 Davidson, "Trade and Politics,"19-20; Little, *The Mende*, 80-82, discusses the labor involved in rice production and describes several institutional arrangements through which households obtained additional labor. See also Jones, *From Slaves to Palm Kernels*, 165-69; Kenneth Little, "The Political Function of the Poro: Part I," *Africa: Journal of the International African Institute* 35, no. 4 (1965): 349-65; and ibid, "The Political Function of the Poro: Part II," *Africa: Journal of the International African Institute* 36, no. 1 (1966): 62-72.

25 Rodney, *A History*, 18-20.

26 Brooks, *Landlords and Strangers*, 53-54. Ibid, *Kola Trade and State Building: Upper Guinea Coast and Senegambia, 15th – 17th Centuries* (Brookline: African Studies Center, Boston University, 1980). More broadly, see Paul E. Lovejoy, *Caravans of Kola: The Hausa Kola Trade, 1700-1900* (Zaria: Ahmadu Bello University Press Ltd., 1980).

27 For estimates of the early West African slave trade, see António de Almeida Mendes, "The Foundations of the System: A Reassessment of the Slave Trade to the Spanish Americas in the Sixteenth and Seventeenth Centuries," in Eltis and Richardson, *Extending the Frontiers*, 63-94; Borucki, Eltis, and Wheat, "Atlantic History"; and David Wheat, *Atlantic Africa and the Spanish Caribbean, 1570-1640* (Chapel Hill: Published by the Omohundro Institute of Early American History and Culture and the University of North Carolina Press, 2016).

28 Brooks, *Landlords and Strangers*, 146-47. Rodney, *A History*, ch. 3. See also Trevor P. Hall, "The Role of Cape Verde Islanders in Organizing and Operating Maritime Trade between West Africa and Iberian Territories, 1441-1616" (PhD diss., Johns Hopkins University, 1992). For the broader transatlantic context of Portuguese expansion, see Philip D. Curtin, *The Rise and Fall of the Plantation Complex: Essays in Atlantic History* (Cambridge: Cambridge University Press, 1990).

29 Quoted in Brooks, *Landlords and Strangers*, 157. Almost two decades earlier, Father Balthasar Barreira suggested that cotton textiles, rather than salt, were at the center of Cape Verde's trade with Sierra Leone. P.E.H. Hair, "Sources on Early Sierra Leone: (9) Barreira's' 'Account of the Coast of Guinea,' 1606," *Africana Research Bulletin* 7, no. 1 (1976): 54-55.

30 In Pereira's well-known *Esmeraldo de Situ Orbis*, for example, which was written around 1505, the author commented that gold was available in exchange for "brass bracelets and basins of the size barbers use, linen, red cloth, bloodstones, cotton cloths and other articles." Quoted in Fyfe, *Sierra Leone Inheritance*, 42.

31 Brooks, *Landlords and Strangers*, 154-55.

32 The comparative insignificance of Sierra Leone is underscored in early records of the Atlantic slave trade, which document a far greater interest among Europeans for exchange in other regions. In addition to estimates in Eltis et al., *Voyages*, see, Adam Jones, ed., *German Sources for West African History, 1599-1669* (Wiesbaden: F. Steiner, 1983); ibid, *Brandenburg Sources for West African History, 1680-1700* (Stuttgart: F. Steiner Verlag Wiesbaden, 1985); and the accounts of William Schouten and Nicolas Villault, reproduced in Fyfe, *Sierra Leone Inheritance*, 54-56.

33 Reproduced in volume one of Kenneth Morgan, ed., *The British Transatlantic Slave Trade*, 4 vols. (London: Pickering & Chatto, 2003).

34 Hilary Jenkinson, "The Records of the English African Companies," *Transactions of the Royal Historical Society* 6 (1912): 185-220.

35 K.G. Davies, *The Royal African Company* (London: Green and Co., 1957), 214-21; Davidson, "Trade and Politics," ch. 3. William A. Pettigrew, *Freedom's Debt: The Royal African Company and the Politics of the Atlantic Slave Trade, 1672-1752* (Chapel Hill: University of North Carolina Press, 2013), provides an updated assessment of the Royal African Company. The British had an agent in the Gallinas in the 1680s, though trade there was of significantly less quantity and value than in Sherbro. See Jones, *From Slaves to Palm Kernels*, 20-22.

36 P.E.H. Hair, Adam Jones, and Robin Law, eds., *Barbot on Guinea: The Writings of Jean Barbot on West Africa, 1678-1712* (London: The Hakluyt Society, 1992), 220. For one of the few extant historical images of a camwood tree, see T.J. Alldridge, *The Sherbro and its Hinterland* (London: Macmillan and Co., Limited, 1901), plate facing p. 75.

37 Jean Barbot, *A Description of the Coasts of North and South Guinea* (London: Henry Lintot and John Osborn, 1746), 106.

38 On Wood and Company, see Fyfe, *Sierra Leone Inheritance*, 59-62. See also, TNA, T70/5, October 24, 1709; TNA, T70/7, April 13, 1721; and Hair et al., *Barbot on Guinea*, 237, where Barbot states that a vessel might obtain fifty tons of camwood over a two-month period.

39 TNA, T70/6, October 17, 1715.

40 TNA, T70/7, July 29, 1723; Rodney, *A History*, 159-61; Hair et al., *Barbot on Guinea*, 236.

41 Rodney, *A History*, 160.

42 TNA, T70/5, August 22, 1706; Rodney, *A History*, 160; *British Parliamentary Papers* (hereafter BPP), *Slave Trade*, vol. 9 (Shannon: Irish University Press, 1968), 6. Although the scope of the early camwood trade was smaller, the figure cited above is nonetheless striking and suggests that a significant number of Africans helped develop the timber trade.

43 Scholars of Upper Guinea have carefully documented the role of African women in the development of trade between Europeans and Africans. See Brooks, *Landlords and Strangers*; ibid, *Eurafricans in Western Africa*; Davidson, "Trade and Politics," ch. 3; Rodney, *A History*, ch. 8; Lynda R.

Day, "Afro-British Integration on the Sherbro Coast: 1665-1795," *Africana Research Bulletin* 12, no. 3 (1983): 82-107; chapters by Carol P. Mac-Cormack, George E. Brooks, and Bruce L. Mouser, in *Women and Slavery in Africa*, ed. Claire C. Robertson and Martin A. Klein (Portsmouth, NH: Heinemann, 1997); and Hilary Jones, *The Métis of Senegal: Urban Life and Politics in French West Africa* (Bloomington: Indiana University Press, 2013).

44   This paragraph and the one that follows is based on Davidson, "Trade and Politics," 60-61.

45   Slave export estimates are based on the estimates page in Eltis et al., *Voyages*, http://slavevoyages.org/assessment/estimates. Although the growth of each of these tropical commodities contributed to explosive increases in slave exports, from an Atlantic-wide perspective, the sugar industry was certainly the most important driver of the system. Scholars have estimated that some eighty or more percent of slaves who crossed the Atlantic did so to support sugar production. See the introduction to David Eltis, Frank D. Lewis, and Kenneth L. Sokoloff, eds., *Slavery in the Development of the Americas* (New York: Cambridge University Press, 2004). On the centrality of sugar and its relationship to slave mortality, see Richardson, "Consuming Goods." Despite sugar's dominance, slavery proved extremely adaptable to local circumstances and demands. Its ubiquity in Brazil, the region to which nearly half of all captives forced across the Atlantic were sent, is illustrated in Herbert S. Klein and Francisco Vidal Luna, *Slavery in Brazil* (New York: Cambridge University Press, 2010). Philip Morgan underscores the dynamic roles that slaves played in non-sugar and urban environments in the Caribbean in his "Caribbean Slavery," in Misevich and Mann, *The Rise and Demise*, 64-99.

46   Paul Lovejoy expresses important concerns about the implications of using European-derived terms and regions – Senegambia, Sierra Leone, the Windward Coast, Upper Guinea – for research on Africa and the transatlantic slave trade. See his careful critique, "The Upper Guinea Coast and the Trans-Atlantic Slave Trade Database," *African Economic History* 38 (2010): 1-27.

47   "A Book of Trade for the Sloop *Rhode Island*, Dec. 1748-July 1749," Misc. MSS., B.V. *Rhode Island*, New-York Historical Society. For a detailed analysis of this voyage, see Philip Misevich, "In Pursuit of Human Cargo: Philip Livingston and the Voyage of the Sloop *Rhode Island*," *New York History* 86, no. 3 (2005): 185-204.

48   Iron bars served a role similar to modern paper currency, allowing traders to buy, sell, or evaluate the value of their merchandise. Fyfe, *A History*, 9; Curtin, *Economic Change*, 312.

49   "A Book of Trade," entry for February 18, 1849.

50   David Eltis, Philip Morgan, David Richardson, "Agency and Diaspora in Atlantic History: Reassessing the African Contribution to Rice Cultiva-

tion in the Americas," *American Historical Review* 112, no. 5 (December 2007): 1339-40. For the increase in slave-loading times, see David Eltis and David Richardson, "Productivity in the Transatlantic Slave Trade," *Explorations in Economic History* 32 (1995): 465-84. On the smaller size of Upper Guinea slavers, see Stephen D. Behrendt, "Markets, Transaction Cycles, and Profits: Merchant Decision Making in the British Slave Trade," *The William and Mary Quarterly* 58, no. 1 (January 2001): 171-204.

51   Bruce L. Mouser, "Iles de Los as Bulking Center in the Slave Trade, 1750-1800," *Revue Française d'Histoire d'Outre-mer* 83 no. 313 (1996): 86.

52   David Hancock, *Citizens of the World: London Merchants and the Integration of the British Atlantic Community, 1735-1785* (Cambridge: Cambridge University Press, 1995), ch. 6. On the slave trade between Sierra Leone and North America in the mid-eighteenth century more generally, see Sean M. Kelley, *The Voyage of the Slave Ship Hare: A Journey into Captivity from Sierra Leone to South Carolina* (Chapel Hill: University of North Carolina Press, 2016).

53   Mouser, "Iles de Los."

54   Hancock, *Citizens*, ch. 6; Mouser, "Iles de Los," 84-85; Kenneth Morgan, "British Merchants and the Slave Trade from Sierra Leone, 1750-1807," presented at Hull University's Interdisciplinary Conference, "Empire, Slave Trade and Slavery: Rebuilding Civil Society in Sierra Leone. Past and Present," September 26, 2008.

55   Mouser, "Iles de Los," 86-87. Walter Charles, the Royal African Company's last factor at Bunce Island in the 1720s, recorded many instances when African traders arrived with produce to sell. See TNA, T70/1465. Although the fort's daily transactions are not recorded for the 1750s, African traders would surely have continued to travel there in search of commercial opportunities.

56   TNA, HCA16/83/2218. The *Crescent* is ID 18040 in Eltis et al., *Voyages*. For Cleveland's relationship with Robert Bostock, a prominent Liverpool merchant, see Denise Jones, "Robert Bostock of Liverpool and the British Slave Trade on the Upper Guinea Coast, 1769-93," in Lovejoy and Schwarz, *Slavery, Abolition and the Transition to Colonialism,* 69-88.

57   British Senegambia was technically Britain's first African colony, though the British never developed colonial infrastructure there. See Paul E. Lovejoy, "Forgotten Colony in Africa: The British Province of Senegambia (1765-83)," in Lovejoy and Schwarz, *Slavery, Abolition and the Transition to Colonialism,* 109-26.

58   Fyfe, *A History.* For more recent work on Freetown's early inhabitants, see Alexander X. Byrd, *Captives and Voyagers: Black Migrants across the Eighteenth-Century British Atlantic World* (Baton Rouge: Louisiana State University Press, 2008); and Ruma Chopra, *Almost Home: Maroons between Slavery and Freedom in Jamaica, Nova Scotia, and Sierra Leone* (New Haven: Yale University Press, 2018).

59　The *Voyages* database includes just one record of a slave vessel purchasing captives from the Iles de Los after 1808. No slavers embarked captives at Bunce Island after that year.

60　Marika Sherwood, *After Abolition: Britain and the Slave Trade since 1807* (New York: Palgrave Macmillan, 2007).

61　In a valuable study of the *Amistad* affair, which I discuss in chapter two, Michael Zeuske characterizes the Gallinas slave trade in the abolition era as part of a "hidden" Atlantic World. He examines the many ways by which slavers and merchants obfuscated their activities in order to continue their participation in the trade. See Michael Zeuske, *Amistad: A Hidden Network of Slavers and Merchants* (Princeton: Marcus Wiener, 2015).

62　The shoals of St. Anne, which form at the entrance to the Sherbro estuary, were exceedingly difficult to navigate. Barbot warned, "you must avoid entangling yourself with the Shoals of St. Anne. There are dangerous breakers and small islands on which the tides can drive you unless you have a strong wind to resist them, but it is rare to have other than dead calm here." Hair et al., *Barbot on Guinea*, 223.

63　Daniel B. Domingues da Silva, "Winds and Sea Currents of the Atlantic Slave Trade," in Misevich and Mann, *The Rise and Demise*, 152-67.

64　Not all slaves who were disembarked in Cuba remained there. A considerable traffic from Cuba to Puerto Rico developed during this period, supplementing a smaller direct traffic to the latter island. Joseph C. Dorsey, *Slave Traffic in the Age of Abolition: Puerto Rico, West Africa, and the Non-Hispanic Caribbean, 1815-1859* (Gainesville: University Press of Florida, 2003).

65　Estimating the volume of the slave trade from African ports requires several steps. The *Voyages* site can be used to generate records of slave exports from southern Sierra Leone ports – Sherbro, Gallinas, and the Banana Islands – and divide them into ten-year intervals: http://slave voyages.org/voyages/5WCIgxjN. It can do the same for slave exports from all of Sierra Leone: http://slavevoyages.org/voyages/6FQhBMoy. Calculating the ratio of the former estimate to the later and applying that ratio to the more comprehensive volume of the slave trade from Sierra Leone on the estimates page of the *Voyages* website (http://slave voyages.org/estimates/6oL4Pvm8) provides the figures for the estimated departures in Table 1.3.

66　Among the last well-documented British citizens involved in the Sierra Leone slave trade was John Ouseley Kearney. Kearney departed from Senegal when it was turned over to the French and resided for some time at Kent, in Freetown. By 1817 he was involved in the Gallinas slave trade. He briefly embarked on a slave vessel to the French Caribbean, having enslaved one of the members of the Cleveland family. He returned to the Gallinas in 1823. That year a rumor emerged that he died when his ship was destroyed off Sugary, on the Windward Coast. Whether or not that was true is unclear. On Kearney, see TNA, CO271/1, *Royal Gazette and Sierra Leone Advertiser* 2, no. 97 (April 15, 1820); ibid, CO271/2, vol. 5, no. 289 (December 6, 1823); Sierra Leone National Archives, Governor's Despatches to the Secretary of State, Enclosures in MacCarthy to Bathurst, February 17, 1820. For the shift to Spanish merchants, see Jones, *From Slaves*, 42-44, especially Table 6, which includes the names of dozens of foreign slave dealers who were active in the Gallinas trade between 1806 and 1849; and more generally, Zeuske, *Amistad*. The Brazilian influx is implied in *BPP, Slave Trade*, vol. 6, enclosure 1 in Fanshawe to the Secretary of the Admiralty, September 9, 1849, 185-91. However, one British naval officer believed that the slave dealers claiming to be Brazilian were really Spanish merchants who feared being charged under the Spanish Penal Act of 1845. *BPP, Slave Trade*, Hook to Fanshawe, December 4, 1849.

67 Jones, *From Slaves to Palm Kernels*, 43-44. Eltis, *Economic Growth*, 161. The life of the notorious slave trader Theodore Canot also underscores the relationship between Cuba and southern Sierra Leone in the nineteenth century. Born of French and Italian parentage, Canot was involved in the slave trade from the Rio Pongo in the 1820s before establishing himself in the Gallinas as one of Blanco's agents. It is possible that more has been published on Canot than any other individual slave dealer in the history of the transatlantic trade. See his *Captain Canot, or, Twenty Years of an African Slaver* (New York: Appleton and Co., 1854); Svend E. Holsoe, "Theodore Canot at Cape Mount, 1841-47," *Liberian Studies Journal* 4 (1971-2): 163-83; Adam Jones, "Theophile Conneau at Galinhas and New Sestos, 1836-1841: A Comparison of the Sources," *History in Africa* 8 (1981): 89-106; and Bruce L. Mouser, "Theophilus Conneau: the Saga of a Tale," *History in Africa* 6 (1979): 97-107.

68 Rediker, *The Amistad*, 43-52.

69 TNA, FO84/268, Spanish Commissioners to Palmerston, February 12, 1839.

70 Jones, *From Slaves to Palm Kernels*, 81-83.

Chapter 2. The Origins of Captives Leaving Southern Sierra Leone in the Nineteenth Century

The growth of the export slave trade from Sherbro and Gallinas pulled the hinterland southeast of Freetown more forcefully into the transatlantic slave system. More than half of the slaves coming from ports in southern Sierra Leone in the nineteenth century originated in the Mende- and Sherbro-speaking parts of Upper Guinea, within about sixty miles of the coast. Consistent with other parts of Africa in the era of abolition, the southern Sierra Leone "slaving frontier" – the internal regions from which the majority of African captives were supplied – receded from deep in the interior to communities nearer to the coast, a pattern that persisted with striking continuity through the suppression of the Sierra Leone trade in the middle of the 1840s. A careful assessment of the homelands of captives pulled into the trade sheds light on slaves as individuals whose encounters with transatlantic slavery were shaped by internal and external factors. Moreover, a rich collection of Liberated African life histories reveals how enslaved people experienced life in captivity.

Despite more than a half century of scholarly research on the Atlantic slave trade, much less is known about enslaved people in Africa than in the Americas. Prior to the abolition of the British trade in 1807, the most detailed information comes from the

New World, where documents often give some indication of slave origins.[1] In Africa, scholars have mined accounts written by European travelers and oral sources to highlight the dynamics of the slave trade within Africa. Among other details, such records provide commentary on warfare – one of the main methods of enslavement – which has enabled scholars to draw conclusions about the likely catchment areas that fed the transatlantic trade.

Scholars of the nineteenth century Atlantic World have a wider variety of sources from which to draw and as a result they have been able to sketch clearer pictures of slave origins for that century. Many have profited from the careful research of S.W. Koelle, a German linguist who spent five years (1847-53) in Freetown as an employee of the Church Missionary Society. While living in the British colony, Koelle gathered vocabularies from among the more than 160 different languages that the Liberated African population spoke. In an article published in 1964, Philip D. Curtin and Jan Vansina used information provided by Koelle's African informants, including their countries of origin and estimates of how many of their fellow countrymen resided in Freetown, to examine the interior sources of the nineteenth century slave trade. They supplemented that data with an assessment of the 1848 Freetown census, which, despite significant gaps in its coverage, provides a broad demographic survey of the colony. In a subsequent article, P.E.H. Hair used similar sources to compile more complete profiles of 179 of Koelle's informants. Suzanne Schwarz has more recently demonstrated the rich potential for Liberated African life histories to reveal individual experiences among slaves and recently freed people in Sierra Leone.[2]

An analysis of the Registers of Liberated Africans, a unique set of documents that have long been known to historians but continue to be under-utilized, provides unrivaled information on individual captives drawn into transatlantic slavery in the nineteenth century. The Registers were maintained primarily in Freetown, Havana, and Rio de Janeiro between 1808 and 1862.[3] They enable scholars to assess the likely ethnolinguistic origins of enslaved people based on evidence given directly by Africans themselves. Over some six decades, British officials engaged in the campaign to suppress the transatlantic slave trade used Vice Admiralty Courts (beginning in 1808) and later Courts of Mixed Commission (beginning in 1819) to process hundreds of vessels and approximately 175,000 "recaptives" – Africans whom the British navy removed from slaving vessels. Africans provided information about themselves including name, age, sex, and, at times, place of habitation. European officials recorded the information in duplicate and at times triplicate form in large ledger books, which they deposited in archival repositories located in countries spread around the Atlantic basin. Often, the ethnic or regional basis of the names is recognizable, making it possible to identify the likely homelands of captives drawn into the slave trade in the final decades before it was fully extirpated.

The value of these records for examining the origins of Africans embarked on slave vessels is by now well established. From their identification of recaptive names among slaves embarked in the Cameroons, for example, David Eltis and G. Ugo Nwokeji concluded that the provenance of the slave trade there was highly concentrated, with just four ethnolinguistic groups accounting for over half of the enslaved people carried from the region over a period of fifteen years.[4] In a preliminary assessment of roughly 1,700 individuals embarked on slaving vessels immediately north and south of Freetown, I found significant contrasts in the catchment areas on which the Rio Pongo and Gallinas slave trades fed. Whereas the former port pulled in a broad mixture of peoples, the slave trade in southern Sierra Leone more closely resembled that of the Cameroons, with a heavy concentration of captives coming from Mende- and Sherbro-speaking areas.[5] Additional fieldwork provides an opportunity to offer a much broader and deeper assessment of captives purchased from Gallinas and Sherbro that draws on records of more than eight thousand Liberated Africans whose details the British recorded in the Registers.

While a fuller explanation of the methods and assumptions underpinning this research are available in the Appendix below,[6]

75

several cautionary comments are necessary. It is important to be clear about what these data can and cannot reveal. Given the fluid and contested nature of identity in precolonial Africa, it is unlikely that a Liberated African with a name that is, for example, distinctly Mende would have self-identified as such. Africans who lived in Mende-speaking areas in the mid-nineteenth century would almost certainly not have privileged ethnicity as a primary form of self-identification.[7] Yet the relative geographic stability of Upper Guinea's language communities over time makes it possible to link names from the Registers with their likely ethnolinguistic origins in Africa. Put simply, a person who in the nineteenth century had a distinctively Mende name would very likely have come from a region where Mende was the dominant language.[8]

Southern Sierra Leone's late entry into transatlantic slaving combined with Britain's heavy policing of the Gallinas and Sherbro trade make the Registers of Liberated Africans a particularly useful source for exploring the origins of African slaves from this area. The information provided in the Registers presents a more complete picture of the trade from southern Sierra Leone than it would for more active slaving ports further east and south. Overall, voyage records exist for the forced departure of roughly thirty-nine thousand Africans from southern Sierra Leone between 1808 and 1844. However, total slave exports were probably closer to eighty-five thousand during the period.[9] If we use this larger estimate, the sample of names in the registers from southern Sierra Leone (8,871) on which this chapter is based constitutes more than ten percent of the total slave trade from the region. Significantly, there is little reason to suspect that the sample is unrepresentative of the remaining ninety percent of captives who slipped through the British antislavery squadron's patrols.

A final important methodological question to address is the extent to which the process of enslavement itself might have influenced the names that recaptives gave to court officials. Is it possible that slaves shipped from southern Sierra Leone during this period took on new names – by force or by choice – at some point prior to their liberation? Answering this question is particularly tricky because of the lack of evidence concerning slave experiences prior to their disembarkation in the Americas. On the one hand, some slaves indeed had their names changed immediately after they were taken captive in the African interior. A rare documented example of this occurred in the Sierra Leone hinterland in the mid-1850s, when a slave owner named Boccari Soonkonokoh asked Momodu Yeli to act as a witness for his purchase of a slave. He paid sixteen dollars for a Kuranko girl named Phena, whose name he then changed to Seerah. Unsurprisingly, when a British official later liberated the girl she chose to identify herself by her birth name rather than the name forced on her by her captor.[10]

Other evidence, however, suggests that slave names were not changed or that, if they were, Liberated Africans returned to using their original names once they were separated from their owners. Records of the individuals carried on board the schooner *Amistad* illustrate this point. The events surrounding the capture of the *Amistad* are by now well known. There is no reason to believe that, at least prior to their successful rebellion, the captives' collective experiences were markedly different from those of other slaves taken from the region in the nineteenth century.[11] The captives were detained in a Connecticut jail beginning in 1839, where over the subsequent year Josiah W. Gibbs, a linguistics professor at Yale University, periodically visited them. Gibbs used the information he collected during these meetings to sketch brief biographies of thirty-six *Amistad* captives.[12] A careful scholar, Gibbs frequently explained the meanings attached to each captive's name. He at times even recorded the names of the captives' children. Had any of the *Amistad* Africans mentioned a name change, Gibbs would certainly have documented it. Moreover, the amount of time spent as a slave in Africa seems to have had no impact on the likelihood of names being changed. Several captives testified that they had been held in Africa for periods ranging between two months and ten years before they were shipped to Cuba.[13] However, in all but a single case, the origins of the names that the individuals provided were consistent with other statements they made about their homelands.[14] It is of course possible that some captives chose to employ new or different names and thus obscure their identities but it is unlikely that this practice was widespread.

The Origins of Recaptives in the Eighteenth and Early-Nineteenth Centuries

The homelands of Africans forced onto slave vessels in Sierra Leone in the pre-abolition era are not well known. Prior to the establishment of the British Vice Admiralty Court in 1808, quantitative evidence allowing for an assessment of African origins is limited. Hints and whispers in the archival record suggest that the catchment area for slaves in the eighteenth and early-nineteenth centuries extended considerably further inland than it would in later decades. Indeed, this was probably true for the entire area between Senegambia and the Windward Coast, where the slaving frontier seems to have reached hundreds of miles beyond the littoral.[15] Given Britain's dominance of the pre-1808 slave trade in Sierra Leone, records on the origins of Africans embarked in this region come overwhelmingly from British slave traders and plantations in the British Caribbean. On the African coast, two detailed accounts from the mid-eighteenth century underscore the long supply lines on which the Sierra Leone trade drew. One comes from John Newton, who took part in three separate slaving ventures around the Banana Islands between 1750 and 1754. Reflecting on his experiences in the trade, Newton noted that the bulk of captives were brought from far away: "I have reason to think that some travel more than a thousand miles, before they reach the sea coast." In his later testimony on the slave trade, Newton revised down his estimate to several hundred miles inland – a far more credible assessment.[16]

An account from the slave trader Nicholas Owen's provides little direct evidence on the origins of slaves but his careful documentation of commercial networks and warfare in the Sierra Leone interior lends support to Newton's testimony. After crisscrossing the Atlantic on several voyages, Owen settled in the Sherbro with his brother, where the two men operated commercial factories in the middle of the 1750s. Woefully unsuccessful as a slave trader, Owen nonetheless offered valuable commentary on how the trade operated. Unlike north of Freetown, where large and powerful Fula and "Mandingo"[17] caravans traveled to the coast seeking trade, in the Sherbro the coastal Bullom people initiated trade with the interior, traveling upcountry to slave markets once each year. Doing so enabled coastal merchants in the Sherbro to purchase enslaved people at reduced prices and sell them for greater profits along the coast. Whereas slaves were sold for between 45 and 50 bars along the littoral, Bullom middlemen purchased them for just twenty bars inland.

Just how far into the interior the middlemen had to go is unclear, but Owens's descriptions of inland warfare suggests that slaves caught up in conflicts traveled considerable distances. Owen describes, for example, the commencement of a battle in February of 1758, led by King Furry Do, a "Mandingo" ruler from "way inland," who went to war with neighboring leaders. The King's campaigns were successful enough to spread fear throughout the region. Within several weeks, Furry Do had subdued all of the headmen in the surrounding districts, enslaving those who opposed him.[18] Though pockets of "Mandingo" settlements existed throughout Upper Guinea, powerful Mandingo communities were more heavily concentrated in the deep interior of Sierra Leone during this period, which suggests that the captives these conflicts affected had homelands well beyond the coast.

The travels of an Englishman named Harrison, who documented his visit to the interior of Cape Mount in the last quarter of the eighteenth century, also lend support to the idea that the Upper Guinea slave trade drew on populations from far inland. In 1808, Governor Ludlam relayed the Englishman's story to the *Sierra Leone Gazette*; the Governor claimed to have heard it years earlier. According to Ludlam, Harrison lived at Cape Mount, where during his youth he journeyed with a party of slave traders as they made their return home after having disposed of captives along the coast. Doubts about the veracity of Harrison's account have made scholars hesitant to use it. Yet separate analyses by P.E.H. Hair and Adam Jones support details from Harrison's journal. Hair and Jones indicate that Harrison likely traveled in 1780 and that the place-names he identifies can be linked to peoples living in the Liberian hinterland at the time. Summarizing Harrison's trip, Hair argues that he passed through the following ethnolinguistic territories: Gola, Loma, Kissi, Kpelle, and possibly Mano and Dyula. Such a route, Hair notes, would have taken him as far as two hundred miles E.N.E. of Cape Mount. The account thus suggests a catchment area for the slave trade from that port of far beyond the coast.[19]

The most comprehensive data on slave origins for the pre-1808 period come from the British Caribbean, where in the 1810s abolitionists pressured the British Government into requiring slave owners to formally register their captives. Abolitionists believed that this process, which in effect created a census of the slave population in British Caribbean colonies, would enable officials to subsequently identify illegal arrivals of Africans in their territories. In his thorough analysis of the registration records, B.W. Higman generated a number of important data tables and observations about the African origins of slaves who resided in the British sugar colonies of St. Kitts, St. Lucia, Trinidad, Berbice, and Anguilla between 1813 and 1819. All of these slaves would have been taken from the African coast before 1808.

Using the registration data to identify the origins of slaves is particularly tricky for Upper Guinea. The data do not identify African ports from which registered slaves were purchased. To get around this problem, Higman linked ethnic terms that appear in the documents with the regions of Africa where they were commonly found. For example, Higman attributes Malinke ("Mandingo"), Bambara, Fulbe (Poulan), and Kassanga slaves to Senegambia. He connects Temne, Bullom, Kissi, Mende, Susu, and Limba slaves to Sierra Leone. These assumptions are reasonable in the vast majority of cases. Yet some groups were so historically dispersed as to make the establishment of such links virtually impossible. Captives originating in Fula and Malinke territories would, for example, have been scattered throughout each of the three regions that make up the Upper Guinea Coast. Nonetheless, the slave registration data indicate that before the abolition of the British slave trade, the networks supplying captives from Sierra Leone tapped into areas located well beyond the littoral. Malinke, Fulbe, Kissi, and Susu captives are well represented. Mende and Bullom (presumably including Sherbro) appear, but not nearly in the same proportion that they would later in the century. Although considerable numbers of Canga/Ganga slaves show up on St. Kitts, Trinidad, and Berbice, the range of ethnic groups that this term covers makes it less useful for an assessment of slave origins.[20] The picture that emergences from these data for the Sierra Leone slave trade is that it drew on diverse populations that were scattered across the interior of Upper Guinea.

The Origins of Liberated Africans from Southern Sierra Leone, 1808-1844

We can now turn to the Registers of Liberated Africans and the British campaign to suppress the transatlantic trade. Between 1808 and 1844, some sixty vessels that took on slaves from southern Sierra Leone ports were adjudicated in British courts. In all, those vessels discharged 8,871 recaptives who survived long enough to have their information recorded in the Registers of Liberated Africans. In a large majority of cases, the names can be linked to modern African equivalents. An assessment of the likely ethnolinguistic origins of the names from the registers reveals a remarkable degree of continuity over nearly four decades. Despite minor differences in the composition of captives embarked on slaving vessels before 1819 when compared to subsequent decades, the overall impression is that the southern Sierra Leone slave trade drew on captives from Mende- and Sherbro-speaking communities in exceptionally high numbers and proportions.

81

As scholars who have worked with these data have already pointed out, the process of identifying names from the registers is not always straightforward. Liberated Africans freed through courts in Freetown had their names written down by British officials who at times clearly struggled to transcribe the names effectively. Spanish-speaking officials in Cuba faced the same challenge, though their transcriptions reflect Spanish spelling conventions rather than English ones. Even a short and seemingly straightforward African name such as "Beah" was rendered in a wide variety of ways ("Bia," "Beer," and "Beeah," to provide just a few examples). Beyond the challenges of decoding the European transcriptions are more basic concerns about the assumptions built in to attributing names to particular ethnolinguistic groups and the implications of doing so. How do we assess names that are common among some language groups but not others? What about names that have contested origins? From a different angle, is it possible to reconcile the emphasis on continuity that this methodology implies with an appreciation for the complex and dynamic nature of African naming systems?

The answers to these questions are complicated. Sierra Leonean informants did not recognize some of the names from the records, an unsurprising occurrence given the sheer size and scope of the data. They identified other names as widely in use among multiple language groups, which led me to code the names as "multilingual" and generally remove them from the analysis below. Even multilingual names occasionally provided other (non-ethnolinguistic) clues about the backgrounds of particular Liberated Africans as, for example, with Musa, a name that transcends ethnolinguistic boundaries, but which is generally given to Muslims. Finally, some names are used among a limited number of language groups – at times even among communities that do not speak mutually intelligible languages. Such names are thus multilingual in a technical sense, but their use is confined to smaller regions. Mende and Sherbro names, for example, are often difficult to disentangle given the steady expansion of Mende speakers toward the Sierra Leone coast over the last century and a half.[21] For that reason, the ethnolinguistic groups Mende and Sherbro were combined. After removing unidentified and multilingual names, some form of ethnolinguistic identification remains for 4,586 of the individuals listed in the registers between 1808 and 1844. Such a large sample size makes this the most thoroughly documented study of the African origins of captives shipped from any Upper Guinea port – and perhaps from any African port – in the entire Atlantic slaving period.

Table 2.1, Ethnolinguistic Identifications of Southern Sierra Leone Liberated Africans, 1808-1844

Ethnolinguistic Community	Number of Recaptives	Column Percentage
Mende/Sherbro	2,457	54
Kissi/Kono/Kuranko	857	19
Temne	416	9
Limba	204	4
Fula	178	4
Mandingo	119	3
Possibly Muslim	108	2
Vai	73	2
Loko	68	1
Outside Sierra Leone	48	1
Susu/Yalunka	39	1
Total	4,567	100

Source: www.african-origins.com (contact author for the spreadsheet)

Table 2.1 provides an overview of the communities pulled most frequently into the southern Sierra Leone slave trade over the four decades for which the Registers provide data. It makes immediately clear the high concentration of Mende- and Sherbro-speaking people, which together represent more than half of all southern Sierra Leone captives. More generally, the table illustrates a high volume of slaves coming from a relatively concentrated area in what today is the nation Sierra Leone and its immediate northern and eastern hinterlands. Taken together, the top three designations, comprising six ethnolinguistic communities – Mende/Sherbro, Kissi/Kono/Kuranko, and Temne - represent eighty two percent of Liberated Africans with identifiable names. The "Outside Sierra Leone" group includes names that contributors recognized as having distant origins, frequently from contemporary Nigeria and often Yoruba or Igbo. Common Muslim names include, among many others, Musa, Abraham, Muhammad, and Fatimata.

Not all Muslims, of course, would have had names that so clearly revealed their religious backgrounds; it is also possible that non-Muslims would occasionally have taken Muslim names. In any case, the table illustrates Islam's slow spread into southern Sierra Leone over the course of the nineteenth century. As might be expected, the concentration of Muslim names during the same period is considerably higher in the Rio Pongo region hundreds of miles to the north, where Islam had penetrated much more widely and played a considerable role in shaping political and economic institutions.[22]

In addition to the concentration of slaving among a limited number of ethnolinguistic communities, the overall impression from the data is that the southern Sierra Leone slave trade drew captives in heavy concentrations from its northern and northeastern hinterlands. Combining Kissi, Kono, and Kuranko names partially disguises this point. Although the distance between coastal southern Sierra Leone and the Kuranko-speaking heartland was several hundred miles, it is likely that the majority of slaves grouped under this combination were taken from Kissi-speaking regions somewhat nearer to the coast.[23] Passing through the Sierra Leone hinterland in the mid-1820s, Gordon Laing noted that "the people of Kissi have no trade except in slaves, which they sell to the people of Sangara for salt, tobacco, and country cloth; and, in such a savage state of wretchedness and barbarism are they, that without the least compunction they will dispose of their relatives, wives, and even children."[24] While antislavery zeal encouraged British officials to make similar statements about nearly all African communities in the nineteenth century, it is worth noting that the size of the Kissi Liberated

African population in Freetown was large enough to merit its own separate village, comprised of "natives of the district of Kissy, lying between Falaba and the sources of the Niger...[who], having been captured from slave ships by British men-of-war, it was considered desirable to locate them in one place."[25]

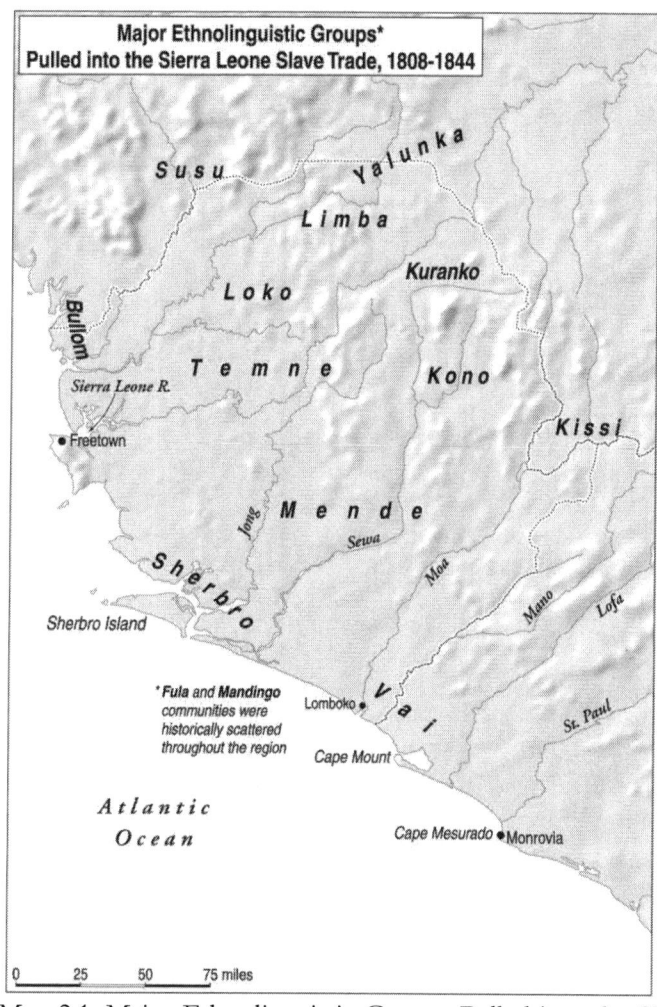

Map 2.1, Major Ethnolinguistic Groups Pulled into the Sierra Leone Slave Trade, 1808-1844

The most striking feature of the table is clearly the number of Mende and Sherbro names among Liberated Africans from southern Sierra Leone. The predominance of slaves from this area is widely supported by nineteenth-century observers. While traveling along the Sherbro coast, the Reverend James Frederick Schön, a missionary who resided in Freetown between 1832 and 1848, witnessed a cargo of slaves being sold to a notorious slaving merchant on the island. Schön claimed that all of the slaves were "Cossoo" (a derogatory word for Mende). When he inquired about the low price the dealer paid for the captives, the man explained that "they were cheap, but that they were Cossoos, and that Cossoos were mere cattle, and more should not be paid for them."[26]

Try Norman, a Yoruba recaptive who was enslaved during a trip to collect a debt from a merchant residing in the Gallinas, also observed a high ratio of Mende captives being held in the region. Before she could settle her financial affairs, Prince Manna, among the most powerful leaders in the region, took Norman prisoner on account of a debt Norman's mistress previously incurred. Prince Manna imprisoned Norman in a slave barracoon, where she was held for three months before a British official liberated her. In a discussion with members of the British Select Committee about her experiences in the barracoon, Norman explained that all of the slaves being held with her were from Mende-speaking territories.[27]

What accounts for such a high percentage of Mende and Sherbro captives coming from southern Sierra Leone ports during this period? A variety of factors shaped the composition of captives. The transportation costs involved in carrying slaves from the hinterland to the coast, for example, played a vital role in linking ports to the particular interior commercial routes on which they relied. Sherbro and Mende speakers dominated the immediate hinterland of southern Sierra Leone. It was easier and less costly to transport a slave from this area to the Gallinas and Sherbro than to journey hundreds of miles north to the Rio Pongo, the next closest slaving center in Sierra Leone.[28] Unsurprisingly then, southern Sierra Leone ports pulled in captives from the areas nearest to them.

Changes in the prices that Europeans paid for slaves also affected the slaving frontier. When prices were high, African merchants could afford to absorb increased transportation costs. During such times, the slaving frontier tended to push further inland. Declining slave prices cut into slave dealers' profits, providing them with less incentive to drive caravans of captives toward the coast. This seems to be precisely what occurred in southern Sierra Leone, where the price of slaves fell considerably during the first quarter of the nineteenth century, as it did elsewhere in Africa.[29] While price data for the slave trade are notoriously difficult to standardize and assess, Adam Jones has demonstrated that between Freetown and the Gallinas, the value of slaves dropped by at least half between1800 to 1825. Converting slave prices from ships' bars to an estimate of their sterling equivalent, Jones suggests that owners paid as much as £23 for an adult male slave from Sierra Leone in 1808. By 1825, the price at the Gallinas had fallen by nearly 75 percent, to just £6.[30] While slave prices after 1825 are scarcer, the increase in the export of Africans living within one hundred miles of the coast into 1835 (see Table 2.3) suggests that prices did not recover over the next decade. By the middle of the 1830s, the southern Sierra Leone slaving frontier began to slowly shift back inland, but Britain's suppression of the trade from southern Sierra Leone interrupted that development.

Yet prices and costs alone do not fully explain why captives from particular communities were drawn into the slave trade in significant numbers. Mende and Sherbro mechanisms of enslavement and methods of slave delivery played equally important roles in shaping the southern Sierra Leone slave trade. Based on a rich corpus of testimony from individuals who had been enslaved in nineteenth century Sierra Leone, it is clear that warfare generated a steady supply of captives to Gallinas and Sherbro slaving centers. Warfare represented one of the primary ways by which young men achieved upward social and political mobility within Mende communities. Successful warriors gained access to the human and commercial spoils of battle and distributed plunder to their dependents. Many war leaders achieved regional fame through their exploits and in some cases town leaders hired them as "war boys" – mercenaries to fight rival leaders – in a process they called "buying war." Successful war leaders used their resources to establish their own towns. In other cases, they were integrated into more prominent settlements under powerful chiefs.[31]

The rise to power of King Siaka, the notorious African leader whose aggressive expansion from his base in Gendema fueled the Gallinas slave trade, illustrates the synthetic relationship between the growth of the Atlantic slave trade, the expansion of African warfare, and the concentration of economic resources in the hands of powerful rulers. In 1808, John Kizell, a former slave from the Sherbro area who cultivated close ties with the British Government in Freetown, described how Siaka rose to power through the support of foreign slave dealers, who began to direct to him the fees they had to pay in order continue their trade activities, even though Siaka was at the time merely one among many ambitious local chiefs. In the context of intense local rivalries at least partially fueled by attempts to access western commercial goods, Siaka clearly outmaneuvered his enemies: by the early 1820s, Europeans were identifying Siaka as "King," for whatever that was worth, and more importantly they widely acknowledged him as one of the key players in the Gallinas slave trade. Siaka had the support of networks of warriors who were feared widely across the region and whose services he purchased through the circulation of foreign textiles, alcohols, and other goods. The leader deployed his warriors into the interior to keep his enemies in line and procure captives for coastal European buyers. Headmen in Siaka's crosshairs took measures to protect themselves and their dependents from military exploits, surrounding their settlements with two or three circular palisades between which armed guards patrolled in pursuit of intruders. Often located within just a few miles of each other, Mende and

Sherbro war towns provided grist for the coastal slaving mills to continue their operations.[32]

Given the significance of the relationship between area of enslavement and coastal embarkation point, Table 2.2 presents the data differently, this time in terms of the distance that recaptives would have traveled before reaching the coast. This calculation is based on a rough estimate of the locations of nineteenth-century ethnolinguistic communities.[33] Given the complexity of this calculation, I have divided the results into very broad categories, distinguishing merely between those recaptives whose homelands were probably less than one hundred miles from the coast and those who likely came from areas more than one hundred miles beyond the littoral.

The catchment area suggested by this table can be refined even further. Many – perhaps most – captives with Mende, Sherbro, Temne, and Vai names would have had homelands that lay within fifty or sixty miles of the Gallinas and Sherbro coasts.

Table 2.2, Location of Liberated African Homelands in Relation to Embarkation Port, 1808-1844

Distance	Number of Recaptives	Column Percentage
Less than 100 Miles	3.014	66
More than 100 Miles	1,553	34
Total	4,567	100

Source: Table 2.1

Assuming that slave caravans traveled between ten and twelve miles per day,[34] we can infer from these data that more than two thirds of southern Sierra Leone captives came from areas located just a few day's journey from the coast. While this proximity would not have made enslavement itself any less traumatic, it would have had at least two significant consequences for captives. First, many enslaved people would have been familiar with the Sherbro and Gallinas and the broader Atlantic World commercial system that enriched the ports – perhaps they even recognized the fate that awaited them. The relatively shallow catchment area also meant a short period of internal transport, at least compared with other parts of West and West Central Africa. Given the close relationship between slave mortality and travel time, Mende and Sherbro captives likely experienced higher survival rates than those that Joseph C. Miller estimated for West Central African captives, for example.[35]

James Campbell, a Mende slave whom the British liberated, provides a useful illustration of captives' experiences during their forced march toward the coast. Campbell was enslaved during a war in the interior and marched to the Gallinas coast over three days. Upon his arrival, he was detained in a barracoon. While Campbell recalled enduring many hardships during the journey toward the coast, including receiving regular whippings and being chained tightly around the neck, he also noted that he remained healthy throughout the affair.[36] We can speculate that, as with Campbell, many Mende- and Sherbro-speaking captives arrived in the Gallinas in at least marginally better physical condition than enslaved people from neighboring regions that drew on deeper slaving frontiers. Alternatively, the one-third of enslaved Africans who lived more than a hundred miles from the coast, endured significantly longer periods of forced transport, which likely resulted in higher rates of mortality within Africa or weakened condition upon arrival along the Gallinas coast.[37]

The sample of Liberated African names is large enough to assess changes over time in the composition of slave shipments from southern Sierra Leone. Table 2.3 divides the data into short intervals. One striking detail is the variation in the ratio of Muslim names, which account for seven percent of Liberated Africans up to 1818 and then fall to just one percent or less for the next three decades. However, the shift is not as pronounced as it seems. The 1808-1818 period preceded the establishment of the Court of Mixed Commission, meaning that Africans liberated during this period were processed through the British Vice Admiralty Court in Freetown. The Vice Admiralty Court records often failed to record the specific port of embarkation for the vessel under adjudication, although most of these vessels had embarked captives from somewhere along the Sierra Leone coast near Freetown. Given the wider range of embarkation ports represented in the Vice Admiralty Court data – particularly including ports north of Freetown – the higher frequency of Muslim names and the slightly lower percentage of Mende and Sherbro names makes sense. Taken as a whole, the table underscores how little the profile of slaves embarked in southern Sierra Leone changed between 1808 and 1844. Despite slight fluctuations in the supply of captives from particular ethnolinguistic communities, the overall pattern is one of striking continuity. Expressed in their simplest form, the results can be characterized as follows: of every ten captives embarked on a slaving vessel from Gallinas or Sherbro between 1808 and 1844, between five and six came from Mende- and Sherbro-speaking regions near the coast; two had homelands in the Kissi, Kono, or Kuranko parts of the hinterland; and the remaining two or three slaves would have lived in a scattered number of other communities throughout the Upper Guinea interior.

Table 2.3, Ethnolinguistic Identifications of Southern Sierra Leone Liberated Africans, 1808-1844 (column or row percentages in parenthesis)

Ethnolinguistic Unit	1808-1818	1819-25	1826-30	1831-35	1836-40	1841-44
Mende/ Sherbro	575 (46.0)	210 (52.9)	323 (51.9)	476 (62.1)	756 (57.1)	117 (56.0)
Kissi/Kono/ Kuranko	253 (20.2)	78 (19.6)	124 (19.9)	124 (16.2)	239 (18.1)	39 (18.6)
Temne	114 (9.1)	32 (8.1)	62 (10)	65 (8.5)	126 (9.5)	17 (8.1)
Possibly Muslim	88 (7.0)	0	6 (1.0)	3 (0.4)	10 (0.8)	1 (0.5)
Limba	75 (6.0)	20 (5.0)	22 (3.5)	17 (2.2)	63 (4.8)	7 (3.4)
Fula	67 (5.4)	18 (4.5)	24 (3.9)	25 (3.3)	37 (2.8)	7 (3.4)
Mandingo	37 (3.0)	13 (3.3)	17 (2.7)	17 (2.2)	32 (2.5)	3 (1.4)
Vai	19 (1.5)	3 (0.8)	14 (2.3)	9 (1.2)	23 (1.8)	5 (2.4)
Loko	8 (0.6)	8 (2.0)	18 (2.9)	10 (1.3)	16 (1.2)	8 (3.8)
Outside Sierra Leone	7 (0.6)	11 (2.8)	10 (1.6)	10 (1.3)	10 (0.8)	0
Susu/ Yalunka	8 (0.6)	4 (1.0)	2 (0.3)	10 (1.3)	10 (0.8)	5 (2.4)
Totals	1251 (27.4)	397 (8.7)	622 (13.6)	766 (16.7)	1,322 (29.0)	209 (4.6)

Source: same as Table 2.2

In geographic terms, these data indicate that the nineteenth century slave trade from southern Sierra Leone fed on a primarily coastal population. The difference between this pattern and the one found in the Cameroons, where the communities pulled into the slave trade shifted considerably over time, is pronounced.[38] Indeed, given on the one hand the violence and upheaval that the slave trade caused and on the other the wide range of peoples that it affected, the continuity in the data is surprising. It suggests that the communities in southern Sierra Leone that were drawn most heavily into the transatlantic slave trade effectively coped with the demographic pressures that trade imposed over some three and a half decades. How long they would have been able to continue doing so remains an open question but as chapter four reveals, Mende and Sherbro communities were targeted for enslavement into the 1880s to provide labor on groundnut plantations in Guinea Bissau.[39]

Conclusion

The majority of southern Sierra Leone's captives came from a relatively concentrated hinterland within about sixty miles of the African coast. The region's shallow slaving frontier distinguishes it not only from other regions of Africa, where slaves were at times marched from hundreds of miles beyond the littoral, but also from Sierra Leone's eighteenth-century trade, which drew on Africans from further inland. The contraction of the catchment area for slaves from Sierra Leone after the Slave Trade Act underscores the dramatic impact that the abolition of the British slave trade and Britain's broader suppression campaign had on the slave trade within Africa. In addition to pushing slave dealers into the Gallinas and Sherbro, Britain's naval campaign and the related loss of British Caribbean markets reduced slave prices along the African coast. For merchants in southern Sierra Leone, this development dissuaded them from making lengthy journeys to and from sources of slave supply far in the interior. Mende, Sherbro, Temne, and a smaller number of Vai captives thus bore the brunt of the transatlantic slaving's reach into nineteenth century Sierra Leone. While chapters one and two have privileged primarily external forces in shaping the timing and pace of Sierra Leone's integration into the Atlantic World, this should not imply that such forces alone were responsible for generating economic, social, and political changes in Africa. Internal pressures interacted with and transformed external ones as southern Sierra Leone communities confronted the challenges posed by the expansion of Atlantic commerce. Chapters three and four thus explore how a variety of communities and individuals exploited new opportunities that emerged as a result of the slave trade, abolition, and colonialism in nineteenth century Sierra Leone.

Notes

1 See, for example, B.W. Higman, *Slave Populations of the British Caribbean, 1807-1834* (Baltimore: Johns Hopkins University Press, 1984). Despite the fact that Higman's data is from the nineteenth century, it is revealing of the British slave trade prior to 1808. Gwendolyn Midlo Hall, *Slavery and African Ethnicities in the Americas: Restoring the Links* (Chapel Hill: University of North Carolina Press, 2005), makes a forceful argument in support of using data on slaves from the American side of the Atlantic.

2 Philip D. Curtin and Jan Vansina, "Sources of the Nineteenth Century Atlantic Slave Trade," *Journal of African History* 5 (1964): 185–208; P. E. H. Hair, "The Enslavement of Koelle's Informants," *Journal of African History* 6 (1965): 193–203. See also P. E. H. Hair, ed., *Polyglotta Africana* (Graz: Akademische Druck- u. Verlagsanstalt, 1963); and Schwarz, "Reconstructing."

3 For an overview, see Anderson et al., "Using African Names." Additional recent work using the registers includes Richard Anderson, "The Diaspora of Sierra Leone's Liberated Africans: Enlistment, Forced Migration, and 'Liberation' at Freetown, 1808-1863," *African Economic History* 41 (2013): 101-38; Lovejoy, "The Registers of Liberated Africans"; and Schwarz, "Extending."

4 G. Ugo Nwokeji and David Eltis, "Characteristics of Captives Leaving the Cameroons for the Americas, 1822-1837," *Journal of African History* 43 (2002): 198.

5 For a preliminary assessment of the Sierra Leone slave trade that treats southern Sierra Leone and the Rio Pongo, see Philip Misevich, "The Or-

igins of Slaves Leaving Sierra Leone in the Nineteenth Century," in Eltis and Richardson, *Extending the Frontiers*, 155–75.

6   For a slightly different methodological approach, see G. Ugo Nwokeji and David Eltis, "The Roots of the African Diaspora: Methodological Considerations in the Analysis of Names in the Liberated African Registers of Sierra Leone and Havana," *History in Africa* 29 (2002): 365–79; and Nwokeji and Eltis, "Characteristics."

7   The problems with making claims regarding African ethnicity and identity in the precolonial period have received increasing attention over the last two decades. See David Northrup, "Igbo and Myth Igbo: Culture and Ethnicity in the Atlantic World, 1600-1850," *Slavery & Abolition* 21 (2000): 1–20; and Peter Caron, "'Of a Nation Which the Others do not Understand': Bambara Slaves and African Ethnicity in Colonial Louisiana, 1718-60," *Slavery & Abolition* 18 (1997): 98–121. For a sophisticated examination of identity in Upper Guinea, see Allen M. Howard, "Mande and Fulbe Interaction and Identity in Northwestern Sierra Leone, Late Eighteenth through Early Twentieth Centuries," *Mande Studies* 1 (1999): 13–39.

8   Hair, "Ethnolinguistic Continuity." David Dalby's contribution, "Languages," in *Sierra Leone in Maps*, ed. John Innes Clarke (London: University of London Press, 1966), 15, lends further support to the stability of the region's ethnolinguistic distribution.

9   Eltis et al., *Voyages*, has evidence of 38,973 slaves embarked at Gallinas and Sherbro between 1808 and 1844: http://slavevoyages.org/ voyages/nV1eZI0n. This represents approximately seventy percent of all recorded slaves purchased in the entire Sierra Leone region during this period: http://slavevoyages.org/voyages/Vkc1aGYW. The more inclusive "estimates" page on the *Voyages* site suggests a total of 120,781 exports from Sierra Leone during this same period: http://slavevoyages.org/estimates/y2OLlGWz. My figure of 85,000 slave departures is derived by multiplying this larger estimate by .7.

10   TNA, C.O. 267/233, Enclosure 7 in Kennedy to the Duke of Newcastle, July 18, 1853.

11   Steven Spielberg's 1997 film *Amistad* popularized the revolt on board this vessel. For an important Sierra Leonean perspective on the historical and contemporary relevance of the story, see Iyunolu Folayan Osagie, *The Amistad Revolt: Memory, Slavery, and the Politics of Identity in the United States and Sierra Leone* (Athens: University of Georgia Press, 2003). More recently, see Rediker, *The Amistad*. It is peculiar that despite much interest among researchers in the *Amistad* case, no original records of the *Tecora*, the vessel that transported the captives to Cuba, have turned up. Michael Zeuske offers an original perspective on this issue in his "Rethinking the Case of the Schooner *Amistad*: Contraband and Complicity after 1808/1820," *Slavery & Abolition* 35 (2014): 156–64.

12   Printed in John W. Barber, *A History of the Amistad Captives* (New Haven:
      E. L. & J. W. Barber, 1840; North Stratford: Ayer Company Publishers,
      2000), 9–15.

13   It is impossible to known the lengths of time that Africans liberated by
      the Mixed Commission Courts remained in Africa prior to being taken
      on board slave ships. Using evidence that S.W. Koelle gathered from 179
      liberated Africans in Freetown around 1850, P.E.H. Hair notes that "few
      of the informants had spent much time as slaves...twenty-nine had spent
      periods of years in Africa, mainly as slaves to Africans. The remainder
      had reached Sierra Leone shortly after enslavement...that is, they were
      enslaved in their home district and immediately taken down to the
      coast...and were shortly afterwards captured aboard a slave ship and
      brought straightway to Freetown." However, these figures include slaves
      drawn from many different parts of West, West-Central, and even South-
      east Africa. See P. E. H. Hair, "The Enslavement," 195.

14   The exception is Kwong, who was born at Mambui, "a town in the Mendi
      country." Gibbs, however, identifies "Kwong" as a Bullom name, not a
      Mende name. See Barber, *History*, 11.

15   See, for example, Curtin, *Economic Change*, 84-91; Hawthorne, *Planting
      Rice*, 78.

16   For the quote, see Bernard Martin and Mark Spurrell, eds., *The Journal of
      a Slave Trader (John Newton), 1750-1754* (London: Epworth Press, 1962),
      108; his later testimony is found in TNA, BT6/9, Examination of Rev-
      erend John Newton, February 15, 1788.

17   Mandingo is an exceptionally tricky term to make sense of in the histor-
      ical literature. It at times refers to an ethnolinguistic group, also at times
      called Mandinka, which had historical origins in the Mali Empire. Euro-
      peans, however, also used the term merely to identify Africans who were
      Muslim regardless of their ethnolinguistic backgrounds. In some cases, I
      use the term without quotes to indicate its ethnolinguistic association,
      such as when I identify a nineteenth century name as Mandingo. In oth-
      ers I use the term in quotes to underscore its more ambiguous usage
      among Europeans defining people as Muslim. On the term Mandingo,
      see Matt Schaffer, "Bound to Africa: The Mandinka Legacy in the New
      World," *History in Africa* 32 (2005): 321-69; and Steven Thomson, "Re-
      visiting 'Mandingization' in Coastal Gambia and Casamance (Senegal):
      Four Approaches to Ethnic Change," *African Studies Review* 54, no. 2
      (2011): 95-121.

18   Eveline Martin, ed., *Journal of a Slave-Dealer: A View of Some Remarkable
      Axcedents in the Life of Nics. Owen on the Coast of Africa and America from the
      year 1746 to the year 1757* (London: G. Routledge, 1930), 93, 101. For ad-
      ditional background on Furry Do, see David E. Skinner, "Mande Settle-
      ment and the Development of Islamic Institutions in Sierra Leone," *The
      International Journal of African Historical Studies* 11 (1978): 43.

19 P.E.H. Hair, "An Account of the Liberian Hinterland, c. 1780," *Sierra Leone Studies* 16 n.s. (1962): 218-26; Jones, *From Slaves to Palm Kernels*, 34-35.

20 Higman, *Slave Populations*, 442-57. David Geggus reaches a similar conclusion for Saint-Domingue, but he too combines each of the three Upper Guinea regions. See David Geggus, "Sex Ratio, Age and Ethnicity in the Atlantic Slave Trade: Data from French Shipping and Plantation Records," *Journal of African History* 30, no. 1 (1989): 32.

21 A list of Sherbro names from 1938 illustrates some overlap with Mende ones. Hall, *The Sherbro*.

22 For the Rio Pongo see Misevich, "The Origins of Slaves;" On Islam in Sierra Leone more generally, see Alusine Jalloh and David E. Skinner, eds., *Islam and Trade in Sierra Leone* (Trenton, N. J.: Africa World Press, 1997). On the diaspora of Muslims from Africa, see Daniel B. Domingues da Silva, David Eltis, Nafees Khan, Philip Misevich, and Olatunji Ojo, "The Transatlantic Muslim Diaspora to Latin America in the Nineteenth Century," *Colonial Latin American Review* 26, no. 4 (2017): 528-45; and Paul E. Lovejoy, *Jihad in West Africa during the Age of Revolutions* (Athens, OH: Ohio University Press, 2016); Manuel Barcia, "West African Islam in Colonial Cuba," *Slavery & Abolition* 35, no. 2 (2014): 292-305, looks specifically at Islam in Cuba.

23 In contrast to the Kuranko heartland, Kissi-speakers are concentrated in a region roughly one hundred and fifty miles from the Gallinas and Sherbro.

24 Alexander Gordon Laing, *Travels in the Timannee, Kooranko and Soolima Countries in Western Africa* (London: John Murray, 1825), 280–81.

25 J. J. Crooks, *A History of the Colony of Sierra Leone, Western Africa* (London: Cass, 1972), 88.

26 *BPP, Slave Trade*, vol. 4, Rev. James Frederick Schön to the Select Committee on the Slave Trade, April 11, 1848, 182.

27 Ibid, vol. 4, Try Norman to the Select Committee, 63.

28 Mende and Sherbro slaves did end up at the Rio Pongo, suggesting that incurring such transport burdens was not out of the question. See Misevich, "Origins of Slaves." This underscores Philip Curtin's point that slave-dealing merchants could adapt their routes to suit local circumstances. Curtin, *Economic Change*, 84–91.

29 The most wide-reaching study of prices for slaves in nineteenth century Africa is Lovejoy, *Transformations in Slavery*, Tables 3.5 and 7.3. See also David Eltis, "The Volume, Age/Sex Ratios, and African Impact of the Slave Trade: Some Refinements of Paul Lovejoy's Review of the Literature," *The Journal of African History* 31, no. 3 (1990): 490-91, who clearly assesses slave prices. More recently, Lovejoy and Richardson have argued that the decline in slave prices on the coast was temporary – that it rebounded in the 1820s but never quite returned to pre-nineteenth century

levels. Paul E. Lovejoy and David Richardson, "British Abolition and its Impact on Slave Prices along the Atlantic Coast of Africa, 1783-1850," *Journal of Economic History* 55, no. 1 (1995): 98-119. Jones' data, however, suggests that for southern Sierra Leone, slave prices did indeed decline throughout the nineteenth century.

30 Jones, *From Slaves*, Table 4, p. 31. To calculate the prices of slaves, I multiplied columns three and four in Jones' table.

31 Several scholars have underscored the role that warfare played in fueling the southern Sierra Leone slave trade. Jones, *From Slaves*, chs. 4–5; Abraham, *An Introduction*, ch. 2; Little, *The Mende*, ch. 1; Rediker, *The Amistad*, chs. 1–2.

32 Jones, 56-73, effectively situates Siaka's history in the context of internal and external pressures within the Gallinas, highlighting the roles that kinship and local political rivalries played in Siaka's rise and the conflicts in which he was engaged. Yet the pressing factor that shaped the southern Sierra Leone slave trade in particular was Siaka's capacity to use his access to European merchandize to wage brutal wars and generate thousands of captives.

33 To calculate the distance I employed two methods. First, the political units from Figure 2.1 were used as the center points from which a measurement to the coast was made. To account for those regions in which languages are particularly widespread – where a distance could vary considerably from one part of a region speaking the language to another – the calculation was then double-checked with the linguistic distribution found in Dalby, "Languages."

34 This assumption is consistent with travel times recorded during the late-eighteenth century. See Bruce L. Mouser, ed., *Journal of James Watt: Expedition to Timbo, Capital of the Fula Empire in 1794* (Madison: African Studies Program, University of Wisconsin, 1994), 12–13.

35 See Joseph C. Miller, "West Central Africa," in *The Atlantic Slave Trade*, ed. David Northrup, 3d ed. (Boston: Cengage Learning, 2011).

36 BPP, *Slave Trade*, vol. 4, James Campbell to the Select Committee, 78–80.

37 Data on shipboard mortality does not shed much light on this issue. Between 1808 and 1844, the *Voyages* database includes information on forty vessels from southern Sierra Leone for which mortality rates are available. The average mortality rate for those voyages was 9.4%. In contrast, the mortality rate for eighteen vessels embarking slaves in the Rio Pongo was 8.2%. Yet slave vessels that embarked slaves in southern Sierra Leone took nine days longer to reach their destinations, which would have resulted in additional losses of life.

38 Nwokeji and Eltis, "Characteristics," 200–202, especially Tables 3 and 4.

39 See ch. 4, below.

CHAPTER 3. THE PROVISIONS TRADE IN THE ERA OF ABOLITION, 1787-1856

Among the many ways that the slave trade and British colonialism transformed Sierra Leone in the nineteenth century, one noteworthy change was how they both concentrated large numbers of people along the coast. From its humble origins in 1787, Freetown was by the 1830s a major urban center with some 30,000 inhabitants, comprised primarily of Liberated Africans. Lomboko was much smaller in scale but it nevertheless contained thousands of people, primarily enslaved. The growth of those two coastal towns required a substantial increase in the production and trade of food and other agricultural commodities. Well positioned to supply both markets and containing rich and productive soils for the cultivation of rice, Sherbro farmers and traders responded actively to meet the needs of hungry settlers, placing southern Sierra Leone at the heart of the clashes between pro- and anti-slavery forces that engulfed West Africa during this period.

In the early 1800s, Freetown's food needs proved especially dire. Aiming to demonstrate the superiority of agricultural commerce over slave trading, the city's founders were shocked to discover that the land on which they established their settlement was poorly suited for commercial farming. The Sierra Leone Company, which financed and helped administer Freetown from abroad, stepped in to help, sending vessels laden with European commodities that enabled settlers to purchase food from neighboring African headmen, but the explosion of trade that Europeans anticipated never materialized. Population growth seriously exacerbated the problem. To combat the extensive costs required to sustain the population, British officials developed a hands off approach, first reducing the rations they provided to newly-freed people and later abolishing the rations system altogether. Instead, officials moved recaptives to inland villages, which provided the recaptives with added autonomy and new responsibilities. As John Peterson explains, the resulting administrative void "was filled by the settlers and Liberated Africans who were able to establish effective control of the political, economic, and social dimensions of their society."[1] By the late-1820s the Liberated African population shouldered most of the burden to feed itself and took initiatives to develop trade with the interior.

While Africans in Freetown tangled with British officials over food and more generally grew accustomed to the rhythms of life in the colony, Sherbro headmen and farmers focused on supplying rice and other commodities to the swarming parade of slave vessels that visited the Gallinas in search of human cargo. Once an active producer of rice, the Gallinas came to depend on the Sherbro's rich soils to feed the captive population that swelled in the barracoons along its coast. Many of the largest Gallinas slave dealers contracted with specific Sherbro headmen to supply food to their factories and for the vessels for which they supplied slaves. In a desperate attempt to break up this intricate commercial network, the British struck at the heart of the system by blockading the paths between Sherbro and Gallinas in the late 1840s. The measure had a profound impact on the slave trade; reports soon emerged of the entire region suffering from starvation. The confrontational British approach seemed to work: By 1850 the Gallinas headmen announced the expulsion of the remaining Cuban and Brazilian traders from the southern Sierra Leone coast.

Competing demands for Sherbro produce led to a booming growth in the supply of foodstuffs from the region in the first half of the nineteenth century. At its height in the 1820s, that trade measured roughly a thousand tons per year – a seismic increase from the eighteenth century and one that had important consequences for African communities in southern Sierra Leone. Food supplies therefore proved vital to the operation of the slave trade and colonialism in Africa – a point acknowledged in the literature on the transatlantic trade but too often neglected in the context of the campaign to suppress it.[2] Moreover, while Padraic Scanlan's analysis of Freetown emphasizes the economic incentives that motivated British naval officers and colonial officials to engage in antislavery activity, an assessment of southern Sierra Leone merchants on the settlement's frontier demonstrates that African traders were equally open to profiting from the opportunities that nineteenth-century Atlantic commerce provided.[3]

The Sierra Leone Company and the Provisioning of Early Freetown, 1787-1807

The Establishment of Commercial Factories North and South of Freetown

The history of Freetown's establishment is well known. In 1787, a British attempt to found what abolitionists called the "Province of Freedom" at Granville Town, on the south bank of the Sierra Leone estuary, ended in disaster. A third of its inhabitants died from exposure to unfamiliar diseases; most of the survivors abandoned the settlement and sought livelihoods elsewhere. In 1790, the few remaining inhabitants were drawn into a conflict between their Temne landlord and an American slave trader, which resulted in the total destruction of the original settlement. The newly established Sierra Leone Company rebuilt the town in 1791, its population considerably expanded in the following year with the arrival of a group of free blacks from Nova Scotia. Abolitionist excitement was in the air. The new settlers arrived singing a hymn of prayer: "The day of Jubilee is come; Return ye ransomed sinners home."[4]

The air of jubilation did not last long. It quickly became clear to settlers that the location of the new site was far from ideal for agricultural production. A report on the state of the settlement in 1794 found that "the land adjoining to the settlement has proved by no means so good as every account received before the inception of the Company had led them to expect." The overall assessment of Freetown's geographic merits, however, kept British financers interested. As one observer commented,

> the site of Freetown is unquestionably the best that can be found, in respect to the salubrity of the air, the goodness of the water, and the convenience of the landing-place; it can hardly fail therefore to continue the chief place of trade, though other parts at a moderate distance, particularly those on the opposite side of the river, will be found the most favorable to cultivation.[5]

Following up on this sentiment, settlers carved out an experimental plantation on the Bullom Shore, on the north side of the Sierra Leone estuary, under the supervision of James Watt, formerly a planter in Dominica. Yet the earlier report on the Bullom Shore's promise proved misleading. The plantation produced little and by 1796 the British had virtually abandoned it.[6]

Poor results on their early agricultural endeavors led Freetown officials to rely even more heavily on commerce to supply the settlement with provisions, as Suzanne Schwarz's analysis of the Sierra Leone Company's history makes clear. But establishing meaningful commercial relationships with local leaders proved no simple task.[7] Recognizing the potentially dangerous implications of Freetown's establishment in a region so heavily engaged in the Atlantic slave trade, slave dealers across Sierra Leone mounted a campaign to oppose the abolitionist project. They spread malicious stories about the new settlers' intentions and warned headmen that British officials intended to conquer and steal African land.[8] To counter the bias building up against them, many of Freetown's most influential settlers organized face-to-face meetings with indigenous headmen. Such efforts, the settlers hoped, would offer them a chance to explain the benefits of legitimate commerce and strengthen relationships by building trust.

Zachary Macaulay worked particularly hard to improve the settlement's relationship with local communities. In July of 1793 he traveled from Freetown south to the Banana, Plantain, and Sherbro Islands. At Sherbro he met William Ado, a powerful headman at Jenkins Town, on the northeast end of the island. The leaders entered into an agreement to increase trade between their settlements. In a classic demonstration of the landlord-stranger relationship that regulated interaction between outsiders and their hosts in this region, Ado promised to protect Freetown merchants who settled in his town – an essential commitment given the limited European presence on the coast and slave traders' widespread hostility toward British aims.[9] The agreement permitted the British to establish a small factory, including a house "in the manner of native houses, a rice house, a yard or inclosure for camwood, and a fowl house."[10] Early the following year Macaulay sent a mission inland to the Fula Country, which led the Almamy of Futa Jallon, the powerful seat of the Fula Empire in the hinterland, to agree to send his merchants to Freetown in the future. To facilitate their interactions with Timbo and attract additional traders, the Sierra Leone Company opened a factory at "Tookey Kerren," which they later renamed Freeport, some twelve leagues up the Rio Pongo, in modern-day Guinea. Despite continued resistance from slave traders north of Freetown, the factory showed promise: it attracted a shipment of 668 pounds of ivory, which Fula merchants brought down in July of 1795 with the promise of future returns.[11]

Yet little ultimately came of the Rio Pongo-based factory during the seven years it operated. Internal and external pressures limited its success. The hinterland northeast of Freetown – the region that supplied the Freeport factory – was at the time going through upheavals that disrupted trade flows. And while Freetown merchants were warned against getting involved in the internal affairs of their landlords, constant skirmishes not only stopped trade along commercial paths but also forced Europeans to choose sides between the parties in conflict, whether or not they wanted to. In February of 1796, less than a year after Freeport was opened, merchants reported that the path to Futa Jallon had been closed for "some time." Anticipating their concern, Thomas Cooper, the Company's factor at the settlement, reassured the British officials that it recently reopened and would bring major commercial benefits.[12]

Cooper's subsequent correspondence underscores the unstable nature of the factory. During the nearly six months following the letter he sent that reported the opening of the path to the interior, Cooper rarely provided positive updates. Perhaps it closed again or did not bring the trade British officials anticipated. The problem, Cooper explained, was that Timbo had been wrecked by a civil war during which the Almamy of Futa Jallon, Alimami Sadoo, was murdered. Domestic struggles continued long after the Almamy's violent removal from power.[13] Under such circumstances it is hardly surprising that trade from Timbo remained unsteady.

Freeport continued its strained existence for another five years, never realizing the benefits the Company hoped it would bring. Its failure demonstrates the limits of Freetown's influence outside of the settlement itself. Indeed, Freeport struggled to attract indigenous merchants away from the more powerful slave traders. As Cooper lamented in early 1796, "I am afraid it will be some time before I shall be able to draw the trade to this river, as all the Foulahs are inclined...to go to Carcundy Path" – a route that led to the slave-dealing parts of the coast.[14] During those few times when Freeport showed glimmers of hope, slave dealers on the coast did everything in their power to disrupt its success. In April 1796, a group of prominent slave traders banded together to implement a policy that refused the purchase of slaves from Fula caravans that had visited Freeport.[15] After an investment of several years and with little to show for it, Company officials concluded "the same obstacles that had prevented trade to the Freeport factory continue. Troubles in the Foulah country continue to prevent free intercourse with those more inland whence the ivory is chiefly brought to the Foulah market, and the same rooted enmity of slave traders to the company continues to thwart its views."[16] By 1802, the Company finally abandoned the factory – an admission of the defeat of legitimate commerce in the area at the hands of slave-trading interests.

In contrast to the centralized organization of trade north of Freetown, commerce south of the settlement drew on several small factories and local leaders that were scattered along the coast between the Camaranca River and Cape Mesurado. Agreements such as the one that Macaulay and William Ado reached in 1793 bolstered Britain's presence across the south. Others followed. James Rooway, a prominent merchant, aimed to settle on the Banana Islands as a host of William Cleveland, the Anglo-African leader. On the Camaranca River, from which a regular supply of rice was obtainable, settlers established a factory in May of 1793. Later, in 1795, John Gray and James Watt entered into negotiations with Furry Cannabas, a "Mandingo" headman on the Camaranca, to establish an additional factory; they opened it the following year under the supervision of Mr. Farel. Further to the south, two additional traders, Mr. Graham and Mr. Ray, who had previously been operating on the Banana Islands, moved their factories to Mesurado, where the American colony of Liberia would later be settled.[17] Spreading trade along many parts of the coast south Freetown appears to have paid dividends. As a whole, Freetown's commercial relationships with Africans in southern Sierra Leone were in the 1790s more advantageous than the ones to the settlement's north.

Two related factors account for the success of early trade between Freetown and southern Sierra Leone. The extremely localized nature of political power in this region meant that the Company had several leaders with whom they could engage, which created better commercial opportunities for British merchants along the coast. The power of the Fula state at Futa Jallon, which inspired Freetown officials to so diligently pursue commercial links with its northeastern hinterland, led to the factory's downfall once domestic struggles discouraged caravans from traveling to Freetown. South of the settlement, there was no inland equivalent to the large Fula Empire that regulated trade in coastwise commerce. Even when wars erupted in the south, as they did intermittently throughout the 1790s, there was no single large path to blockade.

Moreover, unlike in the Rio Pongo, where slave dealers were extraordinarily powerful and worked as a coherent unit to oppose Freetown interests, headmen south of the settlement appeared to recognize that British merchants gave them an opportunity to increase their own prestige against often hostile rival headmen. Given the comparative weakness of Freetown's presence in the interior, the ability to play some headmen against each other proved essential in allowing the British to wield influence that went beyond their limited presence. Commenting on the growing trade between Freetown and the Sherbro, Zachary Macaulay observed, "Our rapid progress in the Sherbro seems to have been considerably owing to the hatered entertained against the name of Clevland, on account of the miseries occasioned by the late Clevland."[18] African opinions about local headmen and British colonizers here were evidently divided.

The Organization of the Sierra Leone Company Produce Trade

One of the most striking features to emerge from recent research on the transatlantic slave trade has been the degree of specialization that the trade fostered: particular European ports had unique links with specific African regions of slave supply; captains of slaving vessels conducted business with trusted slave traders settled along the coast, often building commercial relationships that spanned many years. Given the nature of the trade in which those merchants were involved – and the potential profits and losses of slaving voyages – we might expect such connections to govern the trade. Was the same true for the commerce in non-slave commodities?

Freetown's early history offers a unique opportunity to consider the issue. Sufficient data exist to draw conclusions about the nature of the produce trade from the settlement's earliest years. In 1792, the Sierra Leone Company began sending out vessels laden with European goods for the purchase of legitimate commodities north and south of Freetown. Details for these voyages vary in quality. Some records offer little beyond a vessel name and intended destination of trade; others are documented in great detail through surviving journals. Taken as a whole, these data are strong enough to address many of the issues that scholars of the slave trade have taken up and build on recent research into the Sierra Leone Company's history.[19]

The data indicate that as with the slave traffic, a highly specialized organization underpinned the produce trade under the Sierra Leone Company, which indigenous demands, not European ones, dictated. In their limited commercial sphere along the coast – from the Gambia River in the north to Gabon in the southeast – the extent to which Africans shaped the organization and operation of Freetown's trade is noteworthy. Cargos were carefully sorted based on local preferences, which differed significantly from one port to the next and might unexpectedly change within the same town. Failure to account for such preferences was one quick way to guarantee an unprofitable voyage. Captains of Company vessels, who were entrusted with profitable European cargo, were dispatched to the parts of the coast with which they were most familiar. When a knowledgeable captain was unavailable, merchants or Sierra Leone Company officials accompanied the voyagers and oversaw the excursion. For producer traders, as with their slave-trading counterparts, personal relationships and commercial knowledge mattered.

In the complex riverine networks that carved up the African coast between Gambia and Gabon, one vital step in organizing a trading voyage was selecting a suitable vessel. In 1791, the Sierra Leone Company had three at their disposal: the *Lapwing*, of 35 tons burthen; the *Amy*, of 190 tons; and the much larger *Harpy*, of 380 tons. Within three years, the Company increased its commercial fleet to more than ten vessels, mostly smaller cutters and sloops that Europeans used to collect produce in the adjoining rivers. When a fire in 1793 destroyed the Company's largest vessel, the *York*, of 850 tons burthen – a considerable blow to the young settlement that resulted in a £4,000 loss – settlers transformed the *Harpy* and *Amy* into store ships.[20] Subsequent misfortune further set back the Company's commercial ambitions. A near-fatal strike against the Company fleet came in September of 1794, when a group of French privateers attacked and destroyed large parts of Freetown's infrastructure. In the chaos that followed the assault, nearly three quarters of Company vessels were either taken or destroyed by the French fleet as it proceeded down the coast.[21] However, the Company rebounded and between 1795 and 1801 they employed at least ten separate vessels to carry produce back to the settlement.[22]

In general, captains of Company vessels sailed along well-known and predetermined routes, which they changed up only under pressing circumstances. Alexander Macaulay, one of the most active Sierra Leone Company captains, commanded four separate voyages in 1796 alone – three in the brig *Beginning*. He was transferred to the sloop *Ocean* only once, when his experience with trade much further southeast along the coast required him to switch to a new vessel.[23] William Davis, master of the *James and William* cutter, had extensive knowledge of the trade along the Windward and Gold Coasts, which the Company deeply valued. When Davis was unavailable, Captain Estill, "who has acquired sufficient knowledge of the gold and ackey trade," provided a fallback option. Captains who were capable of trading across multiple regions were most valued. The longest trip the Company organized went between Sierra Leone and Gabon, a trip that lasted six months and passed through diverse territory in which many groups of people lived, each with their own sets of customs and merchandize preferences. Between 1796 and 1797, the Company sent a number of voyages along this route, each one carefully planned, though none of them were profitable. The first two trips were undertaken in the Company vessel *Calypso*, both under the command of Captain Cole. Following Cole's second voyage in 1797, the Company dispatched the Brig *Eliza* on the same route after it received from the *Calypso* a favorable report on trading conditions. In the end, both the *Calypso* and the *Eliza* fell victim to the predations of French privateers. Such was the uncertainty of long-distance trade along the African coast in an era of hostilities between major European powers.[24]

In addition to finding knowledgeable captains and seaworthy vessels, the Company also needed access to suitable cargos. Changing African demands for European goods made this aspect of the trade particularly complicated. Sorting cargos required a comprehensive knowledge of articles Africans in different ports preferred – preferences on which some Company factors reported frequently in their correspondence. Little evidence exists describing the dynamics of the Freetown trade to the Gambia, the northernmost point in the Company's commercial network. In the Rio Pongo, closer to Freetown, Cooper, the Freeport factor, maintained regular contact with Company merchants but his letters are surprisingly vague on local commercial preferences. One article he often mentioned was salt. Indeed, a great scarcity of salt, which he identified in April 1797, led Cooper to conclude that the old supply system that previously brought that item to the coast had been shut down. Cloth, one of the most widely exchanged European products throughout Africa, was unsurprisingly also an article that Africans in the Pongo trade highly valued. Cooper explained that the cloth Africans there most preferred was "blue baft…with satin stripe and chintz."[25]

Journeys south and east of Freetown tended to last much longer and be more complex. Organizing such voyages involved making risky calculations and assumptions about African consumer demands. The sophistication of the trade is underscored by a remarkable document that Mr. Parfitt, a Sierra Leone Commercial Agent during the 1790s, recorded, in which he describes complex trading patterns between Freetown and Cape Lopez. It indicates that some commodities, such as rum and tobacco, circulated widely. American rum found a ready market along the West African littoral, especially along the Gold Coast – a pattern that went back to at least the mid-eighteenth century. "The natives are partial to it, they prefer it to French brandy or Jamaica rum," Parfitt noted.[26] Tobacco was important, too. Unlike along the Bight of Benin, where Africans sought roll tobacco from Bahia, here it was "good, long, broad leaf" tobacco that captured Africans' attention.[27]

It was when dealing with articles other than rum and tobacco that local preferences were most fully expressed. Specific patterns of cloth that sold on one part of the coast might be almost worthless in an adjacent region. On the other hand, introducing new styles could generate higher profits. The balance was a difficult one to strike. As Parfitt explained regarding prospects for the textile trade to the south, "I think if the Pongas or Nunez, blue and high cloths, were cut into their length and sewn together they would be liked, I had not a good opportunity to try them, they must be sewed which might be done by sailors on board." Demand for patterns and sizes of trade beads and beadwork also varied by region: the inhabitants along the Kru Coast were especially fond of "small blue pipe bead bare 3/16 of an inch diameter and ¾ inch long," while as many as seven other color and pattern schemes suited consumers along other parts of the coast. In many cases, in order to obtain this wide and ever-changing variety of goods, captains had to purchase them locally during the early part of their voyage with the intent to sell them later. "From Little or Grand Sesters round Cape Palmas you can sometimes buy a string containing 10 beads about 1 ½ to 1 ¾ in. long for a trifling thing which you can sell at Cape Lahou and to Leeward," Parfitt explained. And "at St. Andrews they are fond of some of the Gold Coast goods, if you have them on board, and their trade will answer, do not spoil it by retaining them, if you can possibly spare them."[28]

The specificity of the demands for goods along the coast often frustrated Sierra Leone Company traders, who relied for the most part on the Directors of the Company to supply them with goods. Moreover, at least if Freetown officials are to be believed, the Directors were slow to send out coveted trade articles. When the vessels arrived, the Company merchants rarely found the assortment they needed to satisfy merchants along various parts of the coast. Upon the arrival of one British vessel, Macaulay commented, "the trade goods which came out in the *Naimbanna* are calculated only for the Gambia."[29] When a particularly valuable commodity was neglected, the Company tried to barter for it with other merchants in the region. They often turned to John Tilley, a slave dealer and agent who operated on Bunce Island. On one such instance Freetown officials lamented that "it appears the Court of Directors have omitted to include iron bars in the trade cargo now sent out on the *Eliza* and such an article being necessary to complete an assortment for the Grain Coast, Parfitt has written to Tilley to know if he can spare some."[30]

For its part, the Sierra Leone Company sought a limited number of commodities that generally were available widely along the coast. Company interests can be divided roughly into two groups: edible goods and luxury goods. Edibles, though of lesser value, enabled settlers to survive. The Company imported huge quantities of rice and supplemented it with yams, fowl, coconut, cattle, plantains, and palm oil. Luxury items included ivory, camwood, gold dust, coffee, wax, gum copal, ebony, and occasionally horses. Some parts of the coast were known for their capacity to supply one good or another; few offered the full assortment. Most vessels dispatched toward the Gambia returned with cargos of ivory, wax, cattle, and rice. Given the length of those voyages, vessels traveling to the Gambia tended to be large.[31] Cattle were also available from Portuguese merchants in Bissau, who traded with Freetown from the time it was first established.[32] Tapping into local rice supplies required close relationships with coastal merchants. Aspinall, a slave trader with over twenty years of experience in Africa who was stationed at Robat, on the Great Scarcies, traded regularly with Freetown merchants, for example.[33] Sustenance trumped moral convictions when rice supplies were at stake.

It is striking to note the number of places at which Company vessels traded and the range of articles that each port supplied. The headmen on the Banana Islands and at Sherbro provided as much rice as did merchants on any part of the coast. Sherbro also supplied camwood.[34] Further along the coast, the trade diversified to include pepper and ivory along the Grain and Ivory Coasts, and gold as vessels reached the forts along the Gold Coast. Palm oil was available "in great plenty" at Old Calabar and in the Cameroons ivory again dominated the trade. Finally, vessels calling at Gabon could load a diverse assortment of goods that included redwood, gum copal, and black ebony – the only place that particular commodity is mentioned. As a whole, Parfitt lists a staggering sixty different points between Cape Mount and Cape Lopez where trade in different commodities could be conducted.[35]

The Volume and Distribution of the Company Trade
Between 1792 and 1801, the Sierra Leone Company dispatched at least sixty-seven vessels to collect produce along different points of the African coast.[36] Table 3.1 shows the number of voyages that departed from Freetown during each of these years. It is clear that the Company's enthusiasm for managing a commercial fleet declined almost as quickly as it emerged. Ninety percent of the produce voyages sailed during the first five years of Company operation and more than half of the voyages left Freetown in a single year. From its highpoint in 1793, the sea-based produce trade declined in each subsequent year with the exception of 1796, when vessel departures more than doubled from the previous year. The drop in voyages from thirty six in 1793 to just one sixth that amount in the following year should not be surprising: the Company lost most of its vessels in the French attack in 1794. Yet other factors were at play, too. The French assault occurred late in September, by which point only a few vessels had been dispatched. At least fifteen produce vessels had sailed out by September of the previous year.

There was no evident preference for when such voyages departed. Data for the month of departure is available for forty vessels, or about sixty percent of the voyages. What is most striking is how evenly dispersed the patterns were: half of the voyages left Freetown in the first six months of the year; half departed in the remaining six months.[37] This pattern of distribution was equally balanced by month of departure. Between three and five vessels departed in eight out of the twelve months of the year. No vessels sailed out in April or June. November, the busiest month for produce-vessel departures, saw six voyages sail out from Freetown. The location to which vessels traveled does not seem to have influenced departure patterns. The top three most frequently visited ports of trade for Company vessels showed similar patterns.

Table 3.1, Number of Sierra Leone Company Voyages, 1792-1801

Year of Departure	Frequency	Percent
1792	5	7.5
1793	36	53.7
1794	6	8.9
1795	4	6.0
1796	9	13.4
1797	2	3.0
1798	1	1.5
1799	1	1.5
1800	2	3.0
1801	1	1.5
Totals	**67**	**100**

Source: *Freetown Trade Database*, available from author[38]

Data on the locations along the coast where Company vessels traded is strong.[39] The evidence for voyages sent north of Freetown is especially reliable. Vessels traveling that route generally stopped in a single location and brought back their merchandize directly to Freetown. The most active northern ports that supplied Company vessels – those locations where at least three vessels conducted trade during the decade – were the Gambia, Rio Nunez, Scarcies, Bissau, and Freeport. Despite deep investment in Freeport and steady communication between it and Freetown, the factory does not stand out as exceptionally busy.

Table 3.2, Places of Trade for Vessels Trade North of Freetown, 1792-1801

Trade Location	Frequency	Percent
Gambia River	5	20.8
Freeport	4	16.7
Rio Nunez	4	16.7
Scarcies	3	12.5
Bissau	3	12.5
Iles de Los	2	8.3
Bullom Shore	1	4.2
Quiaport	1	4.2
Bulama	1	4.2
Totals	**24**	**100**

Source: Same as Table 3.1

Fewer conclusions can be drawn about the Company's southern trade. The designations that officials used to specify intended ports of trade were less precise and most vessels traveling in that direction stopped at numerous points along the coast. Some of the geographic terms that appear in the records – Windward Coast, Grain Coast, and Leeward Coast – might include any number of destinations, as the lengthy list that Parfitt made attests. Vessels sailing along the southeastern route followed the coasting pattern that slave traders in the pre-abolition era had pioneered. It is likely that many of the trade locations provided in Table 3.3, particularly those closest to Freetown, represented the first stop on a longer journey. Other vessels loaded all of their cargo close to Freetown and returned directly there.

In any case, the data indicate that the region south of Freetown was central to the commercial life and ambitions of the settlement.[40] Seventeen produce traders visited the Camaranca, Sherbro, Banana Islands, and Turtle Island, all within seventy miles of Freetown. Vessels dispatched to the Windward Coast would certainly have stopped at one of these nearby locations if only to gather information about the state of commerce further along the coast.[41] The Grain Coast, adjacent to this territory, which includes modern-day Liberia and most of the Ivory Coast, was well known for its cheap supplies of rice. Sierra Leone Company vessels evidently tried to capitalize on them. Provisions were king in early Freetown and southern Sierra Leone proved willing and capable to pitch in to feed the settlement.

Table 3.3, Places of Trade for Vessels Traveling South of Freetown, 1792-1801

Trade Location	Frequency	Percent
Sherbro	8	20
Windward Coast	7	17.5
Camaranca	6	15
Grain Coast	6	15
Gabon	3	7.5
Banana Islands	2	5
Leeward Coast	2	5
Gold Coast	2	5
Turtle Islands	1	2.5
Cape Mount	1	2.5
Cape Mesurado	1	2.5
St. Thomas Island	1	2.5
Totals	**40**	**100**

Source: Same as Table 3.1

Transformations in Agricultural Commerce in Southern Sierra Leone, 1807-1850

Freetown's financial footing under the Sierra Leone Company was never sound. Administrative costs alone averaged over £7,000 a year by the early nineteenth century. In 1800, the British government began providing subsidies to ease Company pressures. By the end of 1807, the Company had received nearly £100,000 toward that end, though that amounted to just half of what its board members paid out of their own pockets. The situation was clearly untenable. Company officials thus opened negotiations for the potential transfer of the settlement to the Crown. After a spirited debate in Parliament, the British Government in August 1807 approved the Sierra Leone Transfer Act, by which in January of the following year the settlement became Britain's first West African Colony.[42]

Many scholars have analyzed Freetown's early colonial history and assessed the fate of its settlers under British rule. An old historiography that dates back to the mid-nineteenth century viewed the colony from the perspective of British political and financial interests. Given the exorbitant costs to the Crown of the African Colony, that historiography approached Sierra Leone's history with a wide eye on its failures.[43] The tradition largely ignored Africans, except to point out their shortcomings – meaning their inability to live according to the plan the British imposed on them. More recent interpretations have privileged dynamics internal to the colony to explain major changes in nineteenth century Sierra Leone. They shine light on the agency of Africans in general and Liberated Africans specifically in the development of Freetown. James Walker describes the period between 1808 and 1815 as one during which confidence among the Nova Scotia settlers was restored. That was followed, he explains, by a short period of "position and prosperity" between 1815-1827. John Peterson outlines a steady movement toward settler "independence," through which "Liberated Africans...were able to establish effective control of the political, economic, and social dimensions of their society."[44] African dynamism has been made particularly evident in work on the colony's commercial affairs, which has emphasized the new trade diasporas that Liberated Africans pioneered into the interior, through which they successfully integrated Freetown with its hinterland. In short, the Liberated African community has increasingly been viewed as the reason for Freetown's success, however uneven it was, and despite profit-seeking motives that recent scholarship on Sierra Leone has emphasized. The Colony's failures, according to this view, were the result of Britain's exploitative policies and its lack of financial investment in the settlement.[45]

What these views share is an "inside-out" view that treats Freetown as the major center of power in Sierra Leone, from which influence and authority emanated inland. With few exceptions, the colony has been conceptualized as a part of European, imperial, and, more recently, Atlantic histories – as a place so unique that it was virtually sealed off from wider regional developments within Africa. Freetown has received far less attention in the context of African history – as a site that shaped and was shaped by the societies that surrounded it. The provisions trade opens space to consider the colony from the perspective of inland communities that helped sustain it. This "outside-in" view makes clear the degree to which the settlement relied on peoples who lived on Freetown's frontier. Highlighting that dependence lays bare the limits of colonial influence in the first half of the nineteenth century. It also allows us to consider how Africans outside of the colony perceived this unusual abolitionist project and the colonization campaign that accompanied it. It is to the provisions trade under colonial control that this chapter now turns.

Freetown and Food Supplies

Freetown's population exploded over the first half of the nineteenth century. In 1807, around the time of the British takeover, it stood at just 1,871 people. In that year the British established in Freetown a Vice Admiralty Court to enforce British maritime and prize law, through which a small stream of Africans liberated from slave vessels entered the Colony. By 1819, when a series of anti-slave trade treaties that Britain signed with other Atlantic powers led to the establishment of a Mixed Commission Court, the colony had grown to nearly 10,000. The courts contributed dramatically to Freetown's growth. By the early 1830s, the settlement surpassed 31,000 people. In a region where the majority of towns ranged between one and ten thousand residents, Freetown represented something unparalleled in the context of Sierra Leone's urban landscape.[46]

Such growth exacerbated many of the problems the Sierra Leone Company had previously faced, most importantly the issue of how to feed so many mouths. Successive officials implemented a variety of policies in an effort to keep on top of this potentially explosive issue.[47] Thomas Ludlam, who governed the colony at the time of the transfer, employed an apprenticeship system to manage Africans that the Vice Admiralty Court freed. For a fee of $20, colonists and government officials gained control over and paid for the upkeep of former slaves – a system that had uncomfortable parallels with slavery. Ludlam's outspoken successor, Thomas Thompson, drew explicit attention to those parallels and as a result fell out of favor with the British Government. Though he did not altogether abolish the apprenticeship system, Thompson set free many apprentices and provided them with land and employment. He expected the Liberated Africans to cultivate the land and feed themselves.

Moral concerns aside, the growth of the Liberated African population made the apprenticeship system difficult to sustain. Governors therefore continued to tinker with it. Lieutenant-Colonel Charles Maxwell required the "strongest" Liberated Africans – about one third of new arrivals – to enroll in the Royal African Corps or the navy. He continued to designate small numbers as apprentices. In the most drastic departure from previous policies, Maxwell founded in April of 1809 a small village, Hog Brook, located some five miles from Freetown, in which he resettled about half of the Africans whom the Vice Admiralty Court liberated. This small town – something of a side-project at the time Maxwell first established it – foreshadowed a prominent change in Freetown's administrative organization that would last throughout the early colonial era. Subsequent officials picked up and ran with the village scheme, as it came to be known, through which Africans were pushed into rural towns on the colony's frontier, where they lived under less direct supervision from colonial officials.

British officials at home and abroad had reservations about the village system. Some feared that, beyond the administration's direct gaze, the Liberated African population would "retrograde in the woods into a state of nature and barbariousness."[48] Others felt the scheme would allow the colonial government to more effectively manage deepening pressures on local resources. For this reason governors generally saw the system as invaluable; over half a century they expanded it farther inland, creating new villages as circumstances required. The scheme's most enthusiastic supporter, Charles MacCarthy, who governed the Colony for nearly a decade beginning in 1814, argued that the villages had a "civilizing" effect on their inhabitants, providing Liberated Africans with a well-structured space where they learned to be industrious and were provided with Christian instruction. Such enthusiasm led him to expand the system. Prior to 1815, the government had officially recognized just three villages: Leicester, founded in 1809; Wilberforce, founded in 1810; and Regent, founded in 1812. Building on this foundation, MacCarthy devoted the better part of five years to strengthening rural districts and increasing the number of settlers who lived in them. By the end of the decade, he had added ten new villages, comprised almost entirely of Liberated Africans. The Church Missionary Society provided each village with a supervisor who provided Christian guidance.[49]

Food production was at the heart of the village settlement initiative. MacCarthy argued that opening districts outside the city to Liberated Africans would encourage them to embrace agriculture. Better soil quality in many of the villages, he hoped, would improve the colony's productive capacity.[50] To foster cooperation among the settlers of particular villages, the government began to concentrate in them Africans from similar backgrounds. Settlements with names such as Kissy Town, Congo Town, and Kossoh Town – each reflecting an ethnolinguistic group found in different parts of West Africa – thus began to dot the colonial landscape.[51]

To further emphasize self-sufficiency among Liberated Africans, the colonial government began to limit its role as a supplier of provisions. The British had provided rations from as far back as when the maroons first arrived.[52] The government expanded the system in 1808, when Liberated Africans started disembarking in large numbers. It provided recaptives with six months of

119

provisions, including rice, salt, and palm oil. Governor Maxwell noted in 1811 that 360 Liberated Africans were receiving government-issued rice; by the end of MacCarthy's term it was estimated that more than two-thirds of Liberated Africans were being fed at least in part on the government's account. MacCarthy's death, however, signaled a switch toward what the British viewed as a more sustainable policy in which the government limited its support for new settlers. Governor Turner, MacCarthy's successor, was sent with explicit instructions to cut expenses. He slashed in half the number of people who were eligible for rations, bringing it down to about 2,000 individuals. The final blow to the rations system came under Governor Campbell, who altogether eliminated government-issued provisions, replacing them with direct payments: three pence per day over six months for men and over three months – or until marriage – for women.[53] From a British perspective, these changes appear to have had their desired effect. Cash payments reduced government spending, increased the circulation of currency within the colony, and improved Liberated Africans' purchasing power. In the rural districts recaptives steadily improved the scale of agricultural production, meeting their own needs and at times cultivating surpluses, which they exported to Freetown. District superintendents praised many of the settlers for their agricultural prowess, even if reports at times bemoaned the subsistence levels at which most settlers produced. One such report in 1825 indicated that the Colony had for the first time cultivated enough produce to feed itself.[54]

From the time Freetown was established under the Sierra Leone Company until the mid-1820s, the trade in provisions underwent several important organizational changes while maintaining a degree of continuity. As its debts increased, the Sierra Leone Company stopped sending vessels to supply Freetown with trade goods. Company-sponsored voyages along the coast, which climbed to as many as 36 in 1793, ceased entirely after 1801. In their absence, the Liberated African population aggressively pursued trade with communities in the interior. Settlers pooled funds to purchase large canoes, which they sent into neighboring rivers in search of new economic opportunities.[55] In short, the colonial government loosened its grip on commercial affairs. Despite these changes, rice continued to dominate the trade and the Sherbro continued to play a prominent role supplying that commodity. While figures are hard to quantify in the post-Company era, one Freetown merchant underscored the agricultural significance of the region south of Freetown in 1820, noting that "the rice upon which our liberated negroes subsist – the palm oil which gives a relish to that simple food – the mats upon which they sleep, are derived principally from the Sherbro."[56]

How did Liberated Africans come to play such an important role in the produce trade during this period? Traditional accounts of their commercial prowess have emphasized the economic and political advantages that recaptives gained through their ties to the British state. Such interpretations are broadly consistent with a wider historiographical trend that emphasizes the coast as a site where African and European cultures fused, creating what has variously been called Eurafrican, Atlantic, or creolized identities.[57] Access to British goods, education, or religious practices allowed Liberated Africans to use their unique status as "King's Boys" to spread their influence into the interior, backed by the might of the British military. Those studies that have examined the interior African dimensions of Liberated African communities have highlighted their connections to peoples that live in modern-day Nigeria. E. Francis White, for example, has explored how Liberated African women – particularly Yoruba – shaped trade with the Sierra Leone interior.[58] In the 1830s, the women traders in rural districts began participating in a small-scale trade bringing produce into Freetown. Over time they expanded their operations, moving beyond the Colony's boundaries and gradually tapping into major inland markets. In this way, Liberated African women turned themselves into a dominant economic force. Their Yoruba identity, according to White, facilitated their success.

This view of Liberated Africans has emerged due to a disproportionate focus on the mid-nineteenth century, by which point the colony was over half a century old, British military power began to emerge as a decisive factor in regional power struggles, and Africans from the Bight of Biafra comprised the largest population in Freetown. An analysis of the first half of the century reveals a different picture. In the first few decades after Freetown became a British Crown colony, Liberated Africans came not primarily from the Bight of Biafra but rather from ports along the coast of Sierra Leone. Moreover, given the limits of colonial authority in the region, Liberated African agency mattered less in these decades than did local leaders' reactions to Freetown merchants. That many Liberated Africans had in the 1810s and 20s been born around Sierra Leone made it easier to forge connections between the colony and its immediate interior. The traders' familiarity with local customs and commercial practices enabled them to complete a commercial circuit that reconnected them with the communities where they were born while also bringing valuable produce back to the settlement.

The nature of British suppression efforts contributed to this process. Prior to the creation of the Court of Mixed Commission, British abolitionist activity along the African coast was extremely limited. With few resources at its disposal, early navy seizures generally occurred in Freetown's vicinity. Of the roughly 15,000 recaptives who were put on vessels that the British intercepted in the decade after the Vice Admiralty Court began operating, nearly a third were embarked along the Upper Guinea Coast and more than one thousand were purchased from Sherbro or Gallinas, in southern Sierra Leone.[59] The mandate of the British antislavery fleet between 1808 and 1818 thus ensured a steady presence in Freetown of settlers from the broader Sierra Leone region. In some cases, those individuals were close enough to home that they made regular trips back to the villages of their birth.

John Kizell provides a clear (if somewhat exceptional) example. The son of prominent Sherbro political leaders, Kizell was enslaved around the age of 12 and forcibly transported to the Americas. He maintained clear memories of his childhood and continued to speak the Sherbro language following his escape from captivity. When he returned to Freetown in the 1790s, Kizell tried his hand as a farmer before turning to trade. He borrowed £5, which he and two other settlers used to build a craft sufficient to carry 12 tons of cargo. By the mid-1790s, Kizell was actively trading in the Sherbro country, where he had established a factory at Camplar, at which he traded for rice and bullocks. In 1811, Kizell was elected president of The Friendly Society of Sierra Leone, the first cooperative commercial society in the Colony, through which settlers could grow or buy produce and market it abroad.[60]

Kizell did not limit himself to opportunities within the colony. Following the creation of the American Colonization Society in 1816, two United States delegates sailed to West Africa seeking a suitable location for an American-run settlement. In Freetown the men befriended Kizell, who recommended they settle down in his homeland. The party traveled together down to Sherbro Island, where Kizell introduced them to several prominent headmen, including King Sherbro, Kizell's father. Although the Sherbro plan never materialized, it is clear from his involvement in it that Kizell had become a powerbroker. Indeed, when warfare broke out and threatened the Sherbro trade, Governor Ludlam dispatched Kizell to negotiate a peace treaty on behalf of the British Government.[61] Such responsibility underscores the significant role that Liberated Africans played in the affairs of the interior and suggests that particular African language and cultural elements were central to the extension of settlers' political and commercial interests.

Shifts in the origins of the Liberated African population may also explain a second change in the provisions trade that began in the mid-1820s. The impression among village supervisors in that decade was that rice was becoming less central to Liberated Africans' diets. While several external factors (see below) shaped rice consumption, one likely reason for the shift was the growing number of Liberated Africans who came from areas outside of the African rice zone. Accounting for as many as one in three between 1808 and 1818, the number of Liberated Africans who grew up consuming this grain as their primary staple dropped steadily in favor of those from yam-consuming areas from the Bight of Biafra. Over the 1820s, Liberated Africans who originated from outside of Upper Guinea outnumbered by nearly ten to one those who came from within the region.[62]

Reports from village superintendents confirm the gradual shift within the colony to other kinds of provisions. That was in part due to the ongoing struggle to produce rice within colonial boundaries. In the early-nineteenth century, Captain Hallowell, who was sent to inquire into the state of the settlement, reported that "our colonists have preferred the cultivation of cassada, yams &c. to that of rice and Indian corn, though a proportion of both the latter has been generally planted."[63] By the second half of the 1820s, however, the superintendents began to specifically link food preferences to the origins of the Liberated African population. One report noted, "at Wellington some rice is grown, but with many natives being Aku, they often prefer maize."[64] As Liberated Africans turned to new crops to satisfy their preferences and that suited local agricultural conditions, the growth of the slave trade in the Gallinas led Sherbro rice traders to turn away from the colony and toward the more lucrative markets that were emerging around slave barracoons.

Sherbro Provisions and the Atlantic Slave Trade

The connection between food supplies and the slave trade has not received the attention it merits.[65] In Upper Guinea, an endless trade in rice fueled virtually every aspect of the slave system. The Sherbro region in particular witnessed a huge spike in rice production and trade to satisfy the demands of nineteenth-century slave dealers. As an American missionary noted in the 1840s, "a slave trader will not buy slaves when he has no means of feeding them."[66] From the 1820s, Sherbro's produce traders thus became the feeders of the slave trade, supplying rice for consumption by captives held in barracoons and for storage by captains of vessels carrying captives across the Atlantic.

Sherbro's role in the provisions trade was not an entirely new one. In the late-seventeenth century, when the British Royal African Company first opened a factory in the region to trade for camwood, agents noted the abundance of rice that local merchants were capable of supplying. By the 1720s, when wood stocks were on the decline and officials began to debate whether to abandon the factory, merchants highlighted the quantity and quality of Sherbro provisions to argue for keeping it open.[67] In addition to supplying food for other British establishments along the Sierra Leone coast, produce traders also sold rice to transatlantic slave traders. John Newton, the famed slaver who later became an abolitionist, purchased large amounts of rice on the Banana and Sherbro Islands during his four voyages to Sierra Leone in the 1750s. His later testimony to the House of Commons provides more detailed evidence on the Sherbro rice trade.[68]

However, as southern Sierra Leone ports became more directly involved in the slave trade in the era of abolition, Atlantic commerce placed heavier demands on local agricultural supplies. Increased numbers of vessels competed with each other in a limited number of ports along the coast to gain access to produce. Slave dealers in the Gallinas entered into agreements with headmen from neighboring areas to secure rice for their captives. Jose Alvarez, a notorious slave merchant at Gallinas, regularly sent his vessels to Lemaignere, a Sherbro-based French associate, to be stocked with food. In 1840, for example, Lemaignere provided sixty tons of rice for the vessel *Eliza Davidson*. Lemaignere also had connections to the house of Blanco and Carballo, of Havana, which financed many of the voyages sent to the Gallinas. Siaka, the notorious Gallinas king, had in the 1820s dispatched vessels to Sam Fish of Sugary, near Cape Mount, for food supplies but in 1840 he noted of the Sherbro and Plantain Islands that "our whole subsistence of rice comes from these ports." Theodore Canot also turned to the Sherbro, among other areas, for provisions.[69]

Rice was thus central to the organization and operation of the southern Sierra Leone slave trade. During raids on prominent slave factories in the Gallinas, British captains discovered large stores of rice meant for the captives. At a small factory called "Dindo," Robert Quin found in a single storage facility eight tons of rice meant for domestic consumption.[70] James Campbell, a Mende Liberated African, explained that he was fed a small portion of dried rice during his forced march to the coast. He also described how he was beaten for taking too long to fetch wood for cooking the rice. Upon reaching the Gallinas coast, he was confined to a barracoon for about a month, where he was given "plenty" of rice and water.[71]

Rarely was the significance of rice more evident than when its supply dried up. A failure of the rice crop in the later half of the 1840s nearly upended the system. Unable to feed their slaves, coastal merchants began turning captives out onto the area beaches, demanding that they feed themselves. One British captain noted with horror that "the beach was strewed with their bones."[72] The inability to secure provisions could ruin a transatlantic voyage, too. Captain Ponz of the slaver *Feliz* canvased the area around the Pongo River for several months in search of rice to feed a cargo of slaves he intended to ship from there to Cuba. Such was his desperation that Ponz even tried to purchase provisions from an officer on a passing British antislavery cruiser, explaining that the vessel's crew was subsisting on cassava and jerked beef. The slaves, who had been prepared for embarkation for months, could not be loaded given the lack of food. Some were dying of starvation; the crew was in a "mutinous" state.[73]

The growth of the direct export trade in slaves from southern Sierra Leone created competing markets for Sherbro rice. Headmen in the Sherbro gradually turned away from Freetown and toward the Gallinas. Several factors account for that decision. A slight difference in transportation costs provides part of the explanation. Gallinas was not just physically closer to the Sherbro; it was also accessible via canoe throughout the year. The Bombotene waterway, which runs nearly parallel to the coast, provided the highway that connected the two regions, allowing travelers to ferry provisions and other goods back and forth over just a few days. That same waterway – and the streams and creeks that fed off of it – made communication between Freetown and Sherbro possible for part of the year, but the journey was longer, more costly, and more arduous. [74]

More importantly, merchants and captains participating in the slave trade consistently outbid Freetown traders to attract Sherbro provisions. Governor Ludlam pointed this out as early as 1802, when he complained that Freetown's rice supplies were suffering at the hands of slave ship captains who offered higher prices for produce.[75] An early trickle of British complaints became a flood as vessels arrived in larger numbers and slaves were held along the coast in larger quantities. By the late 1820s, one district superintendent commented that Gallinas slave dealers monopolized the market for Sherbro rice. Forced to choose between two hungry settlements, prominent Sherbro headmen threw their support behind the Gallinas and began to restrict the sale of rice to Freetown. According to the Reverend Frederick Schön, who resided in the colony for most of the 1830s, "native chiefs prevented their subjects from selling their rice to any but to the slave traders."[76] As a result, Liberated-African merchants were squeezed out of the trade altogether and forced to move their operations into the adjacent and less productive Krim country.[77]

Not all Liberated Africans, however, drew such a fine distinction between "legitimate" and slave commerce. Sierra Leone's governors took note with some alarm of how Liberated Africans blended textiles and other goods with commodities used to fuel the slave trade. John Jackson, a settler who moved regularly between Freetown and the Gallinas to trade in cloth and ivory, indicated that some Liberated Africans purchased large quantities of rice in the Sherbro and sold it in the Gallinas, where higher demand for the crop meant greater profits. More damningly, Jackson noted that two settlers from the colony were living permanently in the Gallinas, where they worked for Pedro

Blanco. He saw many other Freetown residents there.[78] Recaptives used their commercial connections to wade into and out of the networks that slave commerce supported.

Having drawn Sherbro provisions to the slave markets, Gallinas dealers turned their full attention to exporting human cargo. The regional commercial system they created – a coastal settlement dependent on an agriculturally rich hinterland – at least partially resembled that of other parts of the world.[79] Profits from the slave trade and steady supplies of Sherbro rice allowed Gallinas leaders to neglect local agricultural production. When Captain Howland, an American trader, arrived in the Gallinas in 1822, some two decades into the expansion of the southern Sierra Leone slave trade, he painted with evident bias a picture that Europeans had long sketched in their travel accounts of Africa: "The men were all idling about, while the women were doing all the labor of farming, cultivating and raising rice, corn, yuca, tarra, Casava, and other vegetables and roots, including yams." Gallinas's local farming industry appeared at the very least capable of meeting local food demands. Five years later, according to another observer, Gallinas traders were importing all of their food with the exception of cassava, which was comparatively easy to grow. By the 1840s, inhabitants of the Gallinas appear to have turned their collective backs on agriculture.[80]

The merchants who plied the waterways that connected Sherbro and Gallinas were often blamed for undermining British efforts to suppress the slave trade. This included Liberated Africans, who circulated into and out of the colony for commercial purposes and participated regularly in trade in the area's slaving centers. Many, the colonial government suspected, engaged in both slave trading and legitimate commerce, using one to mask the other. Captain Dunlop, a naval officer who oversaw British stations along the entire Upper Guinea coast, complained that merchants used the Bombotene passageway to avoid entering the open sea, through which they "entirely eluded our squadron, and were supplying themselves with goods from our own colony; they were sending large canoes from down the rivers from the

Gallinas, and purchasing their goods at Sierra Leone."[81] That Liberated Africans – individuals who were intimately familiar with the transatlantic trade – might support the traffic underscores the complex realities of slavery and abolition in Africa. As officers on antislavery patrols became more familiar with the organization of regional commerce, their efforts to suppress the slave trade evolved to include disrupting commercial ties between Sherbro and Gallinas. The British navy began to quite literally starve the slave trade. A temporary blockade in 1840 prevented vessels from leaving or entering the region. Its impact was immediate and profound. In a panic, Siaka penned a letter to Governor Doherty in Freetown complaining that "Since Her Majesty's Ships of War have blockaded our port all former correspondence with the Sherbro and Plantain Islands has been entirely cut off; and for a proof several of our boats and canoes have been fired upon by Her Majesty's ships of War, and several taken with cargos of rice in them." The rice, he claimed, was removed from the canoes before the officers returned the vessels. He warned, "interfering with our canoes in such a way will cause a famine in our country" – a calculus the British navy may have deemed worth it in order to shut down the slave traffic.[82]

Although the Gallinas slave trade rebounded once the blockade was lifted, naval officers did not forget the valuable lesson they learned: in the absence of food supplies, the slave trade could not effectively operate. When in 1848 Captain Dunlop led a more ambitious assault on the region's slave trade, he made sure to once again target routes that connected Sherbro and Gallinas. He formally declared war on the Gallinas slave dealers, which facilitated more direct actions against the towns they inhabited. Having done that, Charles Hotham, a prominent British naval officer who patrolled the area around Gallinas, then proclaimed that all vessels carrying goods into that port were subject to seizure. The officers next met with several Sherbro headmen, in particular Thomas Stephen Caulker, who commanded the entryway into the Boom River that lead to the Gallinas, and requested that they destroy or otherwise interfere with canoes that passed from Freetown to the south. The Sherbro chiefs consented to this approach and in the process undermined the foundation on which the Gallinas trade flourished. Within six weeks, the Gallinas was once again in a state of famine. While slaves remained readily available there, merchants expressed concern about how costly it had become to feed them.[83]

In southern Sierra Leone, provisions provided the lifeblood of the Gallinas slave trade in the first half of the nineteenth century. That it took British naval officers some three decades to understand that reality reflects the limits of their suppression campaign and more generally the blinders that abolitionist philosophy imposed on British officials. Commercial food production was, after all, supposed to provide a path away from slavery, not toward it. Deprived through the blockade of the wealth that slave exports generated and unable to purchase provisions for themselves and their dependents, Gallinas leaders finally lashed out against foreign slave traders, expelling them from the territory, often aggressively. Underscoring the contradictory web that abolitionism spun, some forty-four Gallinas-based Cuban and Brazilian slave traders were forced to seek protection on British cruisers and later in Freetown itself before they returned home.[84]

The Volume of Sherbro Rice Exports
Situated between a densely populated new city and a booming slave mart, Sherbro planters played a central role in sustaining both settlements while all the while continuing to feed their own households. The magnitude of produce exports in the first half of the nineteenth century facilitated what must have amounted to an agricultural revolution. While the scale of the Sherbro region's response to new markets for rice seems incredible, studies of other coastal societies indicate how quickly Africans adapted to changes in the demand for produce in the era of the slave trade. In Guinea Bissau, for example, Walter Hawthorne has illustrated how the Balanta expanded the cultivation of paddy rice between the fifteenth and nineteenth centuries, a process that European supplies of iron helped facilitate. In the Senegal River

Valley, James Searing highlights connections between the slave trade and the production of millet. The Sherbro shares a number of characteristics with both of these areas. As with the Balanta, Sherbro societies were decentralized, organized under headmen who held varying degrees of power and influence. And in common with the Senegambia, the rising demand for provisions in Sierra Leone developed in response to the emergence of large urban settlements along the coast.[85] However, the sheer size of Freetown and the scale of the Gallinas slave trade probably resulted in a more dramatic increase in agricultural production in the Sherbro than in Senegambia or Guinea Bissau.

What was the scale of Sherbro rice exports in the first half of the nineteenth century? Estimates below provide an appreciation for African agricultural production and innovation. They are based on a number of assumptions. For example, commercial agents in Freetown did not keep detailed records of the quantity of rice they purchased or the various sources of food supply beyond their borders. At best colonial merchants offer qualitative evidence that allows for an analysis of the comparative significance of particular inland regions to Freetown's food supplies. From a Sherbro perspective, it is not always clear whether rice was produced within the region itself or purchased from deeper in the interior. But the existing evidence suggests that in the majority of cases, the rice that ended up in Freetown and on slave vessels was indeed cultivated within a short distance of the coast. One merchant noted that rice traders came from a maximum of three or four days inland. Governor Ludlam speculated, "the land behind the Sherbro must be rich from the amount of rice they bring down." Other observers singled out the Boom, Kittam, and Bagroo as major producers and suppliers of rice.[86]

Finally, produce merchants did not always specify the type of rice they traded. While this does not affect estimates of rice exports, it limits our ability to consider questions about the relationship between food and cultural change. In general, it seems Freetown settlers and slave traders consumed rain-fed ("dry") rice, which was surely cheaper than the swampland variety culti-

131

vated along the coast. According to John McCormack, a leading Freetown-based merchant who spent decades in Sierra Leone, "Nearly the whole of the rice grown in the neighbourhood of Sierra Leone is on dry ground... dry-ground rice is best and is the principle food consumed by [Freetown] inhabitants."[87] It is also clear that at least in Freetown, both red and white varieties were available.[88]

Despite the limitations of these data, there exists sufficient evidence to estimate the scale of the external trade in Sherbro rice. On several occasions, Freetown officials and merchants provided figures on annual rice consumption. For the years when it is unknown, census data can be used to fill in gaps. For the slave trade, the data is more straightforward. Commercial records of slaving voyages often include details on where and in what quantities provisions were purchased. Statements from captives from the time they were awaiting shipment at the Gallinas allow for a rough estimate of rice consumption in Gallinas barracoons. Taken together, these data underscore the dramatic expansion of agricultural production required to sustain slave and free industries in Sierra Leone.

Freetown
The central factor that dictated Freetown's demand for food was its expanding population. From 1792, when it first became clear that Sherbro was a prominent supplier of Freetown's rice, until 1827, when rice exports become more difficult to estimate, Freetown's population increased by about sixteen thousand. Following the destruction of the original Province of Freedom, some 1,200 people – mostly former slaves from Nova Scotia – arrived in 1792. Scattered data reveals that the population climbed slowly toward 2,000 in the first decade of the nineteenth century. By 1811, with the Vice Admiralty Court in operation, the population had jumped to around 3,500. Once the Mixed Commission Court opened in 1819, Freetown included almost 10,000 inhabitants. Its population surpassed 17,500 in 1827 and by the end of the decade was thought to top 30,000.

Population growth meant more mouths to feed. In August and September of 1793, Zachary Macaulay provided two separate estimates for daily rice consumption in Freetown. In the first, he noted that the settlement consumed half a ton of rice each day; the following month, when provisions may have been less abundant, Macaulay suggested, "3 ½ tons…may with some care serve the colony for ten days."[89] As this implies, food supplies in Freetown, as elsewhere in Africa, varied by the time of the year. In this case, consumption dropped by about thirty percent as the rainy season came to an end. Nevertheless, Macaulay's half-ton estimate represents a surprisingly generous daily food intake for settlers. Although no official population data exist for 1793, the size of the settlement probably did not increase much from the previous year.[90] If we assume the population remained around 1,150 and imagine an equal portion of rice being shared among each inhabitant then, according to Macaulay, each individual settler would have consumed nearly a pound of rice per day. Even taking his lesser daily estimate, .35 tons, would indicate a total daily intake of just under than three quarters of a pound per settler. That rice would have been supplemented with other foods.

Table 3.4, Freetown Population, 1792-1827

Year	Population Estimate
1792	1,150
1802	1,641
1807	1,871
1811	3,500
1814	5,520
1816	9,500
1818	9,565
1820	12,509
1822	15,081
1826	16,510
1827	17,512

Source: Kuczynski, *Demographic Survey*, 154-56; TNA, CO272 (Blue Book) Series for Sierra Leone[91]

133

The next hard estimate for rice consumption, some three decades later, was generated upon the arrival of the new superintendent of the Liberated African Department. In that official's first report on the state of the Liberated Africans, he noted that annual consumption of rice in the colony probably exceeded six hundred tons, or approximately 1.64 tons per day.[92] With a population of 17,512 in 1827, this would amount to a daily intake of a little more than .2 pounds per person per day. The drastic drop in rice consumption by the second half of the 1820s is consistent with changes in settlers' food preferences and the reorientation of rice supplies to the Gallinas described above.

Evidence regarding the consumption of rice between these two years is more difficult to assess. There is little to suggest that Liberated Africans' preferences for rice declined, at least up to 1819, when the Mixed Commission Courts were established. Constraints on rice consumption between the 1790s and 1819 would therefore have been based on supply limitations or purchasing problems within Freetown. Poor harvests, for example, would have affected the availability of rice throughout Sierra Leone. More localized concerns, such as warfare or political uncertainty, would also have strained rice surpluses. Although in general, rice supplies remained steady during this period, colonial officials noted acute rice shortages in three different years: 1803, when warfare among Sherbro leaders produced near-famine conditions; and also in 1811 and 1824.[93]

Table 3.5, Annual Rice Consumption in Freetown, 1792-1818

Year	Population	Estimated Annual Rice Consumption (tons)
1792	1,150	127-183
1802	1,641	182-259
1807	1,871	207-296
1811	3,500	388-553
1814	5,520	612-872
1816	9,500	1,053-1,502
1818	9,565	1,060-1,512

Source: Calculated from Table 3.4; and Suzanne Schwartz, *Zachary Macaulay, 1793-4*, Part I, 46 and 58[94]

134

Table 3.5 provides estimates of annual rice consumption in Freetown between 1792 and 1818 – the years when the highest proportion of Liberated Africans came from rice-consuming regions. The range is based on Macaulay's two estimates. Given that Macaulay generated his figures during the hungry season, prior to the harvest of the rice crop, the figures in the final column are likely lower-bound estimates. The spike in rice consumption over a quarter century is striking. Settlers nearly doubled the amount of rice they consumed over each consecutive estimate. By 1818, annual consumption – virtually all of which came from outside of Freetown – reached some 1,500 tons.[95]

Table 3.6 turns to rice consumption in Freetown between 1818 and 1827, when the colony became less reliant on food from external sources. Although it is impossible to calculate precise estimates, I have assumed a fixed reduction in rice supply of ten percent per settler for each of the four years for which population data exists.[96] From its highpoint of between a thousand and one and a half thousand tons of rice consumed annually in 1818, the colony's rice consumption fell by at least half over the next decade.

Table 3.6, Annual Rice Consumption in Freetown, 1818-1827

Year	Population	Estimated Annual Rice Consumption (tons) [97]
1818	9,565	1,060-1,512
1820	12,509	1,019
1822	15,081	983
1826	16,510	807
1827	17,512	571

Source: Same as Table 3.4

Since Freetown merchants did not carefully document every transaction for rice, determining the Sherbro share of Freetown's rice imports is challenging. Two factors would have influenced the availability of Sherbro rice. Shortages in 1803, 1811, and 1824 would have reduced the provisions trade from the south. And

135

second, over the 1820s, Sherbro merchants gradually pivoted to Gallinas buyers. In productive years the Sherbro likely supplied at least half of the rice that entered the colony.[98] Even during times of famine, some Sherbro produce would still have made it to Freetown, though I have assumed that supplies were halved – in other words, that Sherbro supplied a quarter of the colony's total rice needs. Finally, in the 1820s, as Sherbro headmen began placing restrictions on trade with the British settlement, I have assumed that Sherbro rice accounted for about forty percent of the total supply of produce to the colony instead of fifty.

Table 3.7, Export of Rice from Sherbro to Freetown, 1792-1827

Year	Estimated Annual Rice Consumption (tons)	Sherbro Supply (tons) [99]
1792	127-183	64 – 92
1802	182-259	91 – 130
1807	207-296	104 – 148
1811	388-553	97 – 138
1814	612-872	306 – 436
1816	1,053-1,502	527 – 751
1818	1,060-1,512	530 – 756
1820	1,019	408
1822	983	393
1826	807	323
1827	571	228

Source: Tables 3.5 and 3.6

Table 3.7 allows us to raise a basic but fundamental question: what impact did Freetown's growth have on Sherbro rice exports? The data suggest that over thirty five-years, Sherbro planters produced anywhere between sixty and 750 tons of rice per year for the Freetown market.[100] As a whole, it is feasible that somewhere between 8,000 and 9,000 tons of rice made its way from Sherbro farms into Liberated Africans' bowls. That Sherbro farmers and traders responded so dynamically to the growing need within Freetown for produce is remarkable indeed. And yet, the market in the colony was one part of a much larger system of commercial agriculture.

The Slave Trade

The growth of the slave trade in nineteenth century southern Sierra Leone was built on a foundation of reliable food supplies. Walter Rodney called attention to this point some five decades ago but scholars have in general given limited attention to it.[101] In the Gallinas, where the majority of provisions were imported, the demands the traffic placed on the region's agricultural systems were particularly acute. Slaves were fed with Sherbro-grown produce – and at times less desirable European foods – from the time they were first captured until they arrived in the Americas. While the specific foods that slaves ate depended on what was locally available, captives from the Upper Guinea Coast were almost universally fed a rice-based diet.[102]

How did the supply of rice for the slave trade compare to its counterpart for Freetown? The answer depends on the volume of slave exports in any given year. In evidence he gave to the Lord's Committee on the slave trade, John Matthews estimated that between 700 and 1,000 tons of rice was required annually to feed the 3,000 to 5,000 slaves embarked in Sierra Leone from the time they arrived in factories along the coast until they reached the Americas. That estimate may or may not have included wastage – rice that spoiled or was otherwise inedible.[103] Matthews's calculation of slave exports is surprisingly accurate, as chapter one illustrated: according to the *Voyages* database, some 4,100 slaves left Sierra Leone annually in the mid-1780s, when Matthews resided there.[104] Based on these figures it is possible to derive a simple figure for daily rice consumption among Sierra Leone's captive population. Dividing Matthews' estimate for rice consumption by annual slave exports suggests that slaves received a supply of about 1.25 pounds of rice per day.[105] Such a generous supply of food seems surprising and indeed, given that this is merely an estimate it is worth noting that slaves would not necessarily have been given or consumed this much rice. On the other hand, the profits at stake meant that it worked to a captain's advantage to sustain slaves during the dreaded Middle Passage, if only to ensure that they fetched maximum returns in the Americas.

Given the close ties between the slave and produce trades, any estimate of rice consumption must first address changes in the volume of slave exports. Table 3.8 provides five-year estimates of slave exports from the Gallinas and Sherbro between 1807 and 1856. During this half-century, nearly 240 slaving vessels embarked more than 100,000 slaves at the ports. Slave exports from the region increased gradually up to around 1820, at which point they began to grow in earnest. Between the 1820s and 1850, exports remained steady, removing from southern Sierra Leone some 3,000 and 4,000 captives per annum.

Table 3.8, Southern Sierra Leone Slave Exports, 1807-1856 (Rounded to Nearest Hundred)

Years	Totals
1807-1810	700
1811-1815	900
1816-1820	10,000
1821-1825	20,800
1826-1830	16,000
1831-1835	9,600
1836-1840	26,600
1841-1845	4,000
1846-1850	10,200
1851-1855	2,500
1856	2,300
Totals	103,600

Source: Eltis et al., *Voyages*[106]

Is it possible to estimate the amount of rice needed to sustain this volume of slave exports from southern Sierra Leone? We can begin by returning to Matthews' estimate: 1.25 pounds of rice provided per slave per day. Multiplying that number by annual slave exports provides a figure for daily rice consumption for slaves leaving Sherbro and Gallinas. Distributing the daily figure over a year generates an annual estimate. Table 3.9 shows the results of these calculations spread over five-year intervals. From a low point of just over twenty-five tons between 1807 and 1810, the demand for rice grew substantially over the next two decades. Between 1821 and 1840, in order to meet the daily estimate that Matthews provided, planters in the region would have needed to produce many hundreds of tons of rice. At its height in the second half of the 1830s, the Gallinas imported more than 1,100 tons of produce to feed departing slaves. Given the scale of commercial agriculture required for the continuation of the slave trade, it is unsurprising that Sherbro merchants had ultimately to choose between the Freetown and Gallinas food markets.

Table 3.9, Rice Supplies for the Southern Sierra Leone Slave Trade, 1807-1856

Year	Southern Sierra Leone Slave Exports[107]	Rice Supplies to Sustain Slave Trade (tons)	Annual Average of Rice Supplies (tons)	Annual Sherbro Share of Rice Supplies (tons)[108]
1807-1810	700	145	36	27
1811-1815	900	186	37	28
1816-1820	10,000	2,070	414	311
1821-1825	20,800	4,305	861	732
1826-1830	16,000	3,311	662	563
1831-1835	9,600	1,987	397	397
1836-1840	26,600	5,505	1,101	1,101
1841-1845	4,000	828	166	166
1846-1850	10,200	2,111	422	422
1851-1855	2,500	517	103	103
1856	2,300	476	95	95
Totals	**103,600**	**21,441**		

Source: Same as Table 3.8

We can check these estimates against data from slave voyages that recorded rice purchases and daily food consumption. Table 3.10 lists seven separate vessels that purchased slaves along the Upper Guinea Coast. Each of these vessels sailed before the nineteenth century and most embarked captives outside of southern Sierra Leone. But since they all purchased large quantities of rice to feed slaves during the Middle Passage, it is worth comparing them to the estimates based on Matthews. For each voyage, the amount of rice purchased is recorded along with the number of slaves it embarked. The final column shows the amount of rice carried per slave for each voyage. This should not be read to imply that slaves actually consumed this much food. Slave ship captains would certainly have put aside provisions for extraordinary circumstances, such as an unusually long passage.

Table 3.10, Rice Carried on Slave Vessels, 1684-1790

Vessel Name	Year	Total Slaves Purchased	Total Rice Purchased for Voyage (tons)	Rice/Slave (tons/pounds)
Charles	1684	70	2.1	.03 / 67.2
Speedwell	1688	233	8.3	.036 / 80.64
Little Berkley Castle	1688	150	4	.027 / 60.48
Sherborough Galley	1721	231	6	.026 / 58.24
Rhode Island	1749	120	3.8	.032 / 71.68
Duke of Argyle	1751	156	7.8	.05 / 112
Crescent	1790	268	12	.045 / 100.8

Source: Calculated from TNA, T70/941, p. 47; TNA, T70/943, p. 35; TNA, T70/944, p. 9; T70/957, p. 147; *A Book of Trade*, MSS., B.V. *Rhode Island*, N-YHS; Martin and Spurrell, eds., *Journal of a Slave Trader;* TNA, HCA16/83/2218[109]

A more detailed assessment is available for those vessels for which a provisions manifest survives. The ship *Crescent* is compelling because it purchased the majority of its captives along the coast of Sierra Leone and its records carefully document daily rice consumption. Having arrived on the coast in November of 1789, the *Crescent* cruised back and forth between the Banana Islands and the Iles de Los making arrangements for the purchase of slaves. In March, the vessel loaded its first supplies of rice to feed the small number of slaves it had embarked. William Roper, the ship's captain, continued to purchase slaves and provisions until June, when the vessel departed for Jamaica. By the time the *Crescent* began its passage across the Atlantic, the slaves on board had already consumed more than 300 "crews" of rice, leaving 26,554 pounds of food for the remainder of the voyage.

While the consumption of rice during the period of purchase on the coast is difficult to calculate, several direct estimates of rice usage during the Middle Passage exist. Interestingly, the crew of the *Crescent* fed slaves unevenly. In their first calculation off the African coast, slaves consumed 224 pounds of rice and an equal portion of beans on one day and just half that amount on the following day. Slave portions increased as the vessel neared Dominica, its first port of call across the Atlantic. By the end of June, captives were consuming between 300 and 360 pounds of rice each day. Once the vessel arrived in the Caribbean, consumption stabilized at 324 pounds of rice each day; slaves were no longer given beans. Here we see documented the idea that slave ship captains "fattened up" their human cargo in preparation for American slave markets.

Figures from the *Crescent* and other slave vessels allow us to gain a general sense of food consumption on slave vessels. The 270 slaves embarked on the *Crescent* were fed roughly half a pound of rice per day in the early part of their forced crossing. As they approached the Americas that increased to a daily amount of around one and one-quarter pounds. Generally speaking, we can assume that captains aimed to feed their slaves around a pound of rice per day. This is consistent with the approach that Samuel Bacon, one of the American Colonization Society representatives who explored the Sherbro region in 1820, took. He purchased the schooner *Augusta*, a 104-ton vessel in which he intended to carry a hundred slaves. According to Bacon, his slaves were fed one pint of rice per day – roughly .8 pounds, assuming the rice was uncooked.[110]

It is now possible to estimate the overall supply of rice for vessels involved in the transatlantic trade from southern Sierra Leone. Between 1807 and 1856, the slave trade from southern Sierra Leone was heavily concentrated to Cuba. Of the nearly 100,000 slaves exported during this period, some sixty-five percent – probably even more – were destined for that island.[111] The average length of passage from Sierra Leone to Cuba during this period was 43 days; in one case it took as long as seventy. If we assume that captains planned cautiously for a sixty-day passage, they would have needed between 48 and sixty pounds of rice for each captive. Given the comparatively cheap cost of African provisions, it is safe to further assume most captains would have taken on far more than they needed. Allowing for an extra third suggests that vessels carried between 64 and 80 pounds of rice for each slave on board.[112]

Using that estimate, Table 3.11 provides a breakdown of the volume of rice supplies directed toward the southern Sierra Leone slave trade. A comparison with Table 3.9 indicates that Matthews' estimates are considerably higher. For the five-year period beginning in 1836, the difference between the two estimates is some 4,500 tons. Yet the figures are not as skewed as they at first appear. As chapter one explained, British efforts to suppress the slave trade drastically altered the way slave dealing was organized. Whereas earlier voyages to Sierra Leone confined captives on slave vessels for extended periods of time during the coasting phase of the operation, the fear of capture in the nineteenth century eliminated the coasting strategy altogether. This unique feature of the nineteenth century slave trade had important consequences for provisions supplies. Captains fed slaves for lesser amounts of time. That responsibility switched to operators of coastal barracoons, who in the era of abolition had to be prepared to provide for captives until the coast was clear of naval cruisers. By the 1820s, Gallinas barracoons held as many as two thousand slaves at a time. The Sherbro could have accommodated another thousand. Assuming that the enslaved population in this region consumed rice at a rate similar to what Liberated Africans did would add roughly five hundred tons of rice consumption each year, bringing estimates at least somewhat closer to those provided in Table 3.9.[113]

Table 3.11, Rice Carried on Slave Vessels from Southern Sierra Leone, 1807-1856

Year	Southern Sierra Leone Slave Exports	Rice Production to Sustain Slave Trade (tons)	Annual Rice Production (tons)	Annual Sherbro Share of Production[114]
1807-1810	700	20-25	5-6	4-5
1811-1815	900	26-33	5-7	4-5
1816-1820	10,000	290-363	58-73	44-55
1821-1825	20,800	604-755	121-151	103-128
1826-1830	16,000	464-581	93-116	70-87
1831-1835	9,600	279-348	56-70	56-70
1836-1840	26,600	772-965	154-193	154-193
1841-1845	4,000	116-145	23-29	23-29
1846-1850	10,200	296-370	59-74	59-74
1851-1855	2,500	73-91	15-18	15-18
1856	2,300	67-83	67-83	67-83
Totals	103,600	3,009-3,759		

Source: Tables 3.8 and 3.9

Adding the volume of the rice trade to Freetown and Gallinas provides a window into the scale of commercial rice cultivation in the Sherbro in the nineteenth century. Table 3.12 shows the two estimates side-by-side over a twenty-year period. The data is consistent with observations from Freetown officials. The colony competed effectively into the 1820s for Sherbro rice. However, Sherbro's pivot to the Gallinas had clear effects on Freetown rice consumption. Colony merchants were quite right to fear the growing influence of slave dealers on Sherbro agriculture; naval officers saw clearly that disrupting the rice trade would undermine the slave system.

Table 3.12: Sherbro Rice Supplies to Freetown and Gallinas, 1807-1827 (in tons)

Year	Supply of Rice for Slave Trade	Supply of Rice for Freetown	Total Rice Supplied
1807	27	104 – 148	131-175
1811	28	97 – 138	125-166
1814	28	306 – 436	334-464
1816	311	527 – 751	838-1,062
1818	311	530 – 756	841-1,067
1820	311	408	719
1822	732	393	1,125
1826	563	323	886
1827	563	228	791

Source: Tables 3.7 and 3.9

Conclusion

Food supplies were at the heart of the slave trade, colonialism, and urbanization in nineteenth century Sierra Leone. The dynamic growth of the southern Sierra Leone slave trade would hardly have been possible without a parallel increase of commercial-scale agriculture. This is equally true for Freetown, which would surely have failed if not for rice from the Sherbro. That Sherbro leaders exploited new commercial opportunities should not be surprising. However, a quantification of the rice trade provides a clearer picture of the specific demands that the slave trade and the expansion of colonial cities placed on the local societies that fed these sites. The magnitude of the nineteenth century produce trade, which at its height reached around a thousand tons a year, suggests that Sherbro leaders successfully mobilized labor power even as local peoples were pulled into the slave trade.

The evolution of the Sherbro rice trade has several important implications for West Africa in the nineteenth century. The organization of the trade demonstrates that southern Sierra Leone merchants were still in a position of relative strength when trading with Company and colony officials. In the first few decades of the settlement's operation, Freetown was far more dependent on interior traders than vice versa. African merchants were able to specify precisely the colors, sizes, and quantities of European goods that they desired in exchange for their produce. Company and colony merchants had little choice but to comply with those demands. The targeting by British naval cruisers of the provisions trade to Gallinas in the 1840s also underscores the evolution of Britain's campaign to suppress the slave trade – a new phase of what Scanlan defines as the "militant" nature of colonial expansion in Sierra Leone – and the growing realization of how the slave trade deeply integrated itself into local processes of production and trade.

Notes

1 John Peterson, *Province of Freedom: A History of Sierra Leone, 1787-1870* (London: Faber and Faber, 1969), 13.
2 Walter Rodney, "Jihad and Social Revolution in Futa Djalon in the Eighteenth Century," *Journal of the Historical Society of Nigeria* 4, no. 2 (June 1968): 283.
3 Scanlan, *Freedom's Debtors.*
4 Fyfe, *A History*, 37.
5 *Substance of the Report Delivered by the Court of Directors of the Sierra Leone Company, to the General Court of Proprietors, on Thursday, March 27th, 1794* (Philadelphia: Printed by Thomas Dorson, 1795), 15. It is interesting to note the striking contrast between this more realistic *Report* and the overwhelmingly optimistic one from 1791. The early optimism originated in the faith the Company placed in John Matthews's account of Sierra Leone based on his visits there in the 1780s. The 1791 *Report* drew from Matthews, as did Thomas Clarkson's lengthy assessment of Sierra Leone's general commercial prospects from around the same time. For Clarkson's assessment, see British Library, Add. MS. 12131, f. 1, "Letter Addressed to the Chairman of the Sierra Leone Company by the Rev. Mr. Thomas Clarkson." The disparity between Matthews' observations on the fertility of the soil and the experiences of the early settlers is evident in the 1794 *Report*. John Matthews, *A Voyage to the river Sierra-Leone* (London: Printed for B. White and Son, 1788).
6 The plantation on the Bullom Shore was actually the third and longest lasting British effort to establish large-scale commercial agriculture in this early period. The Company sent out three planters to oversee farms in the area. One farm fell into disrepair following the first rainy season, after which the overseer returned to the West Indies. A cotton plantation also

failed, its supervisor having left for England, which led the British to divide the grounds into small parcels. *Substance of the Report by the Court of Directors*, 46-48.

7   Schwarz, "Commerce." Padraic Scanlan highlights how under Zachary Macaulay, the Sierra Leone Company was forced to come to terms with its reliance on local and regional slave traders for its survival – an acknowledgment that was at odds with the early and clearly naïve idea that the Company could ignore or work around prominent slave traders. See Scanlan, *Freedom's Debtors*, ch. 1.

8   A point about which they were ultimately correct, though those spreading such rumors at the time had no way to know this.

9   V. R. Dorjahn and Christopher Fyfe, "Landlord and Stranger: Change in Tenancy Relations in Sierra Leone," *Journal of African History* 3, no. 3 (1962): 391-97.

10 Suzanne Schwarz, ed., *Zachary Macaulay and the Development of the Sierra Leone Company, 1793-1794* (Leipzig: Institut für Afrikanistik, Universität Leipzig, 2000), Part I: 27.

11 Bruce L. Mouser, "Trade, Coasters and Conflict in the Rio Pongo from 1790 to 1808," *Journal of African History* 14, no. 1 (1973): 45-64. Records on the founding of Tookey Kerren are in TNA, CO268/5, Dawes and Mitchell to the Directors of the Sierra Leone Company, July 13, 1795.

12 TNA, CO268/5, Dawes to the Directors of the Sierra Leone Company, February 6, 1796.

13 TNA, CO268/5, Zachary Macaulay to the Directors of the Sierra Leone Company, July 30, 1796.

14 TNA, CO270/3, February 3, 1796.

15 TNA, CO270/4, July 8, 1796. For the hardships that coastal slave traders imposed on the Freeport factory, see Mouser, "Trade, Coasters and Conflict."

16 TNA, CO268/5, Macaulay and Gray to the Directors of the Sierra Leone Company, June 5, 1798. For an overview of the struggles between the slave traders and Freetown merchants in this period, see Mouser, "Trade, Coasters and Conflict," esp. 58-59.

17 Gray and Watt each kept journals during their mission to Furry Cannabas. They are both held in the British Library, Add. MS. 12131, f. 81, "Mr. Gray's Journal to Furry Cannaba's, Feb 1795;" and f. 122, "Mr. Watt's Journal to Furry Cannaba's between the 31 Jan and 11 Feb 1795." See TNA, CO268/5, Dawes to the Directors of the Sierra Leone Company, February 6, 1796, for the establishment of factories south of Freetown. TNA, CO270/2, May 27, 1793, contains correspondence on the first factory in the Camaranca under Chambard.

18 Schwarz, *Zachary Macaulay*, 52.

19 Several sources recorded the departure and return of Company vessels during this period. The most reliable is the Minutes of Council in TNA,

CO270. Nearly all of the voyages from these records also appear in TNA, CO268/5, or in Zachary Macaulay's journals, which he kept during his time in Sierra Leone. On occasion, one of Freetown's inhabitants records a produce voyage in a separate account. Adam Afzelius, the Swedish botanist who for years lived and conducted research in Freetown, notes several. Peter Kup, ed. *Adam Afzelius, Sierra Leone Journal, 1795-1796* (Uppsala: Studia Ethnographica Upsaliensia, XXVII, 1967). I entered these voyages into a dataset (hereafter the *Freetown Trade Dataset*, or *FTD*), from which the conclusions in this section are primarily drawn. My work builds on Suzanne Schwarz's, particularly her "Commerce."

20 Sierra Leone Company, *Substance of the report of the Court of Directors of the Sierra Leone Company to the General Court, held at London on Wednesday the 19th of October, 1791* (London: Printed by James Phillips, 1791), 45-46; *Substance of the Report Delivered...on Thursday, March 24th, 1794*, 42. For one account of the destruction of the *York*, see Schwarz, *Zachary Macaulay*, 27.

21 For one of many existing accounts of the French attack, see TNA, CO270/3, September 28, 1794.

22 *FTD*, 1795-1801.

23 TNA, CO268/5, Macaulay to the Directors of the Sierra Leone Company, October 7, 1796; TNA, CO270/4, September 4, 1796.

24 On William Davis' voyage in the *James and William*, see TNA, CO270/2, June 22, 1793. For Captain Estill, see ibid, August 21, 1793. A journal of the first voyage of the *Calypso* can be found in the British Library, Add. MS. 12131, f. 272, "Mr. Parfitt's Diary on Board the *Calypso*, W. Cole, from the River Sierra Leone to the River Gaboon & Back, Commencing 17 June and Ending 29 Dec 1796." The subsequent voyage can be found in TNA, CO268/5, Macaulay to Cole, December 2, 1797. The capture of the vessels is recorded in ibid, June 9, 1797 and October 22, 1797.

25 TNA, CO270/4, April 7, 1797.

26 On the significance of American rum along the gold coast see George E. Brooks, *Yankee Traders, Old Coasters and African Middlemen: A History of American Legitimate Trade with West Africa in the Nineteenth Century* (Brookline: Boston University Press, 1970); and Jay Coughtry, *The Notorious Triangle: Rhode Island and the African Slave Trade, 1700-1807* (Philadelphia: Temple University Press, 1981), 106-18. For its role in the Freetown trade, along with that of tobacco, see British Library, ADD. MS. 12131, f. 174, "Mr. Parfitt's Information on Trade between Sierra Leone and Cape Lopez." This valuable document was important not only for the Sierra Leone Company but also other non-Company merchants who traded in this region. Captain Samuel Swan, an American trader who was familiar with this part of Africa, appears to have copied and circulated Parfitt's document some ten to fifteen years later, possibly taking credit for it as his own. Swan's "Memoranda on the African Trade" is reprinted in full in Brooks, *Yankee Traders*, Appendix J.

27 Pierre Verger, *Trade Relations between the Bight of Benin and Bahia from the 17th to 19th Century* (Ibadan: Ibadan University Press, 1976), highlights the unique relationship between the Bight of Benin and Bahia, in Brazil.
28 ADD. MS. 12131, "Parfitt's Information on Trade."
29 Ibid, August 3, 1793.
30 TNA, CO270/3, December 9, 1795
31 TNA, CO270/2, June 18, 1793.
32 Ibid, August 3, 1793.
33 Fyfe, *A History*, 54. The Aspinalls were among the largest Liverpool-based slave traders of this era. They financed nearly two hundred slave-trading voyages to almost every part of the African coast. See *http://slavevoyages.org/voyages/eZ5jNrpp*.
34 See chapter 1, above.
35 ADD. MS. 12131, "Parfitt's Information on Trade."
36 Each of these voyages has been entered into a database with a unique identity number and details from more than forty fields of data. Some voyages are exceptionally well documented whereas others receive only a passing reference. More than fifty percent of the voyages in the dataset were recorded from more than one source, and several were mentioned in as many as four. For each of the voyages, the name of the vessel is known along with the year of departure or return. In all but three cases, the port or ports of intended trade is available. Based on this last piece of data I have added an additional field to indicate whether, broadly speaking, the voyage was dispatched to the north south of Freetown. Data on the cargos purchased by Company vessels is rather less detailed. Although in a small number of cases, the returns of a particular voyage are documented, such evidence is rare. A vessel might be described as carrying "a load" of ivory or "a good deal" of camwood, which is impossible to quantify.
37 ADD. MS. 12131, "Parfitt's Information on Trade."
38 The data for Tables 3.1-3.3 come from the *FTD*.
39 Since the data were generated in Freetown it is possible that the locations to which vessels were sent were not the same as where they ended up. Yet this was surely less common for the produce trade than the slave trade, where many more factors shaped trade patterns.
40 This conclusion runs counter to a heavy emphasis on Freetown's trade relations with Africans in the Guinea highlands. On the latter, see Allen M. Howard, "The Role of Freetown in the Commercial Life of Sierra Leone," in *Freetown: A Symposium*, ed. Christopher Fyfe and Eldred Jones (Freetown: University of Sierra Leone Press, 1968); E.A. Ijagbemi, "The Freetown Colony and the Development of Legitimate Commerce in the Adjoining Territories," *Journal of the Historical Society of Nigeria* 5, no. 2 (June 1970): 243-56; Mouser, "Trade, Coasters and Conflict"; Allen M. Howard, "The Relevance of Spatial Analysis for African Economic His-

tory: The Sierra Leone-Guinea System," *Journal of African History* 17, no. 3 (1976): 365-88; Winston McGowan, "The Establishment of Long-Distance Trade between Sierra Leone and Its Hinterland, 1787-1821," *Journal of African History* 31, no. 1 (1990): 25-41; Brooks, *Eurafricans*, ch. 10. One of the few exceptions that focuses on the south is Davidson, "Trade and Politics," ch. 4. Patrick S. Caulker's, "Legitimate Commerce and Statecraft: A Study of the Hinterland Adjacent to Nineteenth-Century Sierra Leone," *Journal of Black Studies* 11, no. 4 (1981): 379-419, is also focused on the south but is concerned with the mid-nineteenth century.

41 There are several examples of slave-trading vessels stopping at Sherbro to gather information on the state of the trade further south and east. See, for example, TNA, CO267/68, Planta to Horton, July 19, 1825, enclosures on the French slaver the *Deux Soeurs*. Produce traders would surely have used a similar strategy.

42 James W. St. G. Walker, *The Black Loyalists: The Search for a Promised Land in Nova Scotia and Sierra Leone, 1783-1870* (London: Longman, 1976), 246-47 and 257-58.

43 See, for example, F. Harrison Rankin, *The White Man's Grave: A Visit to Sierra Leone in 1834*, 2 vols. (London: R. Bentley, 1836). The debate over Freetown's prospects was polarized from the start. It was often waged between colonial administrators who were attempting to justify their actions and European critics who had never visited the colony. In a December edition of *Blackwood's Edinburgh Magazine*, James McQueen published several pamphlets that were highly critical of the Colony. That provoked an equally spirited defense from Kenneth Macaulay, a former governor and long-time resident of the settlement. See his *The Colony of Sierra Leone Vindicated from the Misrepresentations of Mr. MacQueen of Glasgow* (London: Printed by Ellerton and Henderson for J. Hatchard and Son, and L. Relfe, 1827).

44 Peterson, *Province of Freedom*, 13. See also Walker, *The Black Loyalists*, chs 12-13. Perhaps ironically, by highlighting the agency of Freetown's black inhabitants in the economic, political, and social spheres, recent scholarship has implicitly implicated them in the consolidation of British colonial power in Africa. If the settlers were largely responsible for the development of the colony in the early-nineteenth century, the development path they followed was rather consistent with British interests.

45 On trade diasporas, see originally Abner Cohen, "Cultural Strategies in the Organization of Trading Diasporas," in *The Development of Indigenous Trade and Markets in West Africa*, ed. Claude Meillassoux (London: Oxford University Press, 1971), 266-81. Philip Curtin popularized the concept in his *Cross-Cultural Trade in World History* (New York: Cambridge University Press, 1984).

46 Population statistics are notoriously unreliable for the entire period but can at the very least be checked against records of slaves disembarked

from condemned slavers. Annual population data, often repeated uncritically from year to year until new censuses were taken, are available in TNA, CO267, and also in the annual Blue Book series (TNA, CO272). These data have been carefully compiled and assessed in Robert Kuczynski, *Demographic Survey of the British Colonial Empire*, vol. 1: West Africa (London: Oxford University Press, 1948).

47   The following few paragraphs are based on Walker, *The Black Loyalists*, 275-77. For an early examination of administrative policy from the perspective of one Liberated African, see A.B.C. Sibthorpe, *The History of Sierra Leone*, 4th ed. (London: Cass, 1970).

48   TNA, CO267/71, Turner to Bathurst, January 25, 1826. Though the comment was made after widespread acceptance of the village plan, it nonetheless reflects the concern some administrators had with loosening their control over the settlers.

49   Fyfe, *A History*, ch. 6; Walker, *The Black Loyalists*, 277-78; Peterson, *Province of Freedom*, 93-96.

50   There is a slight tension in reports in Governor despatches on the productivity of particular villages. In 1825, Governor Hamilton noted that Liberated Africans were leaving some of the Mountain Districts for more productive soils around Freetown. In the same correspondence he also explained that the mountain villages were now supplying enough food to feed themselves and provide surplus provisions to Freetown. See TNA, CO267, enclosure in Hamilton to Bathurst, January 31, 1825.

51   Whether these designations reflected the actual makeup of a town – or the way Liberated Africans would at the time have identified themselves – is debatable. According to J.J. Crooks, who wrote one of the earliest general histories of the colony, Kissy Town had its origins in the arrival of freed Africans from Kissy-speaking areas of the interior. Governor Maxwell later explained "several hundreds of this tribe having been captured from slave ships by British men-of-war, it was considered desirable to locate them in one place." Crooks, *A History*, 88. David Northrup argues that while early towns may have been based on ethnic identities, a broader "African" conception came to dominate in the villages. David Northrup, "Becoming African: Identity Formation among Liberated Slaves in Nineteenth-Century Sierra Leone," *Slavery & Abolition* 27, no. 1 (April, 2006): 12. From the perspective of British policymakers, the idea was to foster communal cooperation in the villages. Liberated Africans' self-identification is of secondary consideration here.

52   BPP, *Colonies: Africa*, vol. 1, "Captain Hallowell to the Select Committee on the Settlements of Sierra Leone and Fernando Po," Appendix F, Query XII, 79.

53   On policy changes see Peterson, *Province of Freedom*, 58, 94, and 151-55. Turner's reduction in provisions is noted in TNA, CO267/71, Turner to Bathurst, January 25, 1826. Governor Campbell felt the rations policy

was "decidedly bad," leaving superintendents "engaged in fraud and oc-cupied constantly in purchasing and distributing cassada, which took up much of their time." TNA, CO267/81, Campbell to Bathurst, January 15, 1827. His statement suggests a potential change in food supply from rice to the considerably cheaper cassava, though this may have been driven by a short-term drop in the supply of rice, which officials noted in the previous year. See TNA, FO84/38, Commissioners to Canning, April 10, 1825.

54   TNA, FO84/38, Commissioners to Canning, April 10, 1825.

55   *BPP, Colonies: Africa,* vol. 1, Appendix F, Query XI, "Council to the Select Committees on Petitions of the Court of Directors of the Sierra Leone Company and the Company of Merchants Trading to Africa and on the State of the Settlements and Forts on the Coast of Africa," 90.

56   TNA, CO271/1, *Royal Gazette and Sierra Leone Advertiser,* August 25, 1820.

57   The literature on this topic is extensive. For the Upper Guinea region, see Brooks, *Landlords and Strangers;* and more recently his *Eurafricans.* For West Central Africa, see Linda Heywood, "Portuguese into African: The Eighteenth-Century Central African Background to Atlantic Creole Cul-tures," in *Central Africans and Cultural Transformations in the American Dias-pora,* ed. Linda Heywood (New York: Cambridge University Press, 2002); and Linda Heywood and John K. Thornton, *Central Africans.* This work builds on earlier arguments that Ira Berlin made. Ira Berlin, *Many Thou-sands Gone: The First Two Centuries of Slavery in North America* (Cambridge: Belknap Press of Harvard University Press, 1998). For examples specific to Sierra Leone, see E. Frances White, "Creole Women Traders in the Nineteenth Century," *International Journal of African Historical Studies* 14, no. 4 (1981): 626-42; and Day, "Afro-British Integration."

58   White, "Creole Women Traders." And more broadly, see E. Frances White, *Sierra Leone's Settler Women Traders: Women on the Afro-European Frontier* (Ann Arbor: University of Michigan Press, 1987).

59   Eltis et al., *Voyages,* http://slavevoyages.org/voyages/R0HS6yUt.

60   Fyfe, *A History,* 113. See also Mary Louise Clifford, *From Slavery to Free-town: Black Loyalists after the American Revolution* (Jefferson: McFarland, 1999), 184-85. On Kizell more generally, see Kevin G. Lowther, *The Af-rican American Odyssey of John Kizell: A South Carolina Slave Returns to Fight the Slave Trade in His African Homeland* (Columbia, SC: University of South Carolina Press, 2011).

61   A wonderful sketch of Kizell's meeting with King Sherbro, his father, is reproduced in H.C. Knight, *Africa Redeemed; or, the Means of Her Relief Il-lustrated by the Growth and Prospects of Liberia* (London: James Nisbet & Co., 1851), plate opposite p. 32. For Kizell's account of the Sherbro wars and his role in settling them, see the *Sixth Annual Report of the Directors of the African Institution, Read on 25 March 1812* (London: Printed by Ellerton and Henderson, 1812), 145-53.

62 Eltis et al., *Voyages*, http://slavevoyages.org/voyages/cXOINxtI. While the proportion of Upper Guinea inhabitants who ate rice as their primary food is unknown, it was surely very high. Millet and maize were also available. Rice has received a growing share of attention in studies of the Atlantic slave trade in Africa and the Americas. See, for example, Judith A. Carney, *Black Rice: The African Origins of Rice Cultivation in the Americas* (Cambridge: Harvard University Press, 2001). For an alternative view, see Eltis, Morgan, and Richardson, "Agency and Diaspora." On millet, see especially Searing, *West African Slavery*.

63 *BPP, Colonies: Africa*, vol. 1, "Captain Hallowell to the Select Committee," Appendix F, Query VII, 72.

64 TNA, CO267/91, Sierra Leone Commissioners of Enquiry: Report and Appendix A. The reference to maize is puzzling but may simply note a contrast to earlier rice preferences among the population. Another British official residing in Freetown around the same time described his experiences with Liberated Africans as follows: "Liberated Africans generally have little gardens around their cottages, about 50 feet by 70, for plantains and yams...they produce small quantities for the market." *BPP, Colonies: Africa*, vol. 1, "Mr. George Clack to the Select Committee," 38.

65 For important exceptions, see Hooper, *Feeding Globalization*; and David Eltis, "The Slave Trade and Commercial Agriculture in an African Context," in Law et al., *Commercial Agriculture*, 28-53.

66 Amistad Research Center, American Missionary Association Manuscripts [hereafter AMA], Sierra Leone, Microfilm Reel 2, Raymond to Macdonald, Lieutenant Gov. of SL, Jan. 8, 1846. For the Senegambia region, see Searing, *West African Slavery*.

67 TNA, T70/7, Abstracts, Plunkett, Sept. 18, 1721, ff. 28-29.

68 See Newton's testimony in the *Abridgement of the Minutes of Evidence Taken before a Committee of the Whole House, to Whom it was Referred to Consider of the Slave Trade* (1789), 56. See also Martin and Spurrell, *Journal of a Slave Trader*, 47.

69 For Lemaignere, sometimes called Louis, see TNA, FO84/309, Lewis to Palmerston, November 9, 1840. Siaka's link with Sugary is noted in TNA, CO267/101, Arabic to Ricketts, December 14, 1829. For the 1840 quote from Siaka, see TNA, CO267/160, enclosure in Doherty to Russell, December 7, 1840. For Canot, see TNA, FO84/267, Commissioners to Palmerston, May 13, 1839.

70 *BPP, Slave Trade*, vol. 5, enclosure 8 in Appendix No. 7, "Hotham to Secretary of the Admiralty, Feb. 13, 1849," 164.

71 *BPP, Slave Trade*, vol. 4, "Testimony of James Campbell to the Select Committee on the Slave Trade," First Report, 78.

72 Ibid, "Testimony of George Mansel to the Select Committee on the Slave Trade," Second Report, 70.

73 TNA, FO84/166, Cole to Macaulay, January 5, 1835.

74 See *BPP, Slave Trade*, vol. 6, testimonies of Dunlop and Fanshawe to the Select Committee on the Slave Trade, 133 and 185. Also Jones, *From Slaves to Palm Kernels*, 5.

75 TNA, CO270/8, Enclosed letter from Ludlam to the Council, September 17, 1802.

76 *BPP, Slave Trade*, vol. 4, "Rev. James Frederick Schön to the Select Committee on the Slave Trade" First Report, 182. The district superintendent's comment is in TNA, CO267/109, enclosure in Findlay to Goderich, June 29, 1831.

77 On Liberated Africans being pushed into Krim territory, see *BPP, Slave Trade*, vol. 9, enclosure 3 in Commissioners to Canning, April 29, 1823, 19.

78 TNA, CO267/99, enclosure in Ricketts to Hay, November 4, 1829; TNA, CO267/109, enclosed deposition of John Jackson in Findlay to Goderich, June 29, 1831.

79 For an Atlantic-wide approach to this issue, see Franklin W. Knight and Peggy K. Liss, eds., *Atlantic Port Cities: Economy, Culture, and Society in the Atlantic World, 1650-1850* (Knoxville: University of Tennessee Press, 1991).

80 "Captain George Howland's Voyage to West Africa, 1822-1823," in *New England Merchants in Africa: A History through Documents, 1802-1865*, ed. Norman R. Bennett and George E. Brooks, Jr. (Brookline: Boston University Press, 1965), 109; *BPP, Slave Trade*, vol. 9, Enclosure 3 in Commissioners to Canning, April 29, 1823, 19; TNA, CO267/160, enclosure in Jeremie to Russell, January 4, 1841. It is worth identifying the vested interest that British officials had in representing the slave trade as antagonistic to other forms of legitimate commerce. Gallinas households surely did not altogether stop producing all food. But it seems clear that profits from the slave trade enabled major merchants in the Gallinas to purchase food rather than grow it.

81 *BPP, Slave Trade*, vol. 6, Dunlop to the Select Committee on the Slave Trade, 133.

82 TNA, CO267/160, enclosure 1 in Doherty to Russell, December 7, 1840.

83 See letter and enclosure in TNA, CO267/208, Pine to Earl Grey, October 6, 1849; *BPP, Slave Trade*, vol. 36, Hotham to the Secretary of the Admiralty, December 5, 1848, 287.

84 Enclosure in TNA, CO267/208, Pine to Earl Grey, October 6, 1849.

85 Hawthorne, *Planting Rice*; Searing, *West African Slavery*.

86 *Abridgement of the Minutes of Evidence Taken before a Committee of the Whole House, to Whom it was Referred to Consider of the Slave Trade*, Number 4 (1790), Evidence of Richard Storey, 4; *Rules and Regulations of the African Institution* (London: Printed by William Phillips, 1807), enclosed reprint of a letter from Governor Ludlam, 15; *West African Sketches: Compiled from the Reports of Sir G.R. Collier, Sir Charles MacCarthy, and other Official Sources* (London:

Printed for LB. Seely and Son, 1824), 144-45; George Thompson, *The Palm Land; or, West Africa Illustrated: Being A History of Missionary Labors and Travels, with Descriptions of Men and Things in Western Africa; Also, a Synopsis of all the Missionary Work on that Continent* (Cincinnati: Moore, Wilstach, Keys & Co., 1859), 398.

87 *BPP, Colonies: Africa*, vol. 1, John McCormack to the Select Committee on the Settlements of Sierra Leone and Fernando Po, July 1, 1830, 67; C.B. Wadstrom, *An Essay on Colonization* (London: Darton and Harvey, 1794), 36-38. The rice was also cleaned – removed from the husk – before it was sold in Freetown or to slave traders. See *BPP, Colonies: Africa*, vol. 1, Macaulay's response to Captain Hallowell, Appendix F, Query XXI, 90.

88 TNA, CO267/24, Macaulay to Castlereagh, 8 May 1807; TNA, CO270/12, entry for May 13, 1811. Indigenous inhabitants of Sierra Leone made finer distinctions in rice varieties than red and white. Near the end of the nineteenth century, T.J. Alldridge, the first Traveling Commissioner in the region south of Freetown, listed eight different types of rice that Africans in the region grew. Alldridge, *The Sherbro*, 93.

89 Schwarz, *Zachary Macaulay, 1793-4*, Part I, 46 and 58.

90 Kuczynski, *Demographic Survey*, 154.

91 Censuses were taken in 1818, 1820, and 1822. Annual Blue Book reports also estimated the population with varying degrees of accuracy. See TNA, CO272 for the Sierra Leone Blue Books.

92 TNA, CO267/82, enclosure in Campbell to Bathurst, July 14, 1827.

93 TNA, WO1/352, Day to Thornton, July 8, 1803; TNA, CO270/12, entry for May 13, 1811; *BPP, Slave Trade*, vol. 10, Sierra Leone Commissioners to Canning, April 10, 1825, 8.

94 Macaulay estimated that settlers consumed between .68 and .97 pounds of rice per day. I have used these two figures to calculate the estimated rice consumption in the final column, multiplying them by the population for years for which census data exists. I multiplied total daily rice consumption by 365 to generate annual averages.

95 These figures should be taken as rough and somewhat idealized estimates. It is unlikely, for example, that rice was evenly distributed to Liberated Africans. Although the few available reports on Liberated Africans' diets do not distinguish between different segments of the population, it is likely that men ate more than women and adults more than children. Census data distinguish between male and female settlers but do not organize them by age. While such distinctions were important for Freetown, they matter for assessing changes to production in the Sherbro region.

96 From Macaulay's low estimate of .68 pounds of rice per settler up to 1818, this means a reduction to .5 for 1820, .4 for 1822, .3 for 1826, and .2 for 1827. This brings the final estimate in line with the consumption

of about 600 tons annually for 1827, which the Liberated African Department superintendent noted.

97 Estimated annual rice consumption was calculated using methods described above.

98 A fifty-percent estimate is probably on the cautious side, since the Sherbro was universally known as Freetown's major rice supplier.

99 To calculate the Sherbro supply to Freetown I reduced the overall supply as described above.

100 It is no wonder that when officials of the American Colonization Society first tried to establish themselves in the Sherbro region in the middle of the 1810s, at the highpoint of Sherbro rice imports, British officials came out strongly against the idea, fearing the loss of such a significant part of their agricultural base. See TNA, CO271/1, *Royal Gazette and Sierra Leone Advertiser*, August 25, 1820.

101 Walter Rodney, "Jihad and Social Revolution," 282.

102 Alexander Falconbridge, *An Account of the Slave Trade on the Coast of Africa* (London: J. Phillips, 1788), 21. The list of consumables that slave vessels carried is long but it was almost always cheaper for captains to buy provisions locally. Captives were also more likely to eat what was familiar to them.

103 Of his 1750-51 slaving voyage in Sierra Leone, John Newton noted, "I reckon in the whole I bought 18,600 lb [of rice] of which, clear of expense and waste, I have 17,556." The difference was due to slave consumption, which, though unrecorded, would have been considerable. Newton had been on the African coast for about seven months and had embarked 156 slaves. The fact that he made note of wastage suggests it was an important factor. See Martin and Spurrell, *Journal of a Slave Trader*, 49.

104 Rodney claims that Matthews' estimate for the slave trade is low. Eltis et al., *Voyages*, suggests that 12,295 slaves were exported over these three years. http://slavevoyages.org/estimates/6MmNB98x.

105 Several steps are required to make this calculation. I used the midpoint of Matthews' rice consumption estimate: 850 tons. I then converted that figure to pounds (1,873,927) and divided by 365 to get a daily consumption estimate of 5,134 pounds of rice consumed per day. Dividing that number by 4,100, the estimated number of slaves exported, provides a figure for daily rice consumption per slave of 1.25.

106 Estimates are from Eltis et al., *Voyages*. To estimate the southern Sierra Leone slave trade, I followed the same method described above in Table 1.3. Known slave exports from all of Sierra Leone between 1807 and the mid-nineteenth century can be found here: http://slavevoyages.org/voyages/oa4KmSOR. Documented exports from southern Sierra Leone can be accessed here: http://slavevoyages.org/voyages/hlzLR1wu. I took the ratio of the latter to the former for each five-year interval and

155

multiplied it against the total number of slaves estimated to have been embarked from Sierra Leone during this same period, available here: http://slavevoyages.org/estimates/s3qT1OQO.

107 Taken from Table 3.8.

108 The Sherbro region would have provided nearly all of the rice used to feed slaves exported from southern Sierra Leone after 1830. Though it may be slightly overstating Sherbro's role, I have assumed all the rice listed in the Annual Production column after 1830 was from this region. For the 1820s, I multiplied the total production estimate by .85 to account for rice supplies along the Windward Coast, southeast of Gallinas. From 1807 to 1820, Gallinas itself produced some rice. I have thus assumed that 75 percent of annual production figures were supplied from Sherbro.

109 Each of these vessels is included in Eltis et al., *Voyages*. Their unique identity numbers are in brackets followed by the sources where total rice purchases can be found: *Charles* [9880], TNA, T70/941, 47; *Speedwell* [9835], TNA, T70/943, 35; *Little Berkeley Castle* [9814], TNA, T70/944, 9; *Sherborough Galley* [76371], T70/957, 147; *Rhode Island* [24944], *A Book of Trade*, MSS., B.V. *Rhode Island*, N-YHS; *Duke of Argyle* [90350], Martin and Spurrell, *Journal*; *Crescent* [18040], TNA, HCA16/83/2218. Many thanks to David Eltis for providing these data.

110 *American State Papers, Foreign Relations*, vol. 5, 16th Congress, 2nd Session, Publication No. 346, "Supression of the Slave Trade -- Conference of Foreign Governments on the Subject. Communicated to the House of Representatives, February 9, 1821," Enclosure No. 2, Rev. Samuel Bacon to the Sec. of the Navy, March 21, 1820, 94.

111 Eltis et al., *Voyages*, http://slavevoyages.org/voyages/SRyzg1zv.

112 This ratio falls well within the range of five of the seven vessels listed in Table 3.10.

113 Without any data on daily consumption patterns in slave barracoons, it is not possible to move beyond this basic conclusion. Slaves awaiting shipment were surely the first to be affected by food shortages. A more sophisticated analysis of their diets would have to account for the effects of famine, warfare, naval blockades and other pressures on food supplies.

114 For this column I have used the same assumptions as above in Table 3.9. The data for each of the other columns comes from earlier Tables.

Chapter 4. Commercial Transitions, Islam, and Domestic Slavery and Slave Trading, 1830s to 1860s

The nineteenth century ushered in a series of dramatic changes to western economies that profoundly affected Africa. In this period, the British successfully suppressed the transatlantic slave trade and European and African merchants began to more intensively invest in the production of commercial-scale agriculture across the continent. Historians of Africa have long debated the impact of the transition toward what Europeans at the time called legitimate commerce.[1] But a disproportionate emphasis on the big picture – namely, the link between supplies of African commodities and western industrialization – has at times obscured the unique African responses to the large-scale shift to cash crops.

A regional approach to the commercial transition in Upper Guinea illustrates how African merchants reorganized slaving networks in response to changes in demands for labor. In southern Sierra Leone, owners did not merely put enslaved Africans to work locally once the transatlantic trade ended. Instead, Muslim merchants from north and east of Freetown forcibly moved slaves from southern Sierra Leone to areas around the Pongo, Nunez, and Guinea Bissau – roughly speaking, what the British called the Northern Rivers region – responding to new demands there for labor to expand the groundnut industry. Beginning in the late-1840s, the forced dispersal of Africans in Sierra Leone was thus reoriented: the east to west diaspora that fueled the transatlantic trade was supplemented and later replaced by a south to north one. Undertaken in large canoes, this internal traffic peaked in the 1850s before slowing dramatically in the subsequent decade, when the expansion of the colonial state and growing demand for slave labor in the Sherbro and Gallinas combined to put an end to this domestic slaving network.

The transformation in African slaving networks was undertaken in response to emerging markets for African agricultural products in Europe and to a much less degree, the United States. Over the nineteenth century, the Industrial Revolution increased the demand for vegetable oils and fats, which Europeans used to manufacture soap and candles and lubricate industrial machinery. In West Africa, oil from palm products and groundnuts proved particularly valuable. Yet the collection of these commodities and the extraction of their oils were both labor-intensive endeavors. By the 1840s, even before the transatlantic trade from Upper Guinea ended, several leading suppliers of captives for Atlantic vessels began putting slaves to work locally on northern peanut plantations to increase annual crop yields. However, owners struggled to meet the high demand for labor that the peanut industry created.

With limited access to slaves locally, merchants in the Northern Rivers turned to southern Sierra Leone, where the suppression of transatlantic slaving created a supply of captives far beyond what the region's economy could support. Building on internal commercial networks that had for centuries integrated Upper Guinea, Muslim traders began packing captives into large canoes and sailing them north along the African coast. Uncertain about how to confront this new slaving system – was it, for example, "domestic" or Atlantic? – British officials were forced to redefine and further expand the scope of their campaign against the slave trade. Between the 1840s and 1860s, some colonial authorities took aggressive measures against the trade, capturing "native canoes," prosecuting them in Freetown's Vice Admiralty

Court, and breaking up the vessels upon condemnation, just as they had previously done to transatlantic ships. Others advocated for a more measured approach. In response to British antislavery initiatives, slave merchants adapted the routes by which they transported captives, following a combination of land and sea paths to avoid detection.

How was this new slave trade organized and what impact did it have on southern Sierra Leone? The magnitude of the trade cushioned owners from what to them was the most consequential effect of the suppression of the slave trade: loss of access to foreign goods. However, participation in the new system also came with costs. Local headmen became increasingly dependent on Muslim merchants for access to exotic commodities and accepted credit on terms they could not easily repay. For slaves, the new trade was particularly vicious in its targeting of children – a trend that emerged in the final half century of the transatlantic trade's operation – who were the primary victims of the new slave system. The organization of warfare and war towns seemed almost tailored to the capture of young people, illustrating the flexibility of internal slaving patterns in the era of abolition and, much to the chagrin of British officials, the nonlinear path down which the transition to legitimate commerce traveled.

The Groundnut and Palm Produce Industries in Upper Guinea, 1830s to 1860s

Inhabitants of the Sherbro and Gallinas and their hinterlands experienced the transition to legitimate trade in a unique way. Caught between the groundnut-producing lands of Senegambia and the major palm zones of Lower Guinea, with Freetown representing the rough transition zone between the two, the commercialization of two major commodities shaped the lives of Africans in southern Sierra Leone, rather than just one. Yet production of those staples developed unevenly, beginning with the growth of the peanut trade in the 1830s and by the 1850s and 60s, including palm oil and kernels. The mid-nineteenth century was thus a period of multiple transitions in this region rather than a steady march toward the monotony of mono-cropping.

The Peanut Revolution in Senegambia

Groundnuts have a lengthy history in West Africa. The Portuguese first brought them there from Brazil in the sixteenth century. Local farmers gave the legume little attention over the next two and a half centuries, planting them sparingly among the many other crops that Africans in the region favored. Their primary use was to prevent starvation when rice and millet harvests failed. Indeed, prior to the middle of the nineteenth century, horses probably consumed greater quantities of peanuts in Upper Guinea than did people. Wealthy Africans fed the tops of the nuts to their mounts, believing that they made horses stronger and more durable.[2]

The spark that transformed the value of African groundnuts in global markets came from the West, where industrialization and parallel changes in ideas about hygiene increased the demand among manufacturers for oils and fats. In the first third of the nineteenth century Europeans became more aware of the relationship between personal hygiene and general health. One result was a spike in the use of and demand for soap. Although palm products provided the essential oils used to manufacture British soaps, French consumers found its yellow color unappealing, preferring instead the blue marble soap that peanut oil created. An additional and distinctive demand for West African groundnuts came from the United States, where, unlike in Europe, humans consumed the nuts.[3]

International demands for African peanuts intersected in the 1830s, resulting in an unprecedented growth in Senegambian groundnut exports. Interest in the nuts came from many directions, which made trade in the commodity extremely competitive. Forster and Smith, a London-based commercial firm that traded in palm oil, rice, and various other African commodities supplied early credit to expand production and trade in the crop. Despite early British investments, Americans quickly came to dominate the trade. Between 1837 and 1841, some three quarters of Gambian peanuts ended up in New York and New England, directed primarily to circus and carnival attendees, who bought them in large quantities. Yet an American tariff in 1842 temporarily slowed the Senegambian groundnut trade, which allowed France to step in over subsequent decades and fill the gap.

Data on peanut exports distributed by African port is incomplete, but George Brooks has pieced together statistics to reveal important local and regional trade patterns. In the Gambia, exports increased throughout the 1840s, slowing only briefly in response to the dramatic European revolutions of 1848. The trade rebounded by 1851, when exports reached more than 11,000 tons – nearly triple the amount of the previous few years. Though not to the same degree, Senegalese ports both north and south of the Gambia also expanded peanut exports during this period. In Rufisque and the Petite-Cote, the peanut trade had by the early 1850s reached 3,000 tons. Cayor and the Senegal River exported some 3,000,000 kilos of groundnuts by the late 1840s.[4]

More important from the perspective of southern Sierra Leone was the entry into the peanut trade of regions closer to Freetown. Although statistics for Portuguese Guinea are less precise than for Senegambia, it is clear that in the 1840s the Portuguese zone had stepped up its peanut exports. Bolama was by 1846 a major center of peanut production that supported several large groundnut plantations. According to Adolphe Demay, a French merchant who resided in Bissau, peanut exports had by 1853 reached 320,000 bushels and a decade later they topped 400,000.[5] A similar trajectory emerged in what today would be the coasts of Guinea and northern Sierra Leone, from which peanut exports also expanded in the 1840s. Merchants of many backgrounds contributed to the growth of the industry. George Brooks illustrates the dynamic role that Eurafrican traders played in it. Charles Heddle, for example, operated a groundnut facility in Bathurst in 1835 and later opened factories on the Melakori and Scarcies Rivers. Heddle's success, along with that of several other leading merchants, drew increased attention to the region

161

and attracted other firms and people from Goree and St. Louis, in Senegal. In other cases, European merchants provided the impetus to expand the peanut trade. Nathaniel Isaacs, one prominent British trader, purchased Matacong Island in 1844, inserting himself into a commercial network that linked the Melakori with the rivers that surrounded it. Christopher Fyfe notes that by 1850, Isaacs was able to load with groundnuts some sixteen vessels per year. R.A.K. Oldfield, another English merchant, operated a screw press, used to extract peanut oil, in Freetown in the 1840s. Despite this evident cosmopolitanism, demand for groundnuts from Sierra Leone came almost entirely from Britain. High tariffs in France on foreign oils limited the market for Freetown exports.[6]

The growth of the groundnut trade required steady supplies of African labor. In the Gambia and Senegal, production relied on the seasonal migration of wageworkers, in particular from among Serahuli-speaking communities in the interior. Known among Europeans as "strange farmers," the migrants traveled to the coast from as far inland as modern-day Mali. They took up residence under a local leader, cultivated peanuts, and returned home with a share of the profits from the sale of the crop. As elsewhere in Africa, a series of reciprocal obligations underpinned relationships between the clients and their hosts. Landlords provided security, food, and land and in return received a share of the peanut harvest and labor from the migrants for other community projects and purposes. The scale of this seasonal labor system was large. In 1853, Governor MacDonnell estimated that migrants produced about a third of the peanuts that the Gambia exported.[7]

Further south, peanut production was organized through a combination of enslaved and free laborers. Many of the inhabitants around Portuguese Guinea were disinterested in groundnut cultivation. Plantation owners complained, for example, that they were unable to entice local Biafada and Fula peoples to work for them. Instead they turned to Manjaco men from the Costa de Baixo, who comprised the majority of the area's workforce.

Indeed, Manjaco migrants traveled as far as Gambia and Senegal depending on opportunities for employement there. Joye Bowman estimates that migrant laborers made up two-thirds of the work force on *feitorias*, or local peanut plantations.[8] In the Melakori, Nunez, and Pongo, on the other hand, slaves appear to have provided most of the labor, where peanut cultivation proved quite compatible with the Atlantic slave trade for as long as the two systems operated simultaneously. Slaves worked on peanut plantations during the rainy season and once the dry season commenced, owners sold the groundnut harvest along with the men and women who produced it.[9]

Given the central role that slaves played in groundnut cultivation, commercial production tended to rely on wealthy African owners who could command vast amounts of labor power. In Portuguese Guinea, Caetano Nozolini, a major slave dealer who operated from Bissau, unsurprisingly also came to own the area's largest groundnut plantations. His exploits have been well documented, as have those of his wife, Mae Aurelia, the region's most infamous *nhara*.[10] Together they carved out and operated plantations in the 1830s on Bolama Island, though their influence extended as far as the Pongo River. The Faber and Lightburn families, prominent slave dealers of Eurafrican descent, also developed large groundnut plantations in the Pongo. Upon his father's death in 1851, William Faber became headman in the town of Sangha, where he owned several peanut farms.[11]

By the middle of the 1840s, the peanut trade had thus reshaped the region between Senegal and Freetown. Britain and France's insatiable demand for the legume opened new economic opportunities for many Africans, especially elites and migrant laborers, but also, at times, slaves. Yet the early prospects for the peanut industry were undoubtedly met with skepticism among some owners and wage laborers. While research on the groundnut boom has primarily highlighted the dynamic responses of migrants to it, a careful analysis of the Northern Rivers region indicates that planation owners constantly fretted over access to labor. Shortages in the workforce – whether forced or free – led some dealers to travel hundred of miles in search of new sources of slave supply. It was in this context that Muslim traders turned their attention to southern Sierra Leone. Yet tapping into Sherbro and Gallinas slave markets was made more complicated by the rise of the palm oil and kernel trades.

The Palm Produce Trade in Southern Sierra Leone
Unlike groundnuts, palm produce was a central part of many West Africans' lives prior to the arrival of Europeans. In the seventeenth century, John Barbot commented that "besides its serving to season their meat, fish, etc., and to burn in their lamps to light them at night, it is an excellent ointment against rheumatick pains, winds and colds in the limbs, or other like diseases." But for many of the same reasons described above, the middle of the nineteenth century breathed new value into this commodity, which came to replace slaves as the most important article of commerce that British and African merchants exchanged. Over a forty-year period beginning in 1807, British imports of palm oil increased from 2,233 to an average of 426,087 cwt. per annum. By 1895, when the oil trade reached its height, Africa was supplying to Britain some 1,262,000 cwt. of the commodity.[12]

As with slave and groundnut exports, the palm oil trade varied by region of supply in Africa. The Bight of Biafra was the oil's most prominent exporter, followed by the Bight of Benin and then the Gold Coast. By the 1840s, the Windward Coast and, to a lesser extent, areas south of the Cameroons began supplying palm produce in modest quantities.[13] A single port generally dominated trade within each African region, with areas of secondary importance supplementing the main areas of export. In short, the palm oil trade shared with the slave trade a high degree of concentration along the coast.

The Gallinas and Sherbro were the major suppliers of palm oil in the Sierra Leone and Windward Coast regions. Capital investments from European trading houses facilitated the commercialization of palm produce in Sierra Leone, just as they had in the case of the groundnut industry. Often the same merchants who invested in peanut production north of Freetown became active in the palm oil trade years later. Charles Heddle, for example, began exporting palm products in 1846. In 1850, he sent an agent, Nathaniel Nathan, to Bonthe, in the Sherbro, who opened the first European oil factory in the region. Later in the decade, J.M. Harris, who came to dominate the oil trade from the Gallinas, began operating at Yelbana Island. French and German factories were also scattered across southern Sierra Leone.[14]

The spread of factories provided new opportunities for Africa's small-scale producers to enter the oil trade. Before they were opened, African traders had to bring the oil directly to Freetown. The time and cost of such journeys was often prohibitive, particularly given that enslaved porters had to transport the commodity by foot. Commercial houses provided Africans with bulking facilities, enabling local traders to bring to them small quantities of oil. European traders combined those supplies in large drums and loaded the drums onto British trade vessels, which carried them to Freetown in preparation for shipment to Europe. In the 1850s, a growing number of Sherbro middlemen thus entered the oil trade, bringing palm oil in unprecedented quantities. Late in the decade the British Consul estimated that the palm oil trade had reached a value greater than £35,000 – a vast increase over previous years.

While it was important to the merchants, captives, and communities who traded in it, the significance of the southern Sierra Leone oil trade should not be overstated. In a comparative sense, the region played a marginal role in nineteenth century Afro-European commercial affairs. Despite a noteworthy increase in the volume of Sierra Leone palm oil exports in the 1830s and 40s, during which the trade grew in value from just over £5,000 to nearly £30,000, the region never competed with the more productive zones to its southeast. Indeed, the total supply of the oil between the Gambia River and Cape Mesurado accounted for less than five percent of the entire British oil supply from Africa for each year between 1827 and 1845, and generally its contribution was between just one and two percent of the total.[15] The comparatively minor growth of the palm produce trade in Sierra Leone has presented a puzzle to historians of nineteenth-century West Africa. On the surface, all of the elements were in place to support the expansion of the trade. Palm trees were widely distributed across Sierra Leone, particularly in the south; local knowledge about the collection and extraction of the oil was widespread; and navigable waterways crisscrossed the most productive palm lands in the interior, providing convenient modes of transportation to the coast. Given the knowledge and accessibility of palm production, what accounts for Sierra Leone's limited export of the commodity?

The answer appears to lie in the nature of the palm fruit that grew in Sierra Leone and the quality of the oil the region produced. Compared to oil palms in the Bight of Biafra, the fruit from Sierra Leone trees has a much smaller pericarp and thus provides smaller yields of oil per fruit. Moreover, Sierra Leone traders exported "hard" oil, which was more limited in use than the "soft" variety that came out of Lagos and Bight of Biafra.[16] Why Sierra Leone producers traded in hard oil is uncertain. Susan Martin has analyzed the relationship between oil types and labor inputs. Soft oil, she notes, requires three times the amount of work to extract than the hard variety. Yet this does not fully settle the issue. The fact that slaves were widely available in southern Sierra Leone in the 1840s suggests that the region had the capacity to produce the more desirable soft oil. Perhaps the profits that the internal slave trade was generating were high enough to merit the limited investment in the oil trade.[17]

While its supply of palm oil lagged, Sierra Leone led the way in palm kernel exports from West Africa. Kernels increased in significance over the second half of the century. Following a fall in global prices for palm oil in the 1850s, African merchants found a worthy substitute in the kernel. Kernels required a three-step process to prepare: first, producers had to remove the pericarp from the palm fruit, exposing the inner nut; they then cracked the nut, which revealed a smaller kernel. Crushing that kernel produced a different type of oil, one that was colorless and shared many properties with coconut oil. Palm kernel oil was used to manufacture a higher-quality soap and later also became an essential component in the manufacture of margarine. Exports of palm kernels began early in Sierra Leone but failed to reach significant quantities for nearly fifteen years after they were first shipped. In 1846, Charles Heddle became Sierra Leone's pioneering palm kernel exporter, when he traded £48 worth of the nut. Kernel exports remained trivial over the next decade but began to increase after that. By 1861, the year Britain annexed parts of Sherbro, the value of kernel exports had surpassed £30,000, making southern Sierra Leone a leader in the industry. From that point forward palm kernels became the most significant commodity that Sierra Leone exported. The success of the kernel industry was fueled by traders' abilities to integrate large commercial networks into Freetown's orbit. Sherbro trading houses, for example, drew on merchants from the Gallinas and its hinterland. From his factory on the Moa River, John Harris, a merchant of Anglo-Jewish heritage, tapped large supplies of palm produce from the Gola country. Harris attracted a significant volume of trade along the southern Sierra Leone coast, where he maintained several factories between Sherbro and Cape Mount. By 1867, half of the trade reaching Sherbro came from the Gallinas hinterland.[18]

Similar to the groundnut trade in the north, the commerce in palm products drew on a mixture of enslaved and free laborers. In the Mende-speaking interior, where the largest concentration of palm trees was located, oil plantations exploited large numbers of slaves to cultivate, collect, and transport palm produce. But nearer to the coast, the shipping industry created paid work for men and children. Coastal agents hired boys and girls, paying them a shilling per day to "tut the banga," or carry palm kernels between the store and the wharf. A single agent could hire as many as sixty children. They also employed men in the factories as laborers, measurers, boatmen, and canoemen.[19]

The growth of the peanut and palm produce – especially palm kernel – trades increased the demand for labor throughout Upper Guinea at a time when the Atlantic slave trade was on the verge of being suppressed. For Africans in southern Sierra Leone, the most significant aspect of the commercial transition was its uneven growth. The early emergence of groundnut trading in Senegambia put new stresses on local labor supplies, which rarely met planters' needs. In the Sherbro and Gallinas, slave owners faced the opposite scenario. There, the end of the slave trade glutted the market with captives who, at least prior to the late 1850s, when palm kernels emerged as a valuable export, played limited roles in developing local economies. In response to these labor concerns, slave dealers intensified the domestic movement of slaves between southern and northern Sierra Leone. The result was a new internal diaspora of enslaved Africans from the Sherbro and Gallinas to regions north of Sierra Leone.

The Domestic Slave Trade in Upper Guinea
The internal slave trade that developed as the transatlantic trade was being suppressed represented a blip in Britain's vision for Africa's future. To Europeans, the end of the slave trade marked the first step in a broader "civilizing" mission, a process that included introducing Christianity to Africans and inculcating in them the value of free labor.[20] In southern Sierra Leone, as elsewhere in Africa, however, non-coerced labor was very slow to take root. Instead, slave dealers proved remarkably good at adapting to the changing demands for labor that the commercial transition created. Underscoring this point with a keen eye for comparison, D.K. Flickinger, an American missionary who represented the United Brethren in Christ, noted that

> the Soosoos, who occupy the country North of Sierra Leone, are the great slave traders, and slave owners; they often stint their slaves in food, and work them very hard on their groundnut plantations. The country South-east of Sierra Leone for many miles on the coast, is to them what Virginia is to the

sugar-growing States of this confederacy, viz., the slave-growing region.[21]

How did the new domestic slave trade compare with the transatlantic trade that once flourished in southern Sierra Leone? How did the British confront the new slaving networks that developed in the shadows of legitimate commerce? An analysis of the internal slave trade that fueled West Africa's commercial transition underscores the entangled nature of slavery, abolition, and agricultural production in the nineteenth century.

The "Susu" Canoe Trade
Africans had been forcibly transported along domestic slaving routes in Upper Guinea prior to the nineteenth century, though the volume and significance of the internal trade expanded in the era of abolition. Several scholars have documented the dynamic nature of this south-north commercial corridor, which preceded the arrival of Europeans and continued throughout the era of the Atlantic slave trade. Along these pathways, African merchants carried kola, ivory, other agricultural and textile products, and slaves. In response to Britain's campaign to suppress the slave trade, however, African slave dealers expanded and adapted these networks to better avoid detection and capture at the hands of Europeans – a response that became particularly important during periods when the British navy blockaded slaving ports, as they did in the Gallinas. The resulting movement of slaves along domestic routes thus took on a clandestine nature, mirroring the wider transatlantic trade of the nineteenth century. The volume of slaves pushed along the inland paths was at times considerable. Allen Howard estimates that perhaps forty percent of enslaved Africans embarked on slave vessels along the Upper Guinea Coast – at least a thousand captives per year – were forced along the south-north corridor.[22]

The commercial transition further stimulated the internal slave trade in southern Sierra Leone. As chapter three explained, the suppression of the transatlantic trade caused slave populations along the coast to swell. That many of the captives came from relatively close to the coast made escape an ongoing possibility. Moreover, until the growth of the palm kernel trade enslaved people had limited economic value within the Gallinas and Sherbro. On the other hand, the burgeoning market for labor on northern groundnut plantations created new opportunities for the region's slave traders. In response to these "push" and "pull" factors, merchants turned to internal slaving pathways to integrate the settlements north and south of Freetown. They stuffed thousands of captives in large canoes and forcibly transported them to the peanut-growing regions in the Pongo, Nunez, Scarcies, and Portuguese Guinea. As British colonial officials caught onto the system and began to more aggressively disrupt it, slaving merchants altered their routes to avoid detection.[23]

Although the covert nature of the canoe-based slave trade from southern Sierra Leone makes calculating its volume difficult, it is possible to provide a general overview of the trade's expansion. Beginning in the 1840s, slave dealers began carrying small numbers of captives to Kolente, where the groundnut industry was beginning to take root. Within just a few years, some Freetown officials began intervening in this trade. In 1847, J.S. Palmer, the Assistant Manager of the colony's Western District, seized three vessels with more than one hundred total slaves onboard. Palmer's aggressive approach set a precedent that other inhabitants in the colony were eager to follow. Within a few years of the seizures, British officials were capturing as many as ten slaving canoes per year, many with more than fifty captives embarked on them. Those captures alone suggest that the canoe trade reached a minimum volume of five hundred slaves per year. Given the difficulty of the terrain through which the dealers passed, many other vessels would have escaped detection altogether.

Observations from merchants and colony officials in southern Sierra Leone provide a clearer indication of the magnitude of the canoe trade. According to Nathanial Nathan, the Sherbro-based commercial agent, eight "Soosoo canoes" carrying four hundred slaves departed from the region over just two days in the summer of 1852. A report from two years later suggested that sixty canoes, each capable of carrying forty captives, entered the Boom, Jong and Kittam Rivers in the Sherbro. Though it is unclear whether the canoes in fact embarked so many slaves, the report nevertheless illustrates that the Sherbro continued to be actively involved in supplying captive Africans.[24] At its height in the 1850s, it is even possible that southern Sierra Leone sent as many enslaved people to northern peanut plantations as they had previously dispatched to the Americas at the height of the region's involvement in the transatlantic trade.

Though the British generally referred to them as "Susu," a prominent ethnolinguistic group settled around what today would be northern Sierra Leone and Guinea, the individuals who organized the internal shipment of slaves came from diverse backgrounds and included people from Fula, "Mandingo," and Susu communities – in short, the areas where Islam was most dominant.[25] Merchants from these regions north and east of Freetown had for centuries been involved in long distance commerce throughout Upper Guinea but in the nineteenth century they came to play vital roles in shaping political and economic affairs in southern Sierra Leone. In the 1840s, Susu traders entered in large numbers into coastal Krim communities; by the following decade they established permanent settlements in the Boom, Jong and Bagru, in the Sherbro, and also in the Gallinas, from which they launched canoes loaded with dozens of slaves.[26] Wherever they settled, these merchants generally became the gatekeepers of the domestic slave traffic.

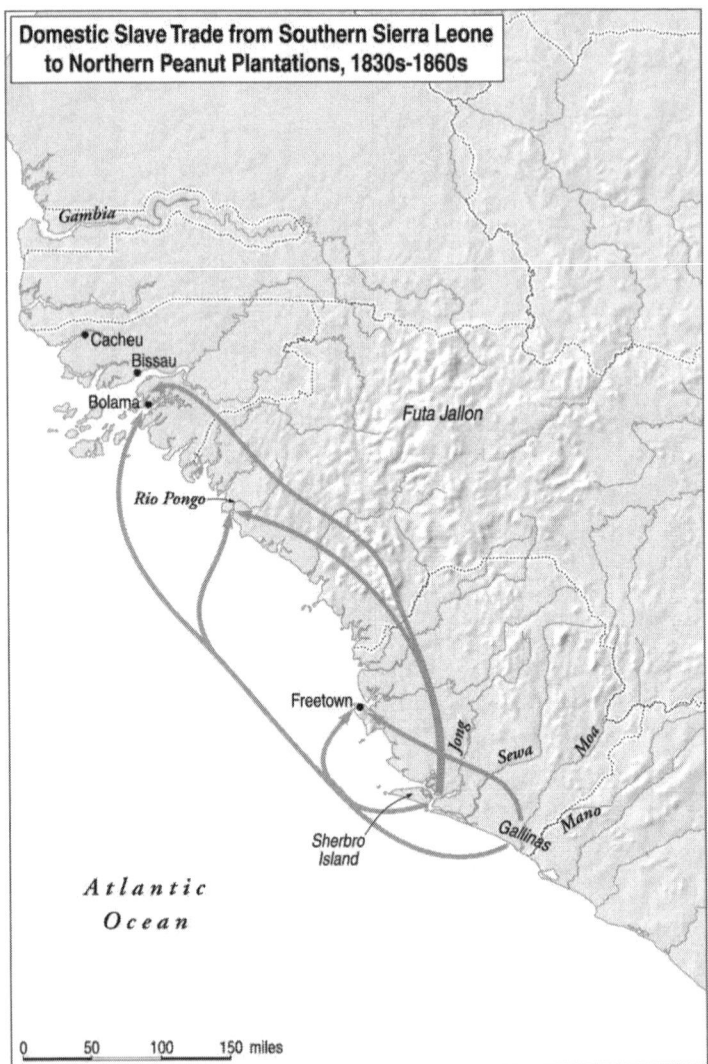

Map 4.1, Domestic Slave Trade from Southern Sierra Leone to Northern Peanut Plantations, 1830s to 1860s

If penetrating southern slave markets represented the first step toward domination over the mid-nineteenth century domestic trade, mastering shipping technologies was a close second. Among the most horrific aspects of the internal slave trade was the employment of large canoes to transport captives to northern Sierra Leone. According to George Thompson, an American missionary stationed in the Sherbro, the canoes

> are made from a large tree dug out, then spread open and timbered as a boat, and a 'raising' put on the top, of from one to two feet high. They are from thirty to sixty feet long, from four to eight feet 'beam' (across the top), and from three to five feet deep, and will carry from fifty to one hundred men. They have from one to three masts and sails accordingly; and from four to ten long oars, with which to row when they can not sail.[27]

For slaves, the experience of forced transport in canoes would have resembled the transatlantic crossing. According to some American missionaries who witnessed the canoe trade, it may even have been worse. They vividly describe how slaves were forced into the bottoms of the canoes, trapped beneath the planks on which their owners stood. As with the Atlantic trade, violence defined the system. As Thompson noted,

> long pieces of bamboo are lashed on over them, to keep them from getting up or rising against the masters – a very uncomfortable situation! And then they are half starved, and often very sea-sick, as many of them were never on salt water before; and often they are cruelly beaten with a whip made of *chain*, instead of cord – a horrid instrument of cruelty.[28]

Merchants stocked the canoes with weapons to prevent resistance. In addition to guns and cutlasses, they used poisoned arrows to maintain control over captives. So dear was this weapon that when Thompson attempted to purchase from one slave dealer a bow and a quiver of fifty arrows, the man replied, "I can not sell it, sir. We can not walk the sea without this."[29]

Captives forced to the groundnut plantations north of Freetown were drawn primarily from Mende- and Sherbro-speaking areas in the southern Sierra Leone interior, as were those who previously ended up in the holds of transatlantic slavers. An investigation into the involvement of the British merchant Nathaniel Isaacs in the slave trade, for example, indicated that the majority of his slaves identified themselves as either "Kossoh" or from Sherbro country. The experience of Bangah, one of his captives, is revealing. Taken as a youth from Mende country, a Susu slave dealer later sold Bangah to Moodoo Sarhie, another Susu man from Fouricariah. Sarhie delivered her to Mr. Parkinson, a merchant in the colony who worked for Isaacs. After several years, Isaacs himself took control over Bangah and forced her to work for him for years without pay. British officials liberated Bangah when she was 22 years old, by which point she had lived almost half of her life as a slave.[30]

Captured as a child, Bangah's story highlights the reality that captives in the nineteenth century – whether bound for the Americas or pushed into the domestic trade – were often very young. Data on the age of slaves embarked on transatlantic vessels suggests that captains increasingly targeted children in the era of abolition. Yet the canoe trade was particularly vicious in this regard. As they had when they captured Atlantic slavers, British officials carefully documented the ages of captives whom they liberated from canoes. While in the final decades of the Atlantic trade the average percentage of children among slaves embarked in southern Sierra Leone reached a staggering 49 percent, the ratio of children forced into slaving canoes was even higher.[31] Summarizing his extensive knowledge of the canoe trade, Governor Kennedy noted that it was "principally confined to children, the vast majority being female, between the ages of 7 and 15. They are usually purchased in countries south of the Colony and conveyed to the Susu and Soombia countries to the north, where they find a ready sale among the Mandingo and Mahomedan chiefs."[32]

What accounts for the increased trade in children in this era? Multiple factors made young captives more attractive and readily available. Children were, for example, easier to capture during wars and raids.[33] They were highly valued because they were more easily incorporated than adults into new kin groups and less capable of violently resisting their captivity. Armed primarily with poisoned arrows, slave traders would scarcely have been able to subdue forty adult men who rose up in rebellion. Finally and perhaps most importantly given the abolition-era context, children were comparatively easy to conceal from British anti-slavery officials. One officer noted, for example, that slave dealers hid captives under bags of rice and other legitimate cargo.[34]

That children were the canoe trade's primary targets – and that the trade operated in support of the groundnut industry – was especially troubling to British officials. At the very least it raised questions about whether legitimate commerce provided a viable alternative to slavery and slave trading, a central tenant of nineteenth century British colonial philosophy in Africa.[35] The canoe trade seemed instead to demonstrate not just the compatibility of the slave trade and commercial agriculture, but perhaps even the dependence that the one trade had on the other. Suppressing the domestic traffic, British officials increasingly realized, would therefore have disastrous consequences for the production of agricultural staples. An analysis of Britain's confrontation with the canoe trade thus exposes tensions between Britain's abolitionist impulses and the on-the-ground realities that they faced.

The Suppression of the Canoe Trade

British officials had two seemingly contradictory reactions to the emergence of the canoe-based slave trade: to some naval officers engaged in the suppression campaign, the internal traffic was something to celebrate – an illustration that Africans had begun to recognize the value of legitimate commerce. One observer from Bissau characterized the shift as a "novel and interesting era in the history of the abolition of Slave Trade, because it clearly proves that a highly important change has taken place in the very locality (Bissao) where an extensive Slave Trade has flourished for more than a hundred years; but where now, many thousands of natives are daily employed in cultivating groundnuts for shipping."[36] That so many of those workers were taken to Bissau by force rather than choice apparently did not merit comment. Missionaries and other colonial officials offered a contrary perspective, highlighting the inhumane nature of the canoe trade and devising schemes to intervene in and disrupt the traffic. To American religious figures such as D.K. Flickinger and George Thompson, there was little difference between the Atlantic system and the canoe-based one.

At the intersection of these two perspectives stood Augustus J. Hanson, a man of mixed Fanti and European descent. Hanson's distinguished career in Africa placed him at the center of debates over the internal slave trade in mid-century southern Sierra Leone. Driven from the consulate in Monrovia after he insulted the Liberian President, Joseph Jenkins Roberts, the British subsequently appointed Hanson the first British Consul in Sherbro in 1853. Yet British faith in Hanson appeared limited from the start of his tenure. The government, for example, made Governor Kennedy the Consul General, which limited Hanson's autonomy and ensured that Kennedy dictated British policy in the south.[37] Moreover, Hanson's responsibilities were ambiguously defined; the consul frequently appeared unclear about his mandate.[38] While they never explained their decision to open a consulate in Sherbro, the British Government presumably did so as a deterrent against the slave trade, though Hanson's capacity to achieve that goal was limited to writing reports and requesting that naval vessels visit and patrol the region. In 1854, Kennedy briefly granted Hanson the authority to seize indigenous slave vessels, following the precedent British officials had set in the previous decade. The consul immediately and decisively exercised that authority: in August, Hanson detained two large slave canoes. Yet he got himself in hot water when he shot one of the slave dealers during a struggle over a seized vessel.[39]

Reactions to Hanson's interventionist approach were mixed, underscoring the unsettled nature of British colonial and anti-slavery ambitions beyond Freetown and exposing the concerns some officials had that his maverick actions would undermine

Anglo-African relations. Authorities in Freetown viewed Hanson as a liability. They were the ones, after all, who were forced to manage the explosive fallout from his activities. Outraged that Hanson targeted their vessels and interfered in their affairs, Susu leaders held the government accountable for the seizures. They threatened violence against British and Liberated African merchants who traveled outside of the colony.[40] In the wake of those threats, Kennedy curtailed Hanson's power to disrupt the canoe trade. At the same time, the consul's actions exposed the fractured nature of political power in the British colony. He inspired copycats within Freetown who aimed to eliminate all forms of slave trading in the region. District Managers and other locals thus continued to seize slaving canoes, particularly when the vessels approached British waters. Suppression efforts seemed at times to snowball beyond the government's control. On one occasion Mamadoo Thomson, a settler in the colony who held no official position, seized a canoe 14 miles outside of Freetown's borders that had 44 slaves onboard. Debates raged in London and within the colony over the legality and potential consequences of such activities. Just how far should the abolition campaign go to stamp out slave trafficking around Freetown?[41]

It was in the context of that central question that British officials developed their response to the canoe trade. Those opposed to direct intervention drew a clear distinction between the transatlantic slave trade and the domestic traffic in Africa, characterizing the canoe system as part of an indigenous institution and therefore beyond the scope of British suppression efforts. That distinction became clear in the reports that naval officers submitted on the effectiveness of their abolitionist activities. In one such report, Commodore Edmonstone claimed that the slave trade north of Freetown was no longer active, even as he described in some depth the robust south-north canoe traffic. Defining the internal trade as an outgrowth of domestic slavery – in effect, identifying it as outside the scope of European anti-slavery interests – allowed the British to settle uneasily on an approach to combat the system. Based in part on directives from

London, they decided to intervene only in cases when slave vessels entered British territory.[42] In a letter to the Colonial Office, Governor Hill confirmed that he "will pay full attention to your instructions regarding the policy of interfering with the domestic slavery existing in the adjacent country," adding that "I shall also be cautious as to seizing canoes carrying slaves excepting within British waters."[43] Yet the governor had clear misgivings about the policy. He expressed in his response disappointment with the directive and noted his regret that the British Government chose to allow slavery and slave trading to flourish so close to the colony.

Individuals such as Governor Hill who favored a more activist approach to the canoe trade did not fall in line quietly. One strategy they deployed was to link the internal and external slave trades, arguing that captives dispatched from southern Sierra Leone were bound not only for northern groundnut plantations but also for transatlantic slavers that, they insisted, continued to operate in the region. The argument was a clever one because it collapsed the neat distinction British officials made between domestic and foreign slave trading. British merchants scattered throughout the Northern Rivers region backed up Governor Hill's claims. Whether their argument had merit is an open question. At least one transatlantic vessel, the American schooner *Catherine*, was captured in the Pongo in 1856, which indicates that the transatlantic trade north of Freetown remained at least marginally active. Yet it seems clear that far more captives were pushed into peanut plantations by the mid-nineteenth century. Perhaps Hill simply knew how to get the Colonial Office's attention.[44]

The government's noninterventionist approach to the canoe trade shifted radically in the next decade, driven by Britain's decision to annex large sections of Sherbro and Quiah territory, in southern Sierra Leone. Though officials had begrudgingly allowed slaving canoes to approach British territory without disrupting them, slavery and slave trading were explicitly banned on British soil. Expanding Sierra Leone's boundaries therefore reduced the regions through which slave dealers could pass without facing detention and possible prosecution. Once it was under British control, Sherbro became fair game in the battle over the domestic slave trade. In January of 1863 alone the manager at Kent seized five canoes in the Sherbro River. The canoe trade was suddenly targeted with the same enthusiasm as the transatlantic slave trade.[45]

How did African leaders react to Britain's increasingly hostile approach to the domestic slave trade? Several British reports detail the immense hostility that some Africans expressed toward British officials. Leaders invested in the trade threatened the colonial government against continued intervention. Following several seizures of canoes in 1848, the king of Sumbia dispatched to Freetown a party of chiefs with a letter that demanded the British return the captured people and seized property. When the government refused his demand, the king threatened to retaliate against colony merchants. After lengthy negotiations, the king settled on a more conciliatory approach.[46] Other merchants and headmen followed this lead. In 1854, the chiefs of Wonkafong sent a letter to Governor Kennedy requesting permission to renew the slave trade from the Sherbro to the northern region. The letter outlined a formal plan to operate the trade for seven years, during which the leaders would invest in and expand their groundnut plantations. The chiefs promised that in addition to increasing peanut exports they would work together to keep open the path between Futa Jallon and Freetown and expand supplies to the colony of valuable African trade goods. The governor refused, however, and insisted that the chiefs already had sufficient labor to invest in ground cultivation.[47]

For slave dealers, British annexation of Sherbro and Quiah lands increased the risks involved in participation in the traffic. Although some dealers continued to organize coastal voyages, others turned to new commercial routes in order to avoid intervention. One common approach was to force captives north via canoe to the colony's southern border and then march them overland, following a path that curved around Freetown's eastern boundaries and thus stayed beyond the reach of colonial officials. The route from Bagroo to Rotifunk, where a large group of Fula merchants were settled, became a notorious slave-trading network. Its success enabled slave owners to virtually abandon the canoe-based slave traffic by the mid-1860s.[48]

Islam, Debt, and Enslavement in Southern Sierra Leone

Shifts in the internal slave trade between the areas south and north of Freetown occurred alongside a major influx into the Sherbro and Gallinas in the mid-nineteenth century of Muslim merchants from the north and east. That migration began in earnest in the 1840s. By the following decade, Muslim migrants had settled in key positions along the Boom, in particular at "Sumbwea" (hereafter, Sumbuya), a large town that commanded the trade of the Big Boom River.[49] The arrival in large numbers of these outsiders transformed southern Sierra Leone's political and economic landscape. The African merchants exploited their access to foreign goods and command over the region's commercial routes to establish themselves as influential political players. Local rulers came to rely on them for access to desirable commodities, which the leaders distributed to their followers in order to demonstrate their prestige and maintain control over their dependents. In exchange for those commodities, the merchants demanded a steady supply of captives whom they sent to groundnut plantations in the Northern Rivers region. The Muslim Diaspora thus lies at the heart of changes to the internal slave trade in southern Sierra Leone.

Islam was not new to southern Sierra Leone. Muslim merchants were likely present there for centuries, though the region was never a major center of Islamic influence. Instead, leaders welcomed the commercial opportunities and medicinal knowledge that individual Muslim traders introduced into their societies. Local headmen and warriors valued in particular the amulets that Muslim visitors fashioned. Powered by select verses from the Koran that the traders either wrote down and enclosed in a cowhide pouch or rubbed into tattooed skin, these charms were thought to bring good fortune to those who used them. War leaders believed that the amulets gave them mystical abilities in battle, such as the capacity to survive a direct hit from a weapon. By the mid-eighteenth century, Islam's influence went well beyond individual merchants and itinerant travelers, reflected in the outbreak of wars that the faith at least in part inspired. Nicholas Owen, a European merchant who opened a commercial factory in the Sherbro, noted in 1758 that King Furry Do, likely Fode Katibi Toure, a Muslim from the interior who would go on to establish the Toure dynasty at Moriah, was driving an army from the interior to confront communities of nonbelievers that were settled along the coast.[50] Islam had by then come to represent a powerful political force in its own right.

The growth of the domestic slave trade reflected a fundamental change in the nature of Islam in southern Sierra Leone. By the mid-nineteenth century, Susu, Fula, and "Mandingo" merchants began carving out permanent settlements south of Freetown, increasing the size and strength of the Muslim presence there. British and American observers explicitly linked this development to the internal slaving system. Reverend Brooks of the American Missionary Association claimed that Susu merchants funneled the trade through their factories at Sumbuya and Momando, drawing captives from the areas that surrounded those towns. Consul Hanson went even further, warning that from these stations the Susu were preparing to conquer the country. Using dramatic prose that was typical for the consul at the time, he explained that the

> wily Mohammedans, who have been able to see a little bit further into the future than the Chiefs of those clans, have been biding their time – when those unwise neighbours shall have effectually broken each other's power – to step in and overrule them all... One thing is certain: their population is on the rise and they maintain a good understanding with each other, and always act in concert.[51]

Though Hanson doubtlessly overstated the power and ambition of Muslim communities in southern Sierra Leone, his emphasis on the unity that Islam provided for Susu and "Mandingo" settlements is important, particularly in contrast to the Sherbro and Mende communities, where war towns continued to provide the primary form of social and political organization.

Unlike previous Muslim traders who served individual headman, the new Islamic settlements represented a threat to some of the established rulers in southern Sierra Leone. Tension between the traditional leaders and Muslim settlers was palpable; violent conflict occasionally broke out as the parties vied for commercial and political influence throughout the region. Such struggles tended to be highly localized, pitting one or two towns or headmen against each other. In 1846, for example, Canreybah Caulker, a prominent headman in the Sherbro, captured and put in chains a small group of Susu slave dealers as they attempted to make off from the Plantain Islands. The cause of the conflict was complex, but one report indicated that Caulker wanted to limit Susu influence in his territory and was more generally "determined to expel [the Susu] from the Sherbro Country."[52] As the Muslim presence increased in size and influence, the newcomers began to attract their own followers, their settlements serving as a magnet, particularly for marginalized men and women who sought new opportunities and aimed to limit the oppression they faced. Concerns among traditional leaders about real and perceived losses of land and dependents fueled other conflicts. In the Kittam Country, locals resisted a Susu initiative to establish new groundnut plantations. The area's settlers complained that peanut cultivation reduced the quality of the soil and negatively affected rice yields. The issue came to a head in November of 1854, when Susu militants pillaged several important towns near Mo Bwavi, burning rice farms and taking captive the settlement's inhabitants.[53]

Not all authorities resisted the growing Susu influence in southern Sierra Leone. Shifting political and commercial sands opened new opportunities for some headmen to enhance their status. This was particularly true for individuals and towns that were deeply invested in the slave trade. Reverend Brooks noted that during the war at Mo Bwavi, the Susu received support from prominent leaders in the Gallinas and at Bompey, a powerful town rather notorious for its militancy.[54] The alliance was a logical one: warriors from Bompey generated a steady supply of captives and reduced risk for the Muslim merchants, since it eliminated the need for them to intervene directly in local conflicts.[55] Bompey, on the other hand, enjoyed the spoils of war, gaining access to human and nonhuman plunder, which enabled its leaders to prosper even as the transatlantic trade was effectively suppressed.

The canoe-based slave trade in southern Sierra Leone reinforced the merchants' alliances with military towns like Bompey, on whom the newcomers relied for supplies of slaves. From their base at Sumbuya, the Susu used the lure of luxury goods to establish bonds with prominent headmen. Trust and credit were the commercial linchpins of the relationship. Thompson explained that the Muslim merchants "passed along in their large canoes, with a variety of goods – guns, powder, tobacco, cloths, &c. – and trusted the various chiefs with from one to ten slave money, for which they promised to return the slaves to the Soo-Soos."[56] The merchants preferred to work with established rulers who, they thought, were more likely to repay debts.[57] Through them Muslim merchants circulated new commodities on which headmen came to rely in order to demonstrate their wealth and power.

How did Susu merchants gain access to foreign commodities at such large scales? Many of the system's observers warned that the goods were distributed through Freetown. Thompson explained that Susu canoes were filled with items from the colony's stores. The profits of the trade meant that some colonial merchants had a considerable stake in perpetuating it. Reverend Brooks went so far as to suggest that Freetown traders were the primary impediment to the suppression of the canoe trade, pinning responsibility on their shoulders for the conflicts that raged south of the settlement. He pointed to the harsh reaction to Hanson's aggressive patrolling of the Sherbro coast to illustrate the complex interconnections between human and nonhuman commerce. "The interests," Brooks explained, "of certain commercial houses in the colony were about to be disturbed so a cry of bloody murder and distraction of lawful trade, etc., was raised. The same houses used certain chiefs as tools to work their own ends, filling their heads with war [and] setting them to plunder factories."[58]

The flow of Atlantic commodities between Freetown and southern Sierra Leone forged a chain of debt that was paid in violence and captivity. Debt was the link that perpetuated the system. Dependents in Sierra Leone assessed the prestige of their communities based in part on whether leaders circulated exotic goods. To gain access to those commodities, headmen and warriors borrowed heavily from Muslim merchants, who demanded enslaved people in return. This sophisticated commercial system had parallels elsewhere in the continent. In West Central Africa, Joseph C. Miller has argued that the circulation of European goods reinforced relationships of dependency within African communities and households. Yet the political economy of nineteenth century Sierra Leone had notable differences with Angola. In West Central Africa, the link between commodity circulation and dependency appears, to Miller, primarily symbolic. It allowed lenders to make abstract claims to future labor and other rights over their debtors should that need should arise. In southern Sierra Leone, the consequences of debt were tangible and often immediate. Muslim merchants demanded quick repayment. Their interest was not in future claims to labor but rather in steady slave supplies. To settle these debts, borrowers had to wage ongoing wars and raids.[59]

Slaves were the ultimate victims of this system. Given the magnitude of the south-north trade, the suppression of the transatlantic system likely brought little immediate improvement to captives' lives. The threat of enslavement continued to stalk southern Sierra Leone communities. Captives bound for the peanut plantations faced many of the same traumas that enslaved people bound for the Americas had, including separations from families, long and difficult passages to unfamiliar destinations, and futures defined by coerced labor. They had to endure long periods of confinement in barracoons, in this case within Susu villages, where they were held before being embarked on canoes. Reverend Brooks provided a rare glimpse into the atrocious conditions inside one of those settlements. While he was returning from a funeral for a European merchant, Brooks stopped at Momando, a prominent Susu slaving village second only to Sumbuya in commercial significance. He was shocked by what he observed. Brooks described high mortality rates among the detained captives. He estimated that there were roughly one hundred slaves being held at the time, primarily comprised of children between six and fifteen years old. In a particularly haunting passage, Brooks noted, "most of them are but little better than walking skeletons, skin dry, whiteish or 'ashy,' wrinkled and glassy, resembling scales."[60]

While a number of scholars have identified the growing exploitation of children in the slave trade, we still have an imperfect understanding of the local factors that contributed to this trend. Demand for young slaves provides one important explanation. As noted above, children were sought after because they lived longer and could therefore be forced to work for more years. They were also easier to hide and subdue, which became particularly important in the context of slave trade suppression. Yet factors internal to Africa also help explain the demographic patterns of the trade. In southern Sierra Leone, the organization of warfare was well suited to capture children. Several scholars have described the centrality of warrior culture, particularly within Mende communities. War towns, which literally etched militancy into the landscape, reflected the region's violent realities. The towns were primarily constructed for defensive purposes, surrounded by between one and three circular stockades, behind which the town's settlers lived. One Sierra Leonean scholar has even suggested that warfare was a defining feature of Mende culture.[61]

The construction of war towns was a reaction to the organization of warfare across the region. In Sherbro and Mende territory, as elsewhere in Upper Guinea, Africans rarely engaged in lengthy pitched affairs. Success in battle was rather based on speed and deception. Bands of warriors secretly surveyed the barricades of rival towns for weeks before they developed a plan of attack. Having prepared for battle, the warriors clandestinely surrounded the town at night and when they were ready used code words to time their raids, which they launched with lightening speed. The element of surprise, the warriors hoped, would enable them to break through enemy fortifications. The warriors' aim was thus to stoke fear and confusion; they attacked noisily and always in the dark. Armies used guns not to shoot at their rivals but rather to increase the overall sense of chaos, ripping communities from their sleeping slumber and driving them out of the safety of their stockaded homes.[62] Success or failure depended ultimately on whether a town's barricades held. If the invaders managed to penetrate the fortifications, the battle was almost always won; inhabitants often did not even violently resist the incursion. They instead fled, leaving behind those less capable of escaping – children, the sick, and in some cases women, who often stayed back to protect their sons and daughters. The nature of warfare in southern Sierra Leone was well tuned for the capture of young people.[63]

Of course, warfare was not the only method of enslavement in the region. Privileging organized raids runs the risk of oversimplifying what was a complex and messy process. Many young people merely suffered the misfortune of being caught alone and unable to protect themselves. Such was the case for Chow Boam, who was enslaved in 1857. Boam, the son of a chief from Kittam, was captured while out fishing in a canoe. A group of Susu men in a large canoe approached him and asked whether he had fish to sell. As he gathered a part of his catch for them the slave dealers seized and forced him onboard their vessel. They held Boam in captivity for three days, when a British naval officer gave chase to the vessel. The Susu men took flight but the naval officers ultimately captured them and brought them to Freetown, with Boam.[64]

By the 1860s, the context of the internal slave trade from southern Sierra Leone had changed drastically. Although the domestic traffic continued, several local, regional, and international factors combined to transform the way slaves in Upper Guinea were exploited and transported. These included not only Britain's increased intervention in the trade in the wake of their annexation of Sherbro, but also the emergence of new demands for labor in southern Sierra Leone itself. By the 1860s, owners had increasingly chosen to put slaves to work locally to collect palm kernels and extract kernel oil. The spiking demand for slaves to support the palm industry was reflected in the increasing prices that people paid for slaves. In a letter in 1854, Reverend Brooks reported that "the very low price at which slaves are sold shows that the trade would be blotted out of existence in a few years...a boy or girl of 12 to 16 years of age is sold among the people of the country for 12 bushels of salt worth no more than £1.16 or for the same quantity of rice worth about the same price, [or] for 12 bars of tobacco and one cutlass."[65] By 1862, Commander Wildman described a "large and increasing trade in Sherbro, Boom-Kittam, and produce enough in Gallinas viz. palm oil, nuts, cotton, wax, etc., to supply many factories." The price of slaves had reportedly risen by this year to between $30 and $40.[66]

The development over the next few years of local industries in southern Sierra Leone made slaves sufficiently valuable locally, such that merchants engaged in the canoe traffic less frequently purchased them in large numbers. In an 1865 report that the Committee to Consider the State of West African Settlements commissioned, John Harris, a prosperous merchant who operated in the Gallinas and Sherbro, extensively described the region's commercial prospects. According to Harris, the suppression of the transatlantic slave trade nearly financially ruined the Gallinas headmen, who had no immediately outlet for their captives. But the expanding prospects for local agricultural production had reestablished slaves' importance in regional commerce, allowing owners to put them to work gathering kernels and manufacturing kernel oil. The value of the palm industry was considerable. According to Harris, slaves could in two months produce enough oil to pay off their purchase price – a line of reasoning so frequently used in the Americas to explain the value of slaves to plantation agriculture. That reality helped put an end to the large-scale traffic in Sherbro and Mende captives to Upper Guinea's peanut zone.[67]

Conclusion

The uneven transition in southern Sierra Leone from the slave trade to the production of commercial-scale agricultural commodities dramatically transformed local and regional patterns of slave trading and use. Rising demand for labor in the Northern Rivers region drove merchants out in search of new sources of slave supply, which they found in southern Sierra Leone. Those merchants organized a massive traffic in enslaved Africans between the areas south and north of Freetown, using land and sea routes to avoid Britain's anti-slavery patrols. The acceleration of this slaving network forced British naval officers and officials to think carefully about the scope of their abolitionist agenda. It required Europeans at home and abroad to make hard decisions about the implications of activist-style interventions in an era when politicians at home scrutinized colonial budgets and warned against "cowboy" colonialism – a term used to characterize the freedom that on-the-ground officials had to make decisions and shape policy in the absence of everyday oversight from the metropole. The contested nature of debates over British policies toward the canoe traffic reveals the deep uncertainties that sat at the heart of the nineteenth century British colonial state and the fractured decision-making process that determined the trajectory of early colonialism in Africa. That process had important implications for Africa as a whole. Indeed, it was on the frontier of Freetown where British officials began to draw hard distinctions between the Atlantic slave trade and domestic slavery and slave trafficking. When scholars characterize slavery in Africa as "benign," they would do well to keep in mind that nineteenth century British officials would have agreed with them, though perhaps only in order to provide moral legitimacy to the non-interventionist approach on which they settled.

An analysis of the internal slave trade also reveals the myriad ways that international commerce and Islam intersected to re-shape politics, economics, and society in nineteenth century Upper Guinea. Slave dealers from north of Freetown flocked to Sherbro and Gallinas slave markets, establishing a lasting commercial and religious presence there, particularly along the Boom River. Exploiting their access to luxury commodities in Freetown, the merchants distributed these goods to headmen and warriors in southern Sierra Leone, forging new relationships of dependency that greased the slave trade's wheels. The resulting chain of indebtedness endured for decades, until the mid-1860s, when new demands for palm kernels enabled headmen to put slaves to work locally. This period underscores the deeply intertwined nature of slavery, slave trading, and commercial agriculture in nineteenth century Africa and the clever ways that Africans adapted to changes in British abolitionist initiatives.

Notes

1 For a review of the literature, see Law, "The Historiography of the Commercial Transition."

2 The following paragraphs are based on Donald R. Wright, *The World and a Very Small Place in Africa* (Armonk: M.E. Sharpe, 1997), 151-55.

3 George E. Brooks, "Peanuts and Colonialism: Consequences of the Commercialization of Peanuts in West Africa, 1830-70," *Journal of African History* 16, no. 1 (1975): 29-54, surveys the international factors that shaped demand for West African peanuts and provides a regional perspective on West African peanut exports. For a more localized approach that focuses on Portuguese Guinea, see Joye L. Bowman, "'Legitimate Commerce' and Peanut Production in Portuguese Guinea, 1840s to 1880s," *Journal of African History* 28, no. 1 (1987): 87-106. For a broader study of trade between the United States and West Africa, see Brooks, *Yankee Traders.*

189

4   Brooks, "Peanuts and Colonialism," Table I, and 34-46.

5   Ibid, 47; Bowman, "'Legitimate Commerce,'" 90. It is curious that in his mid-nineteenth century account of West African commerce, Francisco Travassos Valdez had little to say about groundnuts in Upper Guinea. See his *Six Years of a Traveller's Life in Western Africa* (London: Hurst and Blackett, 1861).

6   Fyfe, *A History*, 239-40 and 258; TNA, CO267/242, Kennedy to Grey, September 16, 1854 and enclosures.

7   On "strange farming," see Ken Swindell, "Family Farms and Migrant Labour: The Strange Farmers of the Gambia," *Canadian Journal of African Studies* 12, no. 1 (1978): 3-17; ibid, "Serawoollies, Tilibunkas and Strange Farmers: The Development of Migrant Groundnut Farming along the Gambia River, 1848-1895," *Journal of African History* 21, no. 1 (1980): 93-104; Brooks, "Peanuts and Colonialism," 43; Wright, *The World and a Very Small Place*, 153-54.

8   Bowman, "'Legitimate Commerce,'" 96. See also Philip J. Havik, *Silences and Soundbites: The Gendered Dynamics of Trade and Brokerage in the Pre-Colonial Guinea Bissau Region* (Münster: Lit, 2004), ch. 4.

9   The compatibility of the slave and produce trades are assessed above, in chapters 1 and 3. David Northrup makes a similar point in "The Compatibility of the Slave and Palm Oil Trades in the Bight of Biafra," *Journal of African History* 17, no. 3 (1976): 353-64. See also the introduction to Law, *From Slave Trade to 'Legitimate' Commerce*. George Brooks describes as symbiotic the relationship between the slave trade and agricultural production with specific reference to Northern Sierra Leone in George E. Brooks, "Samuel Hodges, Jr., and the Symbiosis of Slave and 'Legitimate' Trades, 1810s-1820s," *International Journal of African Historical Studies* 41, no. 1 (2008): 101-116.

10   Known variously as *nhara, signares* and *senoras* by Portuguese, French and British observers respectively, these terms refer to African and Eurafrican women of wealth and influence who often acted as intermediaries between European and African traders. See George E. Brooks, "The *Signares* of Saint-Louis and Goree: Women Entrepreneurs in Eighteenth-Century Senegal," in *Women in Africa: Studies in Social and Economic Change,* ed. Nancy Hafkin and Edna Bay (Stanford: Stanford University Press, 1976), 19-44. The gendered dynamics of coastal trade in Guinea Bissau is a central theme in Havik, *Silences and Soundbites*, especially chs. 3-6.

11   On Mae Aurelia Correia, see George E. Brooks, "A *Nhara* of the Guinea Bissau Region: Măe Aurélia Correia," in Robertson and Klein, *Women and Slavery*, 295-319. Caetano's use of slaves on groundnut plantations was the subject of numerous despatches to Freetown's governors in the 1840s. For an example, see *BPP, Slave Trade,* vol. 36, the Sierra Leone Commissioners to Palmerstone, December 31, 1848, 4. For the Nunez

and Pongo regions, see Bruce L. Mouser, "Women Slavers of Guinea-Conakry," in Robertson and Klein, *Women and Slavery*, 320-39.

12 The quote and export statistics are from Lynn, *Commerce and Economic Change*, 1-3.

13 The similarities between slave and oil trading also extended to British ports. Liverpool, which dominated the slave trade, was also the center of the trade in palm produce, accounting for 96% of British imports. By 1855, Liverpool witnessed a relative decline in significance, with Bristol and London sharing nearly equally some thirty percent of oil imports. See Table 1.8 in Lynn, *Commerce and Economic Change*, 27. This suggests that Stephen D. Behrendt's idea that "human capital" fueled the British slave trade can be fruitfully applied to produce trading. Behrendt argues that Liverpool's dominance of the slave trade developed because of the availability of skilled sailors who had extensive knowledge of Africa. See Stephen D. Behrendt, "Human Capital in the British Slave Trade," in *Liverpool and Transatlantic Slavery*, ed. David Richardson, Suzanne Schwarz, and Anthony Tibbles (Liverpool: Liverpool University Press, 2007), 66-97.

14 This paragraph and the following one are based on Davidson, "Trade and Politics," 96-97.

15 Lynn, *Commerce and Economic Change*, Tables 1.3 and 1.7, 18 and 25.

16 The hardness of the oil is a result of the method by which it is produced. The duration of fermentation is the important aspect that determined oil type. A longer fermentation period reduces the frequency with which the fruit needs to be pounded and boiled and hence minimizes labor requirements for production. It results, however, in the production of harder oil, which fetched lower prices in British markets. See ibid, 46-47. See also M.T. Dawe and F.J. Martin, "The Oil Palm Industry and its Problems in Sierra Leone," in, *Proceedings of the First West African Agricultural Conference* (Unknown Publisher, Lagos, 1927), 7-8.

17 On labor requirements in the production of hard and soft palm oil, see O.T. Faulkner and C.J. Lewin, "Native Methods of Preparing Palm Oil, II," in *Second Annual Bulletin of the Agricultural Department, Nigeria* (1923), 3-22, quoted in Lynn*, Commerce and Economic Change*, 49.

18 Jones, *From Slaves to Palm Kernels*, 104-106.

19 Paul Lovejoy describes the use of slaves in the palm produce trade along the Windward Coast in his *Transformations*, 162-3. On the use of children in the industry, see Alldridge, *The Sherbro*, 14.

20 Mann, *Slavery and the Birth*, ch. 3; Schwarz, "Commerce." For a comparative perspective on the commercial, cultural, and religious motivations that shaped abolitionist projects in Africa, see Everill, *Abolition and Empire*.

21   D.K. Flickinger, *Off Hand Sketches of Men and Things in Western Africa* (Dayton: Published by the Order of the Trustees of the United Brethren Printing Establishment, 1857), 100.

22   On pre-contact commercial routes in the region, see Brooks, *Landlords and Strangers*; ibid, *Kola Trade*. On the internal movement of slaves, see Allen M. Howard, "Nineteenth-Century Coastal Slave Trading and the British Abolition Campaign in Sierra Leone," *Slavery and Abolition* 27, no. 1 (2006): 23-49. For a sample of contemporary observations on the movement of slaves from southern to northern Sierra Leone before the mid-nineteenth century, see TNA, CO271/2, *Royal Gazette and Sierra Leone Advertiser*, 3, no. 174, September 29, 1821; TNA, CO323/148, Reffell to Campbell, December 22, 1826 and subenclosures; TNA, CO267/110, Findlay to Hay, November 11, 1831.

23   Howard, "Nineteenth-Century Coastal Slave Trading," 30.

24   On the 1852 estimate, see SLNA, Colonial Secretary Office Depatches, 1850-1869, Nathan to Colonial Secretary, 21 July 1852. For the larger estimate in 1854, see *BPP, Colonies: Africa*, vol. 41, Consul Hanson to the Earl of Clarendon, December 31, 1854, 77-78.

25   Debates over the meaning of these ethnolinguistic terms have been waged for decades. With specific reference to the Susu and others, see Howard, "Nineteenth Century Coastal Slave Trading," 32; Jones, *From Slaves to Palm Kernels*, 83; Davidson, "Trade and Politics," 81-82; Schaffer, "Bound to Africa"; and Thomson, "Revisiting." For a broader discussion see Howard, "Mande and Fulbe Interaction"; and Northrup, "Becoming African."

26   Jones, *From Slaves to Palm Kernels*, 83-85.

27   Thompson, *The Palm Land*, 186-87.

28   This quote and the one that follows are from Thompson, *The Palm Land*, 187. Flickinger, another American missionary, drew explicit parallels between transatlantic slave vessels and African canoes. In a descriptive account of the domestic slave trade, Flickinger explains, "twenty to forty [slaves] are packed into one canoe, put into the closest possible space as a matter of course. In this condition they often get sick, but they are not cared for, any more than a sick hog would be of the same value." Lambasting his fellow Americans for acting so similar to what he considered less-civilized Africans, Flickinger adds disdainfully, "how similar to the treatment of some slaves in this country, and by *white* men." See Flickinger, *Off-Hand Sketches*, 100-101.

29   Ibid.

30   TNA, CO267/242, Kennedy to Grey, September 16, 1854 and enclosures.

31   I examine the enslavement of children in a different context in the following chapter. "Children" is of course a fluid category – one that Africans and Europeans would have defined differently. In the British case,

children were defined based on their height, with 4 feet 4 inches marking a rough dividing line. Such a rigid definition is problematic, of course. On children in slavery, see Campbell, Miers, and Miller, *Children in Slavery*. For the problem of defining children, see Audra A. Diptee, "African Children in the British Slave Trade during the Late Eighteenth Century," *Slavery & Abolition* 27, no. 2 (2006): 183-96.

32 TNA, CO267/231, Kennedy to the Duke of Newcastle, March 13, 1853.

33 On the enslavement of children and women, see, for example, Nwokeji, *The Slave Trade and Culture*, ch. 6. The 49% rate for children from southern Sierra Leone comes from *Voyages* and covers the final seventeen vessels for which age data is available. See *Voyages*, http://slavevoyages.org/voyages/KDOMSNqJ.

34 *BPP, Slave Trade*, vol. 49, Leetham to Commodore Wilmot, December 30, 1863, 108.

35 Britain's nineteenth-century ambition to transform African economies and societies is most famously laid out in Sir Thomas Fowell Buxton's *The African Slave Trade and Its Remedy* (London: John Murray, 1840).

36 *BPP, Slave Trade*, vol. 36, Sierra Leone Commissioners to Palmerston, December 31, 1848, 4.

37 Davidson, "Trade and Politics," 129-30; Fyfe, *A History*, 274; TNA, CO267/249, Hill to the Secretary of State for the Colonies, November 21, 1855. Hanson's correspondence as Sherbro Consul can be found in TNA, FO2. On the tension between Hanson and the Governor, see TNA, FO2/11, Foreign Office to Kennedy, August 29, 1854.

38 Hanson himself pushed hard to become Sherbro Consul. In March 1853, three months before he was appointed, Hanson wrote a memorandum describing the benefits that opening a consulate there would bring. See TNA, FO2/8, "Memorandum Respecting the Sherbro," March 29, 1853.

39 TNA, CO267/246, Dougan to the Secretary of State for the Colonies, April 18, 1855.

40 Although issued before Hanson arrived, the threat that the King of Sombia Country made in 1848 against capturing slave canoes demonstrates the seriousness of the situation. TNA, CO267/201, Macdonald to Earl Grey, February 9, 1848.

41 TNA, CO267/249, Hill to the Secretary of State for the Colonies, November 21, 1855.

42 The next chapter takes up the issue of how shifts in colonial boundaries affected British policies toward slavery.

43 TNA, CO267/248, Hill to Bart, October 27, 1855.

44 On the *Catherine*, see Eltis et al., *Voyages*, ID 4971. For contrasting positions on slaves from southern Sierra Leone going to the Pongo, see TNA, CO267/248, Hill to Bart, October 27, 1855; and *BPP, Slave Trade*, vol. 47, Commodore Edmonstone to the Secretary of the Admiralty, May 7, 1861, 83.

45 In his testimony to the Committee to Consider the State of West African Settlements in 1865, Colonel Ord specifically linked the annexation policies to the need to suppress the internal slave trade. See TNA, CO267/286, Evidence of Colonel Ord, March 27, 1865, question #481. Davidson notes in general that the "increase in British activity" around Sherbro reduced the canoe trade. See his "Politics and Trade," 82.

46 TNA, CO267/207, Pine to Earl Grey, May 2, 1849.

47 TNA, CO267/220, Dougan to Grey, December 23, 1854.

48 Davidson, "Trade and Politics," 82; Howard, "Nineteenth-Century Coastal Slave Trading."

49 On Sumbuya, see Thompson, *An Account of the Missionary Labors*, 211. The town, in modern-day Sierra Leone's Bo District, should not be confused with the Bullom/Susu capital of the same name, which was located northeast of Freetown and also featured prominently in nineteenth-century colonial correspondence.

50 On the expansion of Islam in Sierra Leone, see Allen M. Howard, "Trade and Islam in Sierra Leone, 18th -20th Centuries," in Jalloh and Skinner, *Islam and Trade,* 21-63. David E. Skinner has written extensively on Islam in the region north of Freetown. See his "Islam and Education in the Colony and Hinterland of Sierra Leone (1750-1914)," *Canadian Journal of African Studies* 10 (1976): 499-520; and "Mande Settlement," esp. p. 43, where he discusses Furry Do. On the role of Islam in the colony, see Cole, *The Krio.* On King Furry Do, see Martin, *Journal of a Slave Dealer*, 95-100; and Skinner, "Mande Settlement," 43. Owen indicated that the Mandingo Muslims had no local place of residence but rather that they wandered as itinerant priests among the coastal Bullom.

51 TNA, FO2/11, Hanson to the Secretary of State for the Foreign Affairs, December 31, 1854; American Missionary Association Archives, Microfilm Reel 4, Brooks to Whipple, Fl-6909-6910.

52 TNA, CO267/193, Macdonald to Gladstone, July 14, 1846. The enclosure to this despatch suggests that Caulker was "determined to expel [the Susu] from the Sherbro Country," but does not explain his motivation.

53 AMA Archives, Microfilm Reel 4, Brooks to Whipple, November 14, 1854, Fl-6910.

54 Ibid.

55 For an alternative approach that highlights the tensions between merchants and warriors, see the influential Meillassoux, *The Anthropology of Slavery.*

56 The quote is from George Thompson, *The National Era* 9, No. 425, p. 29.

57 Ibid. Thompson notes, "the Boompeh chiefs flocked [to Sumbwea] and took money, (goods,) promising to return the slaves."

58 American Missionary Association Archives, Microfilm Reel 5, Brooks to Whipple, Fl-7061, 22 June 1855; Thompson, *The Palm Land*, 186.

59 Miller, *Way of Death*.

60 American Missionary Association Archives, Microfilm Reel 4, Brooks to Whipple, Fl-6909-10, 14 November 1854.

61 Abraham, *Mende Government and Politics*, 8. On war towns, see especially D.J. Siddle, "War Towns in Sierra Leone: A Study in Social Change," *Africa* 38, no. 1 (1968): 47-56. Arthur Abraham has published several essays on the structure and logic of Mende warfare, but in particular see his *Topics in Sierra Leone History: A Counter-Colonial Interpretation* (Freetown: Leone Publishers, 1976). For a broader approach to African warfare, see John K. Thornton, *Warfare in Atlantic Africa, 1500-1800* (London: University College London Press, 1999).

62 There is a substantial literature of the impact of guns on African societies in the precolonial era. For an assessment of the volume of the gun trade, see J.E. Inikori, "The Import of Firearms into West Africa, 1750-1807: A Quantitative Analysis," *Journal of African History* 18, no. 3 (1977): 339-68; W.A. Richards, "The Import of Firearms into West Africa in the Eighteenth Century, "*Journal of African History* 21, no. 1 (1980): 43-59. These essays followed several contributions that more generally assessed the impact of the gun trade on Africa, published in two separate issues of the *Journal of African History*. See vol. 12, Nos. 2 & 4 (1971).

63 For links between the nature of warfare and the gender and age structure of the trade, see Nwokeji, "African Conceptions of Gender;" and Hawthorne, *Planting Rice*.

64 "A Recent Incident of the Slave Trade," *Church Missionary Gleaner*, 7, no 1, N.S. (Jan, 1857): 112-13.

65 American Missionary Association Archives, Microfilm Reel 4, Brooks to Whipple, Fl-6834. In a letter written the following year, Brooks remarked that a man slave was sold for 40 bars of tobacco. See ibid, Microfilm Reel 5, Fl-7061, June 22, 1855.

66 *BPP, Slave Trade*, vol. 49, "Extract from the Journal of Commander Wildman, of His Majesty's *Philomel*," 105.

67 See TNA, CO267/286, for the Report. Harris's contrast between local and transatlantic slave values is found in question number 5015.

CHAPTER 5. COLONIALISM AND SLAVERY, 1790S TO 1860S

Slavery confronted Freetown officials from the time the settlement was first established under the Sierra Leone Company. In a region immersed in slave commerce, Freetown emerged as a site where slaves, owners, and colonists negotiated ideas about slavery, colonialism, and rights-in-people. In contrast to the late-nineteenth century, when European administrators had more clearly defined models and legal frameworks from which to draw to achieve abolition and deal with its potential consequences, the foundation for Freetown's policies toward slavery was set by Company officials a century earlier, when the Atlantic slave trade was near its peak. Indeed, it was Britain's effort to stamp out the export trade in African slaves that pushed colonists to engage with slavery's realities both inside and outside of Freetown. Slaves themselves often forced the issue, sensing that the British suppression movement offered them an opportunity to resist the worst aspects of their treatment and at times even claim freedom for themselves. In the Sierra Leone case, the relationship between the suppression of the slave trade, colonialism, and slavery was time and again re-forged based on actions that slaves, owners, and colonial governors and settlers took over the first six decades of the nineteenth century.

The conflicting pressures that officials faced when dealing with slavery in Africa and the resulting colonial (in)activity against the institution has been well documented.[1] An analysis of the ways that slaves exploited British opposition to the traffic to force colonists to confront the institution of slavery itself helps shift the debate away from European laws and policies and toward the ideas and activities of slaves themselves. Captives in Sierra Leone challenged their status in myriad ways, including especially by escaping to the colony from the interior during forced marches to the coast or from the local societies where they were held. In addition to the small but steady entry into the colony of fugitive slaves, other transformative events more directly led officials to consider the implications of the abolition campaign and colonialism for the future of slavery in Africa. An uprising in 1809 on Bunce Island, the neighboring territory with deep roots in the slave trade, for example, sparked debates in Freetown about the changing nature of the relationship between owners and slaves in the era of abolition and more generally over how to deal with the prevalence of slavery on the colony's borders. Following rumors that British opposition to the slave trade would prevent their owners from disciplining them, a group of captives on Bunce Island rose up in rebellion and briefly seized control of the territory before they were ultimately captured and executed. Illustrating the limits of enthusiasm for radical abolitionism and perhaps also the looming shadow of race-based identity in the region, Freetown officials came to the aid of Bunce Island's British slave owners and helped them suppress the revolt.

More pressing for colonial officials was their concern over the circulation of young captives into and out of Freetown. Between the 1830s and 1850s, administrators uncovered evidence of widespread slave use and slave trafficking among foreign and Liberated African merchants around the colony. In the middle of the century, Governor Kennedy began to catch and prosecute the dealers. However, his efforts raised questions about whether Liberated Africans were in fact British subjects and forced officials to more clearly define the former captives' ambiguous status within the empire. Those discussions led to additional disagreements over whether the government could legally punish individuals who committed crimes outside of Freetown. In acting against slave dealing and slave holding, officials were thus forced to unpack thorny questions about the British colonial project in Africa: what were Freetown's formal boundaries and how did they shape the implementation of policies toward slavery? What status did Liberated Africans and other settlers hold within and outside of the settlement? What were the implications for the future of colonial rule of granting formal citizenship to Liberated Africans? To settle these related concerns the government turned in the 1860s to a more aggressive annexation-oriented approach, seizing parts of Sherbro and neighboring territories and enforcing British law within them. While such actions did not fully resolve the problems of slave use and dealing within British territory, they foreshadowed future tensions and policies that would come to prevail across the continent in the last quarter of the nineteenth century.

Domestic Slavery and the Suppression of the Atlantic Slave Trade, 1790s to 1850s

Fugitive Slaves

Located in the midst of an active slave using and exporting region, Freetown officials faced an immediate dilemma regarding the status of slaves who entered the colony: Recognizing them as slaves was at the very least at odds with the objectives of the new settlement and after British emancipation in 1834, against British law. But freeing slaves who entered Freetown would create conflict between British officials and the headmen around whom they were settled and on whom they relied for provisions. This tension, and a hint at the way it would be resolved, was recognized in the first set of instructions that the Directors of the Sierra Leone Company provided, which explained that settlers were "not to deliver up any persons who are slaves and [the Directors] wish no slavery to exist in the colony. But your own prudence must dictate on the spot the time, and the mode of asserting these principles, in perfect consistency with the safety of our colony."[2] Those guidelines allowed Company directors to maintain the humanitarian face of their settlement while leaving officials on the ground to work out the complex task of putting the directives into action.

Once Freetown was transferred to the Crown in 1808, directives from London more directly and clearly expressed opposition to the existence of slave dealing within the colony, though they said little about slavery itself, which for nearly three decades remained legal within the British Empire. The Sierra Leone Company Transfer Act of 1807 made it illegal for inhabitants to buy, sell, or assist in the exchange of slaves within Freetown.[3] But the Act had a number of evident shortcomings. It left undefined the meaning of the term "inhabitant" and unclear how those who were subject to British law would be punished should they be caught dealing in slaves beyond the settlement's boundaries. Though nobody raised such concerns at the time – indeed, early colonists could scarcely have predicted how large and influential Freetown would become – unresolved questions about the scope of enforcement for the Transfer Act, at least as it related to slavery, periodically emerged throughout the nineteenth century, causing headaches among officials in the Colonial Office and turmoil between governors, merchants, slaves, and slave owners in Sierra Leone.

More important than official legislation against slavery was, of course, the ways that Sierra Leone's politicians interpreted and enacted the laws on the ground.[4] Particularly in the first few decades after Freetown was founded, when administrative infrastructure was underdeveloped and individual personalities and inclinations guided colonial governance, differences emerged in the enthusiasm with which Freetown's policy makers confronted slavery. Under Zachary Macaulay, Freetown's governor in the mid-1790s, opposition to slavery within the settlement appeared unwavering, even as the Macaulay worked hard to establish commercial and political relations with slave traders throughout Sierra Leone. Despite ongoing protests from interior rulers who complained that their slaves were escaping into Freetown to seek British protection, Macaulay refused to return the captives.[5] In contrast, Governor Columbine briefly reversed the policy toward slaves who absconded into the colony. In an 1811 Sessional Paper, Columbine proclaimed that "the Government of Sierra Leone disclaims any such attempt to interfere with the ancient customs of Africa; and therefore any such people running away illegally from their masters and taking refuge in Sierra Leone, will be given up when properly claimed, and the right of the Master made out to the satisfaction of the Government."[6] Just two months later, however, Columbine once again changed his position, reaffirming the government's commitment to welcoming slaves who sought British protection.[7]

Macaulay's willingness to disrupt relations with neighboring headmen, merchants, and slave owners in order to enforce the liberation within Freetown of captives who entered the settlement provides an opportunity to consider British motivations in Africa under Company rule. In his recent study of antislavery in Sierra Leone, Padraic Scanlan emphasizes the coherent vision that underpinned this early colonial project. Fueled by the idea that wage labor was morally and economically superior to its slave-based counterpart, Freetown officials nevertheless doubted Africans' preparedness for immediate entry into this new labor market. What the settlement needed, according to this vision, was greater commercial and military firepower to spread free labor ideology and mechanisms within Freetown to push – even coerce – freedpeople into the labor market. The business of antislavery in Sierra Leone required Liberated Africans to work in support of the British mission in order to illustrate their appreciation and settle their debts for their newfound freedom.[8]

While this may have shaped policies and informed opinions within Freetown and London circles, a view from the colony's southeastern provides a different vision of early confrontations between Company officials, slaves, and slave owners. To Africans who lived on the outer fringes of Freetown's orbit, the key concern was not with British labor ideology and the Civilizing Mission but rather the extent to which the settlement itself and those who were charged with enforcing its laws would interfere with relationships between slave owners and their dependents.

The uneven nature with which Company and later colony officials approached the question of fugitive slaves and even slavery more generally reveals that no matter how developed or misguided British ideas were about how to move Africans along the path from slavery to freedom, on-the-ground realities dictated flexibility in the implementation of their approaches. Slaves themselves were more than mere pawns moved along this path: they seized opportunities to liberate themselves from captivity when circumstances allowed it. Whether or not they intended to, slaves on Freetown's frontier were as a result active agents in shaping the settlement's antislavery vision.

By forcing British officials to clarify their policies toward fugitive slaves who entered Freetown, captives in Sierra Leone effectively thrust slavery onto the colonial agenda as early as the late eighteenth century. Although after 1807 this issue should fundamentally have been a simple matter of applying British laws within a British colony, governors' reactions to the arrival of absconding slaves – both before and after the transfer – varied over time and had effects that rippled far beyond the settlement. By taking advantage of the protection the British Government provided them, fugitive slaves drew colonial officials into conflicts with their former owners and changed the context in which those owners could enforce claims over their dependents.[9] Despite the official claim that British policies toward slavery applied strictly within Freetown, the migration of slaves and former slaves within and around the colony muddied any simple distinction between internal and external concerns. Controversies over claims to enslaved people inevitably turned into complex regional affairs.

The case of Pa For, one of nine slaves who escaped into Freetown in the summer of 1798, illustrates the complexity of this issue during the period of Company rule. Pa For was owned by one of the powerful members of the Cleveland family, in southern Sierra Leone. Cleveland was at the time at war with King Firama, a rival headman. A third influential chief in the area, King Tom, tried to exploit the insecurity that the conflict engendered, announcing that he would accept any slaves who voluntarily gave themselves up to him and would receive the captives as friends, not prisoners. The proclamation provided a welcome opportunity for Pa For and his family, who lived under oppressive conditions, with a chance to change their fortune. They fled and submitted themselves to King Tom, under whose protection they were treated kindly and provided with land. Given the intense rivalry in the region that was rooted in control over dependents, King Tom's actions upset rival leaders, many of whom were invested in the outcome of the war. One such leader, Signor Domingo, confronted King Tom when they met at Robaga and complained that many of King Tom's slaves rightfully belonged to Firama. For Pa For, debates over who asserted claims to him were deeply unsettling. Fearing for his future, he fled the region and made his way into Freetown, where he once again sought the protection of a new authority: the Sierra Leone Company.[10]

This single instance of slave flight illustrates the complex political dynamics that shaped slavery and antislavery in turn-of-the-century Sierra Leone. The disagreement over Pa For involved three separate claims over an enslaved family that lived beyond the colony's boundaries and therefore, as Zachary Macaulay quickly found out, drew him into the politics of the hinterland. The leaders used the debate over Pa For to highlight their own prestige. King Tom lambasted King Firama, "who had sent these palavers to [Macaulay] without first apprizing him."[11] Banna, Firama's deputy, replied that he had been sent to *demand* the return of Pa For and the others, not to "talk palaver." For Macaulay, the case provided a chance to demonstrate Freetown's neutrality. He therefore refused to return the former slaves to anyone. That decision led Firama to storm into the settlement in person, where the headman tried a new approach. Appealing to "country law," Firama argued that it was not permissible to take a man's property for nothing in return. Macaulay, however, turned the tables on the leader, citing his own understanding of country law based on a conversation he had years ago with an

African man named Robin Rasey. According to Rasey, any slave who fled to a new owner became that person's property.[12] Firama's attempt to legitimize his claim based on tradition was therefore rejected.

In addition to revealing how Africans contested rights over dependents, the Pa For incident underscores the interconnected nature of the Atlantic slave trade and slavery. To slaves, the two systems often overlapped. Slaves who escaped to Freetown often did so upon the threat of being sold. Pa For, for example, was briefly owned as a domestic slave and fled only after he heard rumors that King Firama intended to send him off into the Atlantic. In another case, a slave named Corri escaped from the Bullom Shore into the colony, where he sought British protection. Corri was initially a slave of Robanna, a chief in the Rokelle region, from whom he ran away to Yongroo, the town where another chief, King George, resided. Corri lived there happily until 1826, when King George died. The stability that Corri enjoyed under his former owner disappeared with the leader's death. Pa Smart, a relative of King George who lived near Yongroo, constantly warned Corri that he intended to sell him. After one such threat, Corri gathered his wife and three children and together with nine other captives escaped to an island in the Rokelle River. Pa Smart aggressively pursued the group; he recovered Corri's wife, children, and eight of the other fugitives. Corri himself avoided detection and floated on a cork into Freetown, where government officials discovered him.[13]

Slaves also exploited for their own benefit the commercial paths that connected the colony to the interior, along which they regularly passed. It has been well established that by the middle of the nineteenth century, slaves throughout Africa served in large numbers as porters, carrying legitimate goods from the interior to the coast.[14] Less evidence is available to assess the scale of this phenomenon before then, but slaves surely performed similar roles in the first half of the century. Records indicate, for example, that captives almost always accompanied headmen and merchants when they traveled to Freetown.[15] As the colony's influence and reputation grew throughout the region and the volume of the produce trade to it increased, greater numbers of slave porters would have crossed into British territory. Once slaves entered Freetown, they could theoretically make claims for their freedom, though more commonly the former captives merely disappeared within the city, absorbed into the large Liberated African population.

When the Sherbro-based John Cleveland entered the colony in 1801 on a trading mission, he brought with him a slave named Banna, who belonged to Mr. Andow, a prominent merchant at Cape Mesurado, who had organized the excursion. Having completed their business in the city, Banna refused to return with Cleveland and instead expressed his desire to remain in Freetown. Cleveland appealed to the governor for Banna's return but colony officials reminded him that since slavery was not recognized in Freetown, Banna was free to choose his own fate. The government even guaranteed his security once he chose to stay.[16] These occurrences strengthened the impression in the interior that Freetown was a site where captives could break free from the control of their owners. Banna's case surely inspired those who heard about it to consider taking similar actions. Just how widely knowledge about exploits like his circulated remains an open question.

While the evidence is necessarily scanty, one case demonstrates the deep threat that slave flight posed to communities where large numbers of slaves lived. In a memorial to the colonial Governor in 1820, Samuel Samo expressed his frustration over Freetown's policy toward fugitive slaves. An Amsterdam-born merchant with a long history of involvement in the commercial affairs of Upper Guinea, Samo had an intimate knowledge of slavery in the region. He settled in the Pongo in 1797, where he opened a factory and engaged for more than a decade in the transatlantic slave trade. By 1811, Samo had relocated to the Iles de Los, where he had received from local chiefs a large grant of land. He purchased one hundred slaves to clear the ground there for cultivation. Samo actively traded with

Americans and Europeans and over time he became sufficiently wealthy to attract the attention of Liberated Africans merchants. Indeed, Liberated Africans so often visited his establishment that they became close with some of Samo's captives and convinced them to flee to the British territory, where they received certificates of freedom that prevented Samo from reclaiming them. The issue did not stop there. Samo mentioned in his memorial that the deserters kept in contact with his remaining slaves and encouraged them to flee, too. Could the British Government intervene to correct this injustice, Samo pleaded? Charles MacCarthy, the Governor of Sierra Leone at the time, showed little sympathy for the merchant. Indeed, MacCarthy's recommendation must to Samo have bordered on the absurd. Rather than condemn the Liberated Africans for their role in the affair, MacCarthy suggested to Samo that he free his remaining slaves and instead commit them to contracts of indenture to prevent future departures.[17] The gap in perception between slave owners and British officials over this issue had never seemed so wide.

Owners responded to the perceived and real threats that slave flight posed in various ways. The boldest pursued captives within the colony – a dangerous approach that risked provoking the British military. When a family of slaves that Chief Wemba owned escaped to Freetown, the chief immediately lodged a complaint with the governor. Yet colony officials rejected his claim. Outraged by the slight, Wemba dispatched twenty armed men to seize the former captives. The military party identified the fugitive family's house in Granville Town, broke into it, and carried the group off in the middle of the night. Recognizing the danger that this precedent would set, Freetown settlers pursued Wemba's men and ultimately caught and disarmed them. While the aggressors escaped from the settlers' clutches, they never again harassed Wemba's former captives. The government fined the chief $100 for the incursion into British territory, a penalty it later reduced by two-thirds.[18] Yet this instance was exceptional; most chiefs avoided direct confrontation and instead took proactive approaches to prevent the entry into Freetown of their slaves. British settlers, for example, reported that some headmen stationed patrols on the colony's borders hoping to capture slaves in flight. In 1827, Colonel Denham warned Governor Campbell of an "imprudent mulatto fellow," probably from one of the Tuckers' settlements, who had established himself around Kent, in Freetown. The man, Denham explained, was a spy who passed along information about the movement of fugitive slaves into the colony and positioned himself there specifically "to entrap any domestics fleeing from the Sherbro headmen to the settlement to claim freedom."[19]

If the growth of Freetown and the expansion of its abolitionist agenda opened opportunities for slaves to escape from their owners, local and regional developments shaped when and why slaves chose to flee. Consistent with slave societies in many other parts of the world, and as Corri's case above demonstrates, the death of an owner created a major impetus for slave flight. This was particularly true in areas such as Sierra Leone, where slaves could over time bridge the divide within communities between insiders and outsiders, unlike their enslaved counterparts in the Americas. As enslaved people in Africa settled into the new communities that claimed rights over them – as they had children, performed vital social and economic roles, and more generally proved their trustworthiness – they inched along a path toward achieving an "insider" status that theoretically protected them from sale, barring only the most extreme circumstances. Owner deaths disrupted this process of integration and at times even reset it by creating opportunities for other influential community members to assert new rights over the dependents. For captives whose security was based on their capacity to remain valued members of their communities, changes in ownership were both stressful and unwelcome. In those moments, the abstract promise of "freedom," however defined, that emanated from Freetown could prove preferable to other less certain and possibly more menacing alternatives.[20]

The number of slaves who took advantage of that promise through flight is difficult to assess. Until the 1850s, the government did not keep systematic records of the fugitive slave population. Captives only entered into the archival record when their presence provoked conflict between their former owners and the British government. That limited qualitative evidence alone suggests that small numbers of slaves – perhaps a few dozen per year – ran away immediately upon the establishment of the settlement; more continued to seek protection up to the year of the Transfer Act.[21] The growing presence of Liberated African merchants in the Sierra Leone interior and the heavier burdens that the production of rice and other provisions placed on slaves would over time have led more captives to flee into Freetown. How the government reacted to the incoming captives had important ramifications for the colony.

As it had under Company rule, the fugitive slave issue continued to expose divisions between Freetown politicians and their London-based counterparts. Freed from the practical concerns that colonists in Africa faced and charged with overseeing the entirety of the British Empire, Colonial Office officials generally draw hard lines in the sand with respect to slavery. Freetown leaders were on the other hand forced to approach the issue with nuance. A few examples underscore the divide. Following years of hostility between powerful families in the Rokon region, for example, Governor Findlay intervened to secure a treaty of friendship with the parties. A central part of the discussion involved British policies toward fugitive slaves. To satisfy the chiefs, the governor made an abstract distinction between slaves and "domestics," promising to return the latter when they entered the colony. Although Findlay's treaty was approved, when Governor Campbell used it as a model for a new one in 1836 to settle a conflict in the Magbele region, Colonial Office officials refused to ratify it, objecting to the clause that bound Freetown to return runaways. As the Secretary of State, Charles Glenelg, noted, "the convention is obviously formed with the intention of allowing masters of fugitive slaves to claim them as domestics and as the Municipal Law of England can allow of no such compromise between freedom and slavery, there is no alternative but to expunge the whole of the…article."[22]

The British reversal on the issue represented a major blow to the chiefs and led them to renew their suspicion of the settlement. Most alarmingly to colony officials, discontent among headmen raised the possibility that they would retaliate against Liberated Africans who traveled through their territory. Governor Doherty, who succeeded Campbell, expressed concern that the Magbele treaty "indiscreetly revived and agitated" the fugitive slave issue and recommended that future agreements altogether exclude clauses on runaways. The damage, however, seemed to have been done. In 1840, reportedly fueled by anger over the loss of their slaves, inhabitants of the Quiah country joined with chiefs from the Bullom Shore to plan an attack on the colony. Although a British investigation revealed that the conflict had complex origins, officials immediately assumed that control over slaves was the reason for their hostility.[23] Indeed, over the fist half of the nineteenth century the divide between British and African leaders over the future of slavery seemed to color in some way virtually every interaction between Freetown and its hinterland. Even those captives who remained with their owners saw in Britain's abolitionist rhetoric and ambitions an opportunity to recapture some of the rights that they lost in captivity.

Revolt on Bunce Island

Not all slaves wanted or had the capacity to flee from their owners. But even for those who remained outside of the colony, British suppression efforts seemed at times to fracture the authority that owners claimed over them. Although scholars have not carefully studied the ways that slaves in Africa understood and exploited growing western opposition to the transatlantic slave trade,[24] one dramatic occurrence in the first decade of the nineteenth century – rare for the fact that it was documented – demonstrates that slaves in Sierra Leone were well aware of the abolition movement's potential to transform their lives. Drawing their own conclusions about the implications of abolitionism, a group of plantation captives rose up and for a week seized control of Bunce Island, in the Sierra Leone estuary. Their rebellion was violently suppressed and the leaders of the revolt were summarily executed. An assessment of this powerful abolition-inspired moment provides a unique window into African views on slavery and antislavery.

Bunce Island had, of course, for centuries been involved in the transatlantic slave trade. For more than five decades while under the control of the Royal African Company the island remained at the center of the British traffic from Sierra Leone. The fort was burned down in 1728 and subsequently abandoned following a dispute between Walter Charles, the island's newly appointed British governor, and Senior Domingo, an influential Afro-Portuguese settler.[25] It then passed into private hands under which the island remained the most prominent point of slave embarkation in the Sierra Leone region throughout most of the eighteenth century.

In addition to exporting captives, private European merchants on the island carved out plantations on which their slaves produced provisions and other commodities for export. Bunce Island was thus not merely a fort or a slaving port; it was a small-scale slave society. That reality troubled early British and African settlers in Freetown, given their antislavery leanings. Slaves on Bunce Island were also well aware of the abolitionist impulses that radiated out from Freetown. Indeed, captives on plantations there understood that the suppression of the British export trade limited their owners' ability to use the threat of sale as leverage to extract additional labor. Without that crucial disciplinary tool, some slaves reasoned, owners could lose control over the plantation system they operated.[26] Captives saw clearly the threat that abolitionism posed to slavery even in the absence of direct British intervention in the institution.

With this sentiment in mind, a group of slaves on Bunce Island rose up in 1809 and seized freedom for themselves. Their rebellion began on the morning of October 13 when, according to the island's superintendent, Samuel Walker, the slaves began behaving in a "riotous manner." They had forcibly removed from confinement one of the island's captives whom the superintendent had previously isolated as punishment for a misdemeanor. The following day, Walker gathered the slaves to identify the people who had undermined his authority. But as they stood in single-file, the group consistently ignored his orders. They then turned hostile, Walker claimed, and aggressively chased him away, overtaking the island in his absence. With few allies around to support him, Walker turned to officials in Freetown for help, appealing to their shared British identity and underscoring the instability that the revolt could provoke across the region. Given their contrasting motivations, one might expect that the colony government would welcome the overthrow of the superintendent. Yet it chose instead to support him and at least implicitly the slave system he represented, noting that "it is the duty of the government of this colony to render every possible assistance at all times to any British settlement upon the coast, and particularly to one whose interests are so closely connected by local circumstances with the welfare of this Colony as are those of the Settlement of Bance Island."[27] Just three days after the revolt commenced, Governor Thompson dispatched a military force that successfully captured the rebels. He assembled a court martial in Freetown that convicted fourteen slaves for their involvement in the affair. The court sentenced the two leaders of the rebellion, Banna and Morrey, to death; other participants were banished to the neighboring Gold Coast.[28]

This brief analysis offers important insights into slavery and abolition in the early nineteenth century. Though Britain insisted that it had no ambition to undermine slavery in Africa, slaves saw foreign intervention in the slave trade as an opportunity to transform the slave system. Summarizing the incident to the Colonial Office, Governor Thornton got to the heart of the matter when he indicated that the revolt had arisen "from the persuasion of the inhabitants that as the abolition of the slave trade had deprived the superintendent of the island of the power of punish-

211

ing acts of insubordination by selling the offender, there remained no method of enforcing subordination."[29] Freetown's response to the affair was equally telling: it exposed to enslaved Africans the limits of British support for radical abolitionism and reminded captives that the governor valued regional stability above the unchecked application of universal freedom. Finally, while archival correspondence about this affair avoids thorny questions about race and identity, participants in the revolt would have understood clearly one important message from the British government's violent reaction to it: British people protected their own.

Slave Dealing, Citizenship, and the Expansion of Colonialism

Confronting Slavery in Freetown

Few points better illustrate the complexity of Britain's confrontation with domestic slavery than the continued circulation of captives within the colony and on its outskirts throughout the nineteenth century. Slave dealing around Freetown was transformed by the large internal slave trade that the previous chapter described, by which primarily Muslim merchants transported captives from southern Sierra Leone to the peanut-producing regions north of Freetown. Merchants who traveled along this route often entered Freetown itself and in some cases clandestinely offered to sell to Liberated African families enslaved boys and girls.[30] Dealers also occasionally kidnapped vulnerable children within the settlement and marched them north toward the groundnut fields. Confronting the circulation of enslaved children into and out of the British colony pulled Britain into broader internal conflicts and, just as the fugitive slave issue had, limited the colony's ability to seal itself off from regional concerns over its policies toward slavery. The government's interference in networks of domestic slave dealing also provided captives with new opportunities to break free from their owners and seek British protection.

Although the purchase and trade of slaves in Freetown was not widespread in the first few decades of the nineteenth century, concerns about these two related issues occasionally emerged. George Nicol, a European carpenter that the Sierra Leone Company once employed, was twice questioned about whether he had bought slaves. In the first instance Nicol confirmed that he had in fact purchased three children but explained that he did so merely to save them from being loaded into the hold of a transatlantic slave vessel – a justification that was suspicious at best. Several years later, Nicol was once again put on the defensive after he was caught asking a merchant at Robanna to purchase for him a seven-year old girl from Pedro Naimbanna, the town's headman.[31] While these anecdotes underscore the limited scope of the problem, they serve as an important reminder that not all settlers in Freetown embraced antislavery principles.

The scale of slave trading within the colony amplified over time, as did concerns about how to effectively combat it. In 1830, Chief Justice Jeffcott grew suspicious over what he perceived to be the small size of Freetown's Liberated African population. Digging into recent census counts and comparing them to estimates of the number of Liberated Africans who entered the colony from condemned slave ships, the justice identified large discrepancies in the data – even after he accounted for the high rates of mortality in the settlement.[32] Something of a polemicist and also a dedicated antislavery activist, Jeffcott immediately concluded that slave trafficking was the cause of the population drain, warning that "the slave trade is either directly carried on, altho' of course not openly and ostensibly, or...is aided and abetted in this Colony."[33] His bold proclamation generated a stir in Freetown and the Colonial Office, in Britain. To examine the claims, the Secretary of State formed a board of enquiry whose investigation confirmed that Liberated Africans were indeed being held in captivity in the interior in large numbers.[34] One witness testified that as many as five hundred recaptives were enslaved in the Mandingo country alone. Another believed that 250 had over three years been marched from Freetown to the Pongo and Gallinas. Colonial officials reacted with shock to the findings. They began to aggressively pursue individuals whom they suspected were involved in trafficking in the colony. Over a three-week period in 1830, the colonial government handed down 26 indictments for slave dealing.[35]

While pursuing people who were suspected or accused of kidnapping Liberated Africans, colonial officials were forced to confront the interior headmen to whom the victims were sold. When Governor Findlay received a report that five Liberated African boys had been forcibly removed to the Lower Boom River in the Sherbro, he dispatched a representative there who demanded that they be returned. Yet as the boys' experiences illustrate, the complex network of slave circulation in the region made it difficult to hold accountable any specific leaders. The boys were first sold to Kony Tom, a nephew of James Tucker, the chief of the Lower Boom. Kony Tom then transferred them to a French slave trader named Sabatier, who resided at Yealla, one of Tucker's towns on the Boom. Shortly after their arrival there, the boys were once again on the move after a war in the area destroyed the town and forced the Frenchman to flee with them, first to Kittam and then toward Gendema, in the Gallinas, where he intended to sell some of his captives to King Siaka. The boys' journey was unfortunately not over. As they approached the Gallinas, Mahmadoo Seacy, one of Cleveland's most trusted warmen, intercepted the party. Seacy unloaded the Liberated Africans to a passing group of Susu slave traders, who removed them farther inland. It was at this point that the British Government entered the picture. Under heavy pressure from Freetown, Cleveland successfully tracked down and helped recover the boys, whom he released to colony officials on York Island.[36]

Excursions into the interior such as these not only resulted in the freeing of Liberated Africans; they also provided slaves in the region with opportunities to seek protection from their owners. Some captives simply lied about their origins and claimed to British officials that they were recaptives. "Becoming" a Liberated African – taking on that identity – was made easier by the often-scattered records that the government maintained of the recaptive population. Confused and frustrated British officers were as a result unsure how to assess the veracity of such claims. When in doubt they seemed to use familiarity with the English language – or Krio, its more widely spoken local counterpart – as their benchmark. When the condemned slave schooner *Enganador* arrived in Freetown in 1840, Governor Fergusson noted with alarm that three people "who spoke the broken English of Sierra Leone with great fluency" were found onboard.[37] Based on that point alone he expressed suspicion that the trio had previously been liberated. But given the lengthy history of entanglement along the Sierra Leone Coast between British and African peoples, familiarity with English was common.[38] Indeed, southern Sierra Leone merchants generally conducted business with Freetown traders in the language; translators were abundant; and Krio itself had its origins in the mingling with English of indigenous African languages. Linguistic grounds were therefore a misleading and unnecessarily inclusive indicator of who should be considered a Liberated African.

Governor Doherty explicitly identified this problem in 1840, in the wake of a report he received from James Kennedy, a commissioner in the Havana Court of Mixed Commission, which warned that Liberated Africans had frequently turned up on vessels that the Caribbean-based court processed. Kennedy highlighted in particular the case of Daniel Speck, an English-speaking captive found onboard a slave ship that the British navy had captured. While Kennedy confirmed that Speck himself was a former recaptive (he was thus twice liberated), he nevertheless took the opportunity to contradict Kennedy about the scale of Liberated African enslavement. Familiarity with English was a problematic way to assess the issue, the governor warned. Many indigenous Africans – people who had not previously been liberated – knew English. The regular entry into the colony of outside merchants helped make it the language of business throughout the region.[39] Though the governor was demonstrably correct about this particular point, we should not discount the likelihood that he made it merely to calm concerns over the safety of the Liberated African community. It was to the government's benefit to downplay insecurity.

But Liberated Africans were at times victims of re-enslavement, particularly when they traveled outside of the colony. During the investigation into the captured slaver *Enganador*, court officials in Havana spoke with several Africans who claimed that they were recaptives who had previously lived in Sierra Leone. According to their testimony, they had been seized and sold in the interior during a commercial excursion. Tom Peters, one of the victims, explained in his deposition that he was a Sherbro man who was previously brought to Freetown as a boy on a condemned slave vessel. Upon his liberation Peters was sent to a school at York under the supervision of superintendent Pratt. The administrator expressed an interest in sending Peters to England but Peters refused. Fearing he would be dispatched abroad against his will, he fled to Kissy, where he found work as the captain of a canoe that Mahamadoo, an Aku Liberated African, owned. On one excursion up the Bompey River to Tiama, in Mende country, Mahamadoo unexpectedly sold Peters to Sanasee, the town's headman, to settle a debt. Peters was then sold several additional times: to a man named Tayack, in the Boom country, under whom he spent three months in captivity; and then to Luiz, a well known Spanish slave dealer stationed in the Gallinas.[40] Colony officials were further outraged to hear from the three men about the abuse they witnessed of Elizabeth Eastman, a Liberated African who worked as a washerwoman for Luiz, in the Gallinas. When the recaptives arrived in Luiz's settlement, Eastman recognized them from the time they had spent together in the colony. She took pity on the detainees and secretly provided them with additional food and water. When Luiz discovered what she had been doing, the slave dealer became enraged and severely beat Eastman. He placed her in shackles and submitted her to additional abuse.[41]

Outraged by these graphic depositions, Governor Fergusson immediately dispatched Commodore Jones to Seabar, in the

Sherbro, where Eastman was first abducted, to confront Harry Tucker. Jones called a meeting with the chiefs of the region, who agreed to organize a palaver to settle the affair. In June, four months after the three recaptives first passed along information to the government of Eastman's abuse, the chiefs concluded their gathering. They levied a fine against Harry Tucker valued at ten slaves as punishment for Luiz's indiscretions.[42] Tucker paid half of the fine in trade goods; he offered five enslaved children to settle the rest of it. The "payment" put the governor in an uncomfortable bind: on the one hand, the colony could of course not accept payment in slaves; on the other, rejecting the captives would doom them to lives lived in captivity. Governor Fergusson ultimately accepted the payment and immediately liberated the children.[43]

In addition to slave dealing around the colony and the kidnapping of Liberated Africans from within it, British officials faced the growing problem of slave use among Freetown settlers. Concern over this issue emerged in earnest in the 1850s under Governor Kennedy, but slaves clandestinely circulated throughout the settlement much earlier. The secrecy of the trade was undermined only after the governor sought and received assistance from Momodu Yeli, a Muslim "Mandinka" man from Jolof country, who helped document many instances of slaveholding. At the governor's encouragement, Yeli testified in 1852 against several well-known slave dealers in return for a small reward. He did so at a considerable personal cost: in a letter of commendation written to the British Colonial Office in London, Kennedy warned that Yeli "will never again be able to go beyond the precincts of the colony without danger and his personal safety is questionable even within it."[44]

With Yeli's help, the government uncovered an intricate network that helped circulate captives around the colony. Most incoming slaves arrived through the same route that integrated southern Sierra Leone and the Northern Rivers region. During that lengthy journey, slave merchants snuck small numbers of enslaved Africans into Freetown itself, separating them from the larger caravan bound farther north. This colonial branch of the trade was defined by the extremely young age of its victims. Dependent children were in high demand in Freetown, where they were put to work as domestics within households. Because of their age, the children were easily disguised and more likely to be absorbed over time into households.[45]

Yet enslaved children rarely became fully accepted members of Freetown communities. They were instead generally disposed of as they grew older - removed from the colony before they had time to fully integrate. Given the insatiable demand for labor in the interior, colonial slave owners found plenty of buyers for these maturing captives. They sold them in exchange for cattle and other commodities from inland.[46] The organization of this clandestine traffic ensured a continuous cycle of alienation for its victims, who rarely had time to acculturate into any society at all and thus remained permanent outsiders open to ongoing exploitation.[47]

Precisely how long captives in the colony could remain before they challenged their status is an open question. Owners in Freetown knew all too well that as slaves were exposed to British colonial officials and the abolitionist rhetoric they spread, they would gain a clearer sense of the options they had at their disposal to free themselves. For owners, maintaining slavery in Freetown was a constant juggling act. A young slave who had been in the colony for ten years was, for example, unexpectedly sold to Susu slave dealers from Mabelly who immediately shipped him by canoe to Medina. "He would have kept me," the boy later explained, "had I not known so much English fashion," which the owner felt would enable the boy to run away and seek British protection.[48]

The steady movement of captives within and beyond Freetown exposed them to divergent worlds that the confrontation between slavery and antislavery at least partially shaped.[49] Snippets culled from the life histories of captives whom the British Government freed in the interior in the mid-nineteenth century help bring those worlds to life. Koota, one young captive, testified in 1853 about her wide-ranging experiences under slavery and in freedom. During a war in the Mende country, she was captured and sold to a Susu slave dealer who marched her to Wonkafong, where for several years she was forcibly detained. Koota was sold a second time in 1853 to Peter Wilson, a Liberated African man, who snuck her into Freetown, where she performed domestic chores under the supervision of Wilson's wife. Two years later, Koota, then just 14 or 15 years old, was removed from the colony with a small group of enslaved children and sent to Romatangoh, a town on the Bullom Shore. She was eventually freed with help from Momodu Yeli.[50]

Among other issues, stories such as these highlight the centrality of gender to the organization of the internal slave trade in nineteenth century Sierra Leone. Slavery scholars have long recognized the high demand in Africa for female captives but they have at times disagreed over what caused it. Suzanne Miers and Igor Kopytoff, for example, emphasize the value of women's reproductive roles, which enabled them to increase the sizes of African households and the number of dependents leaders controlled. Claude Meillassoux, Martin Klein, and other generally Marxist scholars point primarily to women's productive capacities, highlighting the important tasks that women performed in African agricultural regimes. More recent works have aimed to synthesize these two views by underscoring how gendered aspects of slavery and the slave trade varied across time and space.[51]

What does an analysis of slaveholding in Freetown and on its outskirts add to the conversation? Given the secretive context in which slaving within the colony operated, it is difficult to identify owners' motivations. They surely desired girls for many reasons. In some cases, settlers sought women as wives. Yet the issue was not always so straightforward. Under pressure from the British Government, an owner might, for example, merely claim that a woman was his wife to avoid criminal punishment. Here again a life story that a former captive provided is instructive. In the mid-1850s, Boccari Soonkonokoh obtained a young Kuranko slave named Phena for $16. He changed her name to See-rah and kept her for several years in his household, which was within the colony. Upon hearing that he was suspected of slave-holding, Soonkonokoh had his wife remove the girl from Free-town and hide her from British officials. But the plan did not work and he was eventually arrested and tried for slaveholding. In his defense, Soonkonokoh first testified that he bought the girl not as a slave but only to help his family fetch water and perform other chores. He then amended his story, adding that he found Phena while he was in Kono country, where he "fell in love with her and redeemed her for a wife." A witness to the case confirmed that Soonkonokoh had paid kola to the girl's previous owner to secure her release. Interestingly, even Phena herself seemed unsure of her status: asked directly by an investigator whether she was held in captivity, the girl merely replied that she was never called a slave.[52] Such testimony helps draw attention to the complex spectrum along which slavery and freedom ex-isted in nineteenth century Africa and the challenges officials faced when trying to define, confront, and eliminate the institu-tion.

Slavery's ambiguity and seeming ubiquity provided Freetown officials with the flexibility to choose when to intervene in cases of slave dealing and slaveholding. From a legal perspective, the situation should have been clear. Slavery within British colonies was made illegal in 1833 and a subsequent law passed in 1843 made it an offense for British subjects to own or trade slaves anywhere in the world. But applying that law proved difficult both because of the complex range of coercive practices that prevailed across the region and the hostility from local leaders that strict enforcement would have provoked. For those reasons, it took Freetown officials a decade to begin to aggressively im-plement the law against slave owning and dealing.

Governor Kennedy spearheaded the transition. During his first year in charge, Kennedy had rescued 268 children – 138 male and 130 female – including many who were carried into the settlement and some who were removed from it. To combat the trafficking in young slaves, Kennedy pushed through several measures that restricted access to liberated girls and boys and monitored children's movements inside of the colony. In December of 1853, he passed the "Ordinance for the Better Protection of Alien Children within the Colony of Sierra Leone," which required all children under 21 years old to register with the government within 24 hours of their arrival in Freetown. Two years later, the government amended this ordinance, adding provisions that required all incoming children to attend school for four hours per day and made it illegal to remove children from the settlement without permission from the government.[53]

Passing ordinances requiring the registration of alien children dragged Kennedy into a contentious issue over which settlers, administrators, and the region's interior inhabitants vehemently disagreed. At the heart of the problem was the British Government's inclusive definition of slavery. Some Liberated Africans argued that the children whom the ordinance targeted were not slaves at all but rather were members of the recaptives' extended families who were deliberately sent from the interior to be raised under supervision in the colony. A memorial that they circulated in 1854, signed the "citizens of Freetown," dismissed outright the existence of child slavery. Kennedy's investigations, they argued, merely demonstrated that "free African children of free African parents residing in the neighboring territories are placed, in accordance with long usage, under the guardianship of their friends or connections for education and training in useful occupations."[54] The authors of the memorial further warned that rescuing children whom the government suspected were slaves once they entered Freetown risked scaring away prominent merchants and disrupting the flow of goods into the colony. Liberated Africans knew that such language stood a strong chance of capturing the officials' attention.

In addition to these ordinances, the government began to compile information about fugitive slaves who escaped into Freetown from their owners inland. As they had in the Registers of Liberated Africans, which documented captives who were removed from slave vessels, officials identified each fugitive slave's name, sex, and age. They also noted ethnicity and other relevant data. Freetown officials maintained the fugitive slave registers only sporadically into the middle of the century. But in 1858 they began to more systemtically record the information, which they enclosed in reports that were sent back to the Colonial Office. Although the registers likely capture a small fraction of the total number of fugitive slaves who escaped into the colony, they nevertheless suggest a steady increase over the 1850s in the volume of slave flight. While just 35 captives were documented entering Freetown in 1858, the number of entries in the ledgers for the following year more than tripled, reaching 117. Between 1858 and 1861, when Britain annexed the Sherbro and other neighboring areas and drastically transformed patterns of slave flight, 288 enslaved men, women, and children entered the colony.[55]

What do these registers reveal about slaves who fled from their owners and sought protection in the colony? The composition of the former captives is heavily concentrated to areas nearest to Freetown, as we would expect given the dangers or traveling for long distances through the interior as a slave. Table 5.1 illustrates that nearly half of the escaped slaves were identified as Temne, the ethnolinguistic community that surrounded Freetown. Mende and Sherbro, and to a lesser extent Susu, Kuranko, and Loko peoples also sought British protection. The Temne entries stand out not just by their volume but also because of their even distribution between males and female. While Mende and Sherbro slaves entered the colony at a rate of roughly three men to each woman, more Temne females than males arrived in Freetown. This suggests a direct correlation between the sex of the captive and the distance of travel. The unique vulnerability that slave women faced would have been exacerbated the longer they spent in flight. The data underscore that females were willing to risk those dangers on Freetown's immediate frontier but less likely to do so from farther away.

Table 5.1, Fugitive Slaves Entering Freetown by Ethnicity and Gender, 1858-61

Ethnicity	Male	Female	Total
Temne	61	63	124
Mende	50	16	66
Sherbro	20	7	27
Susu	8	6	14
Kuranko	8	4	12
Colony Born	3	9	12
Loko	5	6	11
Outside Sierra Leone	6	2	8
Limba	1	2	3
Kono	2	0	2
Toma	1	1	2
Fula	1	0	1
Vai	1	0	1
Totals[56]	167	116	283

Source: Registers of Escaped Slaves Database

By the middle of the nineteenth century, Freetown's administration had begun to appreciate two points that slaves from the region had been making clear through their actions for six decades: British policies that targeted the slave trade had important implications for the institution of slavery itself, whether or not Britain wanted them to; and slave migration between the colony and the interior made the application of antislavery laws within the colony difficult to isolate from wider concerns in the hinterland. Questions about how best to intervene in slave-related issues had by the mid-century commanded attention at the highest levels of the colonial administration. Aggressive implementation not only raised the ire of headmen and some Liberated Africans but also opened thorny questions about the legality of pursuing beyond the borders of the British territory any recaptives who were accused of slave dealing. Where did Liberated Africans fit in the context of defining British citizens and subjects? Did British laws apply to them wherever they went? A clear policy against

223

slave dealing required Britain to formally address these types of concerns.

Slave Dealing and Defining Colonial Subjects
The second phase that Governor Kennedy launched in the 1850s against slave dealing within and around Freetown leaned heavily on the courts to prosecute guilty parties. Grand Juries tried those whom the government caught or suspected of slave dealing. Those juries convicted 17 individuals over two sessions early in 1853. But the jurors came under suspicion, including from Kennedy himself, who claimed that they were often too closely related to suspects to be impartial. Aku jurors, he warned, were particularly reluctant to convict people who shared their background. Kennedy took the drastic step of undermining the existing legal system to sidestep his concerns. He passed an ordinance that altogether abolished Grand Juries and restricted the pool of petty jurors to those who owned property. The settlers were outraged. A group of more than 550 of them sent a petition in protest to the Secretary of State, which was rejected.[57]

These debates and the broader context of prosecuting Liberated Africans for slave dealing in which they took place raised new questions about how and where recaptives fit within the framework of the British Empire. The problem stemmed from disagreements over their legal status. Some lawyers and officials from the Colonial Office argued that since Liberated Africans were never officially declared to be colonial subjects, they could not legally be pursued for crimes outside of Freetown. Leading administrators in the colony desparately sought clarificatiom.[58] The resulting correspondence exposed differences of opinion over how to approach the question. Given the size of the recaptive population, Governor Macdonald asked the British Government to pass an Act of Imperial Parliament that would establish Liberated Africans as British subjects. Dragging his feet, the Secretary of State replied that local legislation would be sufficient. As the debate wore on, recaptives began to actively and cleverly exploit the legal loophole. In a pointed letter to Earl Grey, Macdonald warned that "We should either allow [Liberated Africans] to be amenable to country law (which in our treaties is strictly prohibited) or we should make them amenable to our own law...Liberated Africans currently claim British citizenship when it suits their interests and disown this right when it would render punishment."[59]

To further complicate things, confusion over the legal status of Liberated Africans was by this point not limited to Sierra Leone. In the late-1830s, a wave of recaptives emigrated to Nigeria, where they established themselves as traders and missionaries. Decades later – around the same time that Freetown administrators anxiously awaited advice from abroad on how to settle the Liberated African question – officials in Lagos also sought clarification about the legal status of the emigrants. The situation was particularly unclear for the earliest arrivals, many of whom were born around Lagos or in its hinterland, had lived for a few years in Freetown, and then returned close to their homelands. The Treaty of Cession that the British signed in 1861 declared that all the city's inhabitants were "the *Queen's* subjects" but that was not quite the same as being British subjects and it offered settlers few guarantees. In 1865, Sir John Glover, the Lieutenant-Governor of Lagos, took decisive action on the issue when he determined that the colony would treat any non-"British" inhabitants as British subjects while in the city but would not should they leave.[60]

Despite Glover's clarity, disagreements between Freetown and London persisted and the issue remained unsettled. The Colonial Office baulked at requests to deal formally with questions about citizenship. The Secretary of State continued to push for solutions at the local level. Treaties, he advised, might in the future be more inclusively worded as "British subjects or Liberated Africans" but that change would require the government to renegotiate old treaties. London was evidently keen to embrace the uncertainty.[61]

Colony officials ultimately won the day by doubling down on their warning that clarifying the status of Freetown's settlers was the only way to effectively suppress the colonial slave trade. In

August of 1853, the British passed an Imperial Act that formally made all Liberated Africans British subjects.[62] The Act made it possible to more aggressively prosecute individuals involved in slaveholding and dealing within and around the colony. It also provoked debates about how officers should respond to indigenous leaders in the interior who held Liberated Africans in captivity. What types of punishments could the government legally impose on them? That question was indirectly answered when Britain turned to a more aggressive policy of annexation, which added to the colony large parts of Sierra Leone that immediately became subject to British law. The final section explores the relationship between abolitionism and the growth of Freetown.

Abolition and Colonial Expansion

By the 1850s, Africa's colonial landscape was beginning to take shape, even if the well-known Berlin Conference, through which Europeans formally implemented a plan to partition the continent, was still more than a quarter of a century away. The six decades that had passed after British activists founded Freetown brought growing numbers of European peoples and powers to Africa who competed to carve out spaces over which they could claim control or influence. But that process was uneven and deeply contested, not only by Africans who defended their land from the incursion but also between European governments at home and the settlers who represented them abroad. Though popular narratives of imperialism suggest that western powers shared a universal enthusiasm for conquest, the reality was that at least prior to the 1870s and 80s, British and French officials frequently rejected proposals from men-on-the-spot for even marginal increases to the size of their colonial landholdings. Few settings illustrate this point more clearly than Freetown, where clashes between officials in Africa and London occurred early and often. In the face of mounting debts and widespread concern over high mortality rates for European and Liberated African settlers, the Colonial Office worried that new territories would bring new troubles. Restraint was the mantra.[63]

The challenges of implementing antislavery policies further limited administrative enthusiasm for conquest. This was true not only in Sierra Leone, where colonialism and abolitionism had complicated each other for decades, but across large parts of coastal West Africa. Scholars of the Gold Coast have examined this issue with particular care, revealing the pains the British took to avoid intervening in slavery. Before formal conquest, councils of merchants administered the forts along the littoral. They openly supported and often benefitted from the region's slave system and even returned fugitive slaves to their owners. But in 1843, the British Government assumed responsibility over the territory, transforming the legal context in which the settlement operated. To minimize the disruptive impact of the transition, the government drew a distinction between the thin coastal strip that they formally colonized and the larger interior over which they claimed a protectorate. Slavery was outlawed within the colony, in which British laws applied, but not the protectorate, where officials adopted a more flexible approach. Practical concerns trumped ideological ones.[64]

But Sierra Leone and the Gold Coast had a few prominent differences. The most important, at least as it related to the evolution of the relationship between abolition and colonization, was how early Freetown became British. The settlement took shape at the height of the Atlantic slave system, when Liberated African and European settlers faced concrete threats from merchants and headmen who were invested in the continuation of the slave trade. Recaptives were occasionally re-enslaved and deported across the ocean, as the previous section illustrated. The thriving external slave trade added a layer of danger to Freetown's existence and colored the way the government approached internal slavery and questions about additional conquest. By the time the British formally absorbed the Gold Coast, on the other hand, it had largely suppressed the transatlantic trade from the region. Colonization there occurred in the context of widespread slave holding but with little concern about Atlantic slave trading. That difference was important: officials along

227

the Gold Coast effectively defined slavery as a domestic institution in which they did not need to intervene; in Sierra Leone, the slave trade and slavery itself were so tightly bound together that European policies had implications for both. Some activist governors went so far as to argue that more widespread conquest was the only way to achieve their abolitionist agenda.

That logic first emerged in 1825, under Governor Turner. An uncompromising Scottish veteran of the Peninsular War, Turner approached his responsibilities as governor as he had previous military assignments. He was particularly passionate in his opposition to the transatlantic slave trade. The simplest solution to end the traffic, he argued, would be to extend British control over any coastal regions from which captives were embarked. In a series of dispatches to the Colonial Office, Turner outlined a plan that advocated for British conquest of all of Upper Guinea, from Senegambia to the Windward Coast. He at the same time proposed widespread military intervention in the interior to put an end to the wars that fueled the slave trade. In that context, the governor sailed to the Sherbro to mediate a long-standing and messy dispute between the Caulker and Cleveland families, which involved dozens of warriors whose allegiances were unclear. The treaty that Turner offered, without approval from London, required chiefs to cede to Freetown the land between the Camaranca River and the town of Camalay, in the Lower Kittam, and commit faithfully to the suppression of the slave trade. The leaders agreed, but by the following year rivals reopened the traffic, infuriating the notoriously short-tempered governor. Turner launched a military excursion to the Sherbro, where soldiers effectively blockaded the entire coast between Seabar and Cape Mount.[65] His campaign succeeded in the short term at reducing the slave trade but Turner paid a heavy price for participating in the affair: he died shortly after the expedition, likely from a disease he caught while in the Sherbro.

The governor's actions were not well received back home. Writing to Turner's successor, Secretary of State Bathurst explained that his office would not support "anything which might be construed into a desire of territorial aggrandizement."[66] He revoked Turner's treaty of annexation, sending a clear message about the limits of radical abolitionism in Africa. Denied the option of further conquest, subsequent governors tried to retain informal control over the Sherbro through a combination of treaties of friendship, the distribution of stipends to loyal headmen, and at times direct military intervention. Though these approaches lacked Turner's raw aggression, they over time drew Sherbro rulers deeper into the orbit of the British colonial state and opened space for Freetown administrators to more directly shape African affairs. In 1849, the British signed a treaty with several Sherbro chiefs that among other things required the leaders to submit disputes for arbitration to the colonial government, whose decisions could not be challenged. In return the governor promised to protect the signatories and provide them with stipends of 400 bars per year.

Why would southern Sierra Leone headmen agree to such terms? This is a complex question that lacks a simple answer. But one important factor was the military protection to which the treaties committed the British Government. Warfare had long shaped the area south of Freetown. Waging it successfully brought material wealth and provided an avenue to absorb greater numbers of people into local households. Prominent chiefs distributed their resources to their followers to establish loyalties within their towns. They also "bought war," paying for the services of the region's mercenary war boys, whose exploits were notorious throughout the Sherbro and Gallinas. Perhaps some chiefs calculated that the British Government offered a more secure guarantee of protection against the growing militancy of the interior. Alternatively, fear over the impact of abolition led others to sign in order to ensure a reliable supply of British goods for redistribution. Whatever the case, it seems clear that the British viewed the treaties in a very different light than did African signatories. Europeans famously used them to open up land for exploitation and strip locals of their capacity to make decisions for themselves and their dependents. Africans likely signed on to cement their own legitimacy to British and African locals in the face of widespread instability. Ceding land to the British Government might have seemed like a price well worth paying in order to maintain their authority.

These varying contexts and motivations revealed themselves when the British took formal control over the Sherbro in the mid-nineteenth century. By the late 1850s, several French firms had established themselves at Bonthe, on Sherbro Island, where they engaged in trade for palm products. The Frenchmen fell out with Thomas Stephen Caulker and, fearing for their factory, they called for protection from the French Government. Naval officers arrived in the *Grondeur*, a man-of-war, ordered Caulker to strip the palisades and other fortifications from his town, and demanded that he sign a treaty that would protect French commercial interests in the area. As he considered the proposal, a larger French force arrived and burned down Caulker's settlement at Bendu. In the face of such aggression, Caulker appealed for help to Governor Hill in Freetown, offering to cede Bendu to them in return. He reminded the British of the timber supplies in the Bagroo that they would lose if the French were to seize control over the area. Hill was persuaded. He immediately dispatched a naval force to the region and ordered the acting consul to hoist a British flag at Bendu. Later in the year, Hill formalized through a treaty the cession of that town and many others. Illustrating Sherbro's fractured politics, William Tucker and other rival headmen quickly contested the annexation treaties. They argued that the original signatories lacked legitimate claims to the land they gave to the British. Tucker and his allies explained that while they did not object to putting themselves under British protection, they were unwilling to give up their sovereignty. The governor forged ahead, ignoring those protests. Perhaps due to the growing French presence in the Sherbro, the Colonial Office approved the treaty without expressing any reservations.

The treaty added to the British Empire hundreds of miles and thousands of primarily Sherbro and Mende subjects. It also reestablished the legitimacy of using conquest to settle local problems – a policy that dated back to Turner's expedition. And while the Colonial Office previously denied that approach, it did not hesitate to exploit Turner's treaty when the circumstances called for it. In the 1860s, the British and Liberian Governments began a protracted debate over the border between the two territories. They established a Boundary Commission to investigate the issue but before it met, Governor Rowe shocked the Liberian Government when he dusted off and revived the 1825 treaty, asserting British rights over trade along strategic parts of Turner's Peninsula and at the mouth of the Boom. The Colonial Office supported Rowe's move in 1881 and over the next two years approved additional measures that expanded the size of British Sierra Leone. In the years preceding the Berlin Conference, British officials had therefore asserted rights over the entire region between Freetown and the Gallinas. That they drew on a treaty from nearly six decades earlier that was drawn up in an effort to suppress the slave trade provides a stark reminder of the link between colonialism and abolitionism.

The impact that British expansion had on slavery in southern Sierra Leone was complex. The last transatlantic slave vessels that embarked slaves in Sierra Leone had sailed in 1856.[67] Annexation of Sherbro therefore occurred in a context that more closely resembled the 1840s Gold Coast than early-nineteenth century Freetown. As they had along the Gold Coast, British officials justified non-intervention in affairs relating to slavery in the newly colonized Sherbro by tiptoeing around the institution, emphasizing its ancient and benign nature. In a despatch to the Earl of Carnarvon that explicitly draws on the Gold Coast example, Governor Kortright noted of slavery

> it is of a very mild form...I can scarcely accept that the people of Sherbro are unaware that it is in their power to break the chain at any time should they choose to. I believe in a majority of cases their position is voluntary. I request permission to adopt the course taken at the Gold Coast, to let it be known by proclamation that all men are free in British territory and

that it is not in the power of any one to retain their services against their will.[68]

Yet the British put little effort into publicizing the freedoms to which captives were suddenly eligible. The new realties of colonial expansion required a quietist approach to abolitionism.

Not all slaves awaited advice from British officials on whether and how to seek freedom. As they had since the 1790s, some captives sensed that colonial expansion mildly cracked the system that kept them in captivity and began to flee to British colonial stations in the Sherbro. Others stayed with their owners but submitted complaints of mistreatment to officers in British Sherbro and requested support to improve the conditions under which they lived. While Sierra Leone never witnessed the massive waves of slave flight that occurred in French West Africa, an assessment of slavery, resistance, and colonialism in the nineteenth century underscores how attuned some captives were to the prospects for freedom that Freetown's growth offered.

Conclusion

Although British officials drew careful lines separating their policies toward the slave trade and slavery, enslaved Africans took actions that undermined any such neat distinctions. Abolitionist activity over the first half of the nineteenth century was premised on the idea that British colonizers could seal themselves off from the wider world in which they operated, establishing an antislavery settlement where the productivity of free labor would inspire Africans to turn their backs on the transatlantic trade and invest in the production of agricultural commodities. Yet slavery proved so complex and enduring – and captives themselves so dynamic – that Freetown officials were constantly drawn into broader debates about slavery and slave ownership in and around the settlement. Resolving those debates required the British to answer basic but central questions about their colonial ambitions: just how far would they go to confront slavery and slave dealing? Who could they subject to British laws? What rights did former captives have as they moved into and out of British colonies? And how ambitious did the British intend for their colonial project in West Africa to become? British officials seldom had ready answers to such deep questions. Their policies were instead worked out without precedent or models from which to draw, at least in Africa, and in response to pressures from slaves, slave owners, and Liberated Africans, whose activities helped shape the abolition campaign in this corner of the continent. On the southern frontier of Freetown, Europeans and Africans waged an ongoing struggle over the scope and direction of colonialism in Sierra Leone.

Notes

1   See especially the introduction to Miers and Roberts, *The End of Slavery*. The tightrope that officials walked trying to satisfy various transatlantic lobbies is a central theme in John Grace, *Domestic Slavery in West Africa with Particular Reference to the Sierra Leone Protectorate, 1896-1927* (New York: Barnes and Noble Books, 1975); Miers and Klein, *Slavery and Colonial Rule*; and Mann, *Slavery and the Birth*, ch. 5.
2   SLNA, "Orders and Regulations from the Directors of the Sierra Leone Company to the Superintendent and Council for the Settlement." Fyfe, *A History*, 54.
3   TNA, BT6/70. The Transfer Act is reprinted in C.W. Newbury, *British Policy Towards West Africa; Select Documents, 1786-1874* (Oxford: Clarendon Press, 1965), 477-79.
4   Tension between colonies and metropoles has reemerged as a theme in colonial studies over the past two decades. See, for example, Frederick Cooper and Anne Laura Stoler, eds., *Tensions of Empire: Colonial Cultures in a Bourgeois World* (Berkeley: University of California Press, 1997); and Jane Burbank and Frederick Cooper, *Empires in World History: Power and the Politics of Difference* (Princeton: Princeton University Press, 2010).
5   TNA, CO270/3, September 13, 1794.
6   TNA, CO270/12, February 26, 1811.
7   TNA, April 29, 1811. Columbine noted that the earlier proclamation was misconstrued but he did not provide a specific reason for the formal change in policy. It is likely, however, that officials at home felt his previous statement came dangerously close to condoning slavery within British territory.
8   Scanlan, *Freedom's Debtors*, esp. ch. 1 and 210-12. Scanlan's argument is a sharp critique of Britain's nineteenth-century vision of its antislavery

campaign as rooted strictly in humanitarian impulses. Instead, Scanlan suggests that British naval and colonial officers profited in myriad ways from their involvement in the antislavery campaign. His point is well taken, yet serious profits were surely limited to a small number of officials. Moreover, humanitarianism and economic self-interest are not, of course, necessarily contradictory.

9   A point more generally made in Miers and Klein, *Slavery and Colonial Rule*, 6, but for later in the century.

10 TNA, CO270/4, 16 July 1798.

11 Ibid.

12 TNA, CO270/4, August 9, 1798. Macaulay often used statements from elders to demonstrate his familiarity with country law. In this instance he cited conversations he had with Mr. Aspinall, a prominent merchant in the Scarcies, and Mr. Richards, of Bunce Island, who both informed his position on fugitive slaves. Macaulay also appealed to King Firama's practical side by posing a hypothetical scenario: were a group of Temne slaves from Firama's settlement to flee to Freetown, Macaulay asked, would it be appropriate to return them to Mr. Cleveland, a Sherbro man? Fyfe alludes to Macaulay's use of country law to suit his own purposes in *A History*, 54.

13 TNA, CO267/81, Reffell to Campbell, February 23, 1827.

14 This point is generally made in literature on the commercial transition. See Law, *From Slave Trade to "Legitimate" Commerce*. On the changing position of slaves in nineteenth century Africa more generally, see Lovejoy, *Transformations*; and Stilwell, *Slavery and Slaving*. Freetown officials also noticed the increased use of enslaved porters in the mid-nineteenth century. Milan Kalous, *Cannibals and Tongo Players of Sierra Leone* (Trentham: Wright & Carman Ltd., 1974), 3.

15 See ch. 2.

16 TNA, CO270/6, September 11, 1801.

17 TNA, CO267/52, Individuals, Samo to Bathurst, "The Memorial of Samuel Samo, of Factory Island, One of the Iles de Los – on the Western Coast of Arica – Merchant;" See TNA, CO267/51, MacCarthy to Henry Eonlburn, September 30, 1820, for the governor's reply.

18 *Substance of the Report, Delivered, by the Court of Directors of the Sierra Leone Company, to the General Court of Proprietors, on Thursday the 29th March, 1798* (London: Printed by James Phillips & Son, 1798), 32.

19 TNA, CO267/81, Campbell to Hay, March (N.D.), 1827.

20 The idea that slavery in Africa served primarily to incorporate outsiders into new communities comes from the introduction to Kopytoff and Miers, *Slavery in Africa*. Many scholars have criticized the coauthors' vision, highlighting among other problems its timelessness, neglect of the dynamic economic roles that slaves played in African societies, and the antithetical nature of enslavement, slavery, and kinship. The most well

known critique is Meillassoux, *The Anthropology of Slavery*. For an overview of the early models that scholars of slavery developed and their short-comings, see Frederick Cooper, "The Problem of Slavery in African Studies," *Journal of African History* 20, no. 1 (1979): 103-125. While these criticisms highlight important problems with the Kopytoff and Miers model, the relatively small size of slaveholdings in Sierra Leone made the incorporation of outsiders an important – if not the defining – feature of slavery in the region.

21 In 1840, Governor Doherty noted that 41 slaves had sought refuge in Freetown over the previous three years: 22 men, 11 women, and 8 children. See TNA, CO267/159, Doherty to Russell, April 22, 1840.

22 TNA, CO267/140, enclosure in Campbell to Bart, November 21, 1837. For the context of the Magbele and Rokon conflicts and subsequent British intervention, see Fyfe, *A History of Sierra Leone*, 185-86 and 206.

23 TNA, CO267/159, Doherty to Russell, April 22, 1840; ibid, Doherty to Russell, July 29, 1840.

24 In one of the only major volumes dedicated to African strategies of resistance to the slave trade, no contributions specifically address the impact of the suppression movement on African resistance to the transatlantic trade. See Sylviane A. Diouf, *Fighting the Slave Trade: West African Strategies* (Athens: Ohio University Press, 2003). Several slave rebellions occurred in the Sierra Leone hinterland in the late-eighteenth and nineteenth centuries, though their causes are complex. See Bruce Mouser, "Rebellion, Marronage and Jihad: Strategies of Resistance to Slavery on the Sierra Leone Coast, c. 1783-1796," *Journal of African History* 48, no. 1 (2007): 27-44; Ismail Rashid, "Escape, Revolt and Marronage in Eighteenth and Nineteenth Century Sierra Leone Hinterland," *Canadian Journal of African Studies* 34, no. 3 (2000): 656-83; Bronislaw Nowak, "The Slave Rebellion in Sierra Leone in 1785-1796," *Hemispheres* 3, no. 3 (1986): 151-69.

25 Fyfe, *A History*, 4-5. For a first-hand account of the destruction of Bunce Island, see TNA, T70/1465, which includes Walter Charles' diary and minutes of the transactions he completed up to the point of the attack.

26 TNA, CO267/27, Thornton to Castlereagh, February 4, 1810.

27 Ibid.

28 Documents describing the Bunce Island revolt are included in TNA, CO270/11, October 14, 1809 and its enclosures; and TNA, CO267/28, Walker to Thompson, November 4, 1809. Fyfe, *A History of Sierra Leone*, 108, also briefly mentions the rebellion.

29 TNA, CO267/27, Thornton to Castlereagh, February 4, 1810.

30 See Mann, *Slavery and the Birth*, 163-89, for a similar treatment of children and slavery around Lagos.

31 TNA, CO267/24, August 29, 1808 and September 14, 1808. See also *[Review of] the Trials of the Slave Traders, Samuel Samo, Joseph Peters, and Wil-*

liam Tufft: Tried in April and June 1812, before the Hon. Robert Thorpe, L.L.D....: with two letters on the slave trade/from a gentleman resident at Sierra Leone, to an advocate for the abolition in London (London: Longmans, Green & Co., 1813).

32 Jeffcott later admitted that he miscalculated mortality and fertility rates but he remained convinced that nearly three thousand Liberated Africans were missing. See TNA, CO267/109, Findlay to Goderich, June 29, 1831, and enclosures.

33 Ibid.

34 Investigators also explained that Sherbro and Mende Liberated Africans, whose homelands were near to the colony, returned home in small numbers, which accounted for some of the discrepancy in population estimates. TNA, CO267/109, enclosure 3 in Findlay to Goderich, June 29, 1831.

35 TNA, CO267/105, Murray to Findlay, May 15, 1830.

36 CO267/103, enclosure 1 in Findlay to Hay, July 17, 1830.

37 TNA, CO267/187, Fergusson to Stanley, February 15, 1845. On the *Enganador*, see Eltis et al., *Voyages*, ID 3884.

38 Day, "Afro-British Integration."

39 TNA, CO267/260, Doherty to Russell, October 18, 1840.

40 TNA, CO267/187, Fergusson to Stanley, February 15, 1845 and enclosures.

41 Ibid.

42 Slaves served in some cases as a unit of value, similar to the bar in Upper Guinea. On the bar trade, see Curtin, *Economic Change*, 312; and Fyfe, *A History*, 9; and Grace, *Domestic Slavery*, 13.

43 TNA, CO267/187, Fergusson to Stanley, February 15, 1845; and ibid, enclosure in Fergusson to Stanley, June 16, 1845.

44 Fyfe, *A History*, 270-72, briefly mentions Yeli's role in undermining the slave trade within the colony. For additional detail, see TNA, CO267/229, Kennedy to Parkington, December 23, 1852. For the quote, see *BPP, Slave Trade*, vol. 90, Kennedy to Parkington, January 6, 1853, 343.

45 On the organization of the trade and its relationship to the broader internal traffic, see TNA, CO267/231, Kennedy to the Duke of Newcastle, March 14, 1853. For a similar treatment of British concerns in Lagos about the use of slave children, see Mann, *Slavery and the Birth*, 163-78.

46 TNA, CO267/229, Kennedy to Pakington, December 23, 1852; TNA, CO267/234, Kennedy to the Duke of Newcastle, December 9, 1853.

47 Such constant movement fostered the "institutionalization of marginality" that Miers and Kopytoff describe in their introduction to *Slavery in Africa*.

48 *BPP, Slave Trade*, vol. 90, Enclosure 3 in Kennedy to the Duke of Newcastle, March 15, 1853, 351-52.

49   Inspiration for the idea that the slave trade created unique "worlds" comes from the subtitle in Robert Harms, *The Diligent: A Voyage through the Worlds of the Slave Trade* (New York: Basic Books, 2002).

50   TNA, CO267/233, enclosures in Kennedy to the Duke of Newcastle, July 18, 1853.

51   Local and regional studies addressing the relationship between slavery and gender in Africa are numerous. The broadest works include Kopytoff and Miers, *Slavery in Africa*; Meillassoux, *The Anthropology of Slavery*; Robertson and Klein, *Women and Slavery*; Martin A. Klein, "The Study of Slavery in Africa: A Review Article," *Journal of African History* 19, no. 4 (1978): 599-609. More recent gendered approaches to slavery in Africa include Gwyn Campbell, Suzanne Miers, and Joseph C. Miller, eds., *Women and Slavery, Volume 1: Africa, The Indian Ocean World, and the Medieval North Atlantic* (Athens: Ohio University Press, 2007), esp. Paul E. Lovejoy's chapter, "Internal Markets or an Atlantic-Sahara Divide? How Women Fit into the Slave Trade of West Africa."

52   TNA, CO267/233, Enclosure 7 in Kennedy to the Duke of Newcastle, July 18, 1853.

53   TNA, CO879/1, African, XXVI, Memoranda on the British Settlements on the West Coast of Africa," 15-16, explains the context of the ordinances. The printed texts can be found in see TNA, CO267/234, Kennedy to the Duke of Newcastle, December 9, 1853; and TNA, CO267/249, Hill to Labouchere, December 18, 1855. These ordinances seem to have provided models for later ones passed in other British territories in Africa. See, for example, Mann, *Slavery and the Birth*, 182-83.

54   TNA, CO267/239, Kennedy to the Duke of Newcastle, February 10, 1854.

55   The complete Registers of Escaped Slaves cover the period between 1858 and 1894. I have entered these materials into a database on which the next few paragraphs are based. The annual lists for the period between 1858 and 1861 can be found in TNA, CO267/261, Hill to Sytton Bart, July 13, 1858; TNA, CO267/264, Fitzjames to the Duke of Newcastle, August 19, 1859; TNA, CO267/267, Fitzjames to the Duke of Newcastle, August 27, 1860; and TNA, CO267/271, Hill to the Duke of Newcastle, July 18, 1861.

56   I have eliminated five entries for which the sex of the captive was unclear. Interestingly, the ethnic makeup of escaped slaves changed significantly in the 1860s. Mende and Sherbro captives became far more numerous in that decade, a result of the extension into the Sherbro of formal British rule. The presence of colonial infrastructure – buildings, towns, and soldiers – in the south provided local slaves with new ways to obtain their freedom.

57   Fyfe, *A History*, 271.

58 BPP, *Slave Trade*, vol. 90, Macdonald to Earl Grey, August 10, 1851 and reply, 331.
59 Ibid, Macdonald to Earl Grey, November 27, 1851, 332-33.
60 Jean Herskovits Kopytoff, *A Preface to Modern Nigeria: The "Sierra Leonians" in Yoruba, 1830-1890* (Madison: University of Wisconsin Press, 1965), 204-5.
61 BPP, *Slave Trade*, vol. 90, Macdonald to Pakington, June 14, 1852, 340.
62 Crooks, *A History*, 189.
63 On diseases, see the classic article, Philip D. Curtin, "Epidemiology and the Slave Trade," *Political Science Quarterly* 83 (1968): 190-216. Naval officers complained that Freetown was too far removed from the major sources of slave supply in the Bights of Benin and Biafra. The lengthy journey that detained vessels took back to the colony resulted in extremely high mortality rates. A short-lived initiative to transfer the courts to Fernando Po to address the problem failed. See Robert T. Brown, "Fernando Po and the Anti-Sierra Leone Campaign, 1826-1834," *The International Journal of African Historical Studies* 6, no. 2 (1973): 249-64; and David Northrup, "African Mortality in the Suppression of the Slave Trade: The Case of the Bight of Biafra," *Journal of Interdisiplinary History* 9, no. 1 (1978), 47-64.
64 Dumett and Johnson, "Britain and the Suppression of Slavery"; Grace, *Domestic Slavery*, 25-29; Dumett, "Pressure Groups"; McSheffrey, "Slavery, Indentured Servitude"; John Parker, *Making the Town: Ga State and Society in Early Colonial Accra* (Portsmouth: Heinemann, 2000).
65 Davidson, "Trade and Politics," 123.
66 Quoted in Fyfe, *A History*, 159.
67 Eltis et al., *Voyages, http://slavevoyages.org/voyages/RociQjaA*.
68 TNA, CO879/8, African Number 82, Part I, Kortright to the Earl of Carnarvon, June 28, 1875.

Epilogue: Transatlantic Slavery and Colonialism on Freetown's Frontier

In 2013, I joined colleagues Marcus Rediker, Konrad Tuchscherer, and a film crew on a trip to Sierra Leone. Our group traveled with the intention to explore sites and memories that had historical ties to the *Amistad* story. While we uncovered some new and exciting connections between the past and the present,[1] doing so proved an uphill battle. Unlike Bunce Island, which commanded the slave trade in the Sierra Leone estuary for more than a century and whose remains continue to cast shadows over the country today, virtually everything about the infrastructure of the slave trade from the nineteenth-century Sherbro and Gallinas, through which the *Amistad* captives passed in the 1830s, was built to be forgotten. The contrast between the two locations today could hardly be starker: whereas Bunce Island continues to attract well deserved attention from organizers of heritage tours and related interest in its preservation, few Sierra Leoneans and even fewer non-Africans are familiar with coastal southern Sierra Leone as a region that was central to the history of transatlantic slavery. Even King Siaka's burial site in Gendema was at the time we arrived badly neglected, the grounds overtaken by dense vegetation. While many factors contributed to the decline of the town, including especially the brutal civil war in Sierra Leone in the 1990s that destroyed so many people and places, our group was nevertheless surprised by the site's comparative desolation and the disconnect between it and other areas in Sierra Leone with historical ties to the slave trade. Two centuries earlier, southern Sierra Leone was central to African and European entanglements with the slave trade, abolition, and colonialism. Rising as major ports of slave embarkation in the era of slave trade suppression, the Sherbro and Gallinas were among the first areas in Africa to be squeezed between the forces of transatlantic slavery and antislavery. Their proximity to Freetown made the persistence of the slave trade in southern Sierra Leone an ongoing source of embarrassment to British officials invested in demonstrating the superiority of free over slave labor. Indeed, reliance by British colonists on provisions and other non-human commodities produced and supplied in these slaving areas undermined this central tenant of abolitionists' economic philosophy. Rather than reconsidering their assumptions about the linear path from slaving to freedom and "civilization," Freetown and London officials doubled down on their vision, disrupting the slave trade with increased intensity by sea and land. The last known slave vessel to leave southern Sierra Leone for the Americas did so in 1856; formal annexation of the Sherbro in 1861 signaled not only the end of southern Sierra Leone's engagement with transatlantic slavery but also the logical outcome of a militarized style of antislavery that had been taking shape over previous decades.

The unique nature of Freetown's history in Africa has triggered serious scholarly attention for more than half a century. Over the last seven decades, research into the settlement's history has drawn on increasingly wide-ranging collections of sources that have been used to develop a richer understanding of nineteenth century African and Atlantic history. While the nature of the questions scholars have asked and the type of evidence they have utilized has changed significantly over time, interpretations have tended to emphasize the expanding role that British colonial officials and policies played in determining the futures of inland communities. Padraic Scanlan's recent book, *Freedom's Debtors*, effectively represents this vision.[2] Sweeping in scope and informed by previously untapped and underutilized archival evidence, Scanlan positions Freetown as a site from which colonial and capitalist forces shaped antislavery practices within and, at least eventually, beyond the settlement's boundaries. Individual administrations created profit-driven incentives to motivate officials involved in slave trade suppression and imposed from above a coercive system of wage labor on Liberated Africans. That system was spread through militarized colonial expansion, enforced with support from the British navy. British colonialism in Sierra Leone over the first half of the nineteenth century appears, from this perspective, undeniably powerful; its effects resemble those that followed the notorious Scramble for Africa and can even be read as providing the foundation for more mature forms of colonial rule.

To what extent does shifting the focus to Freetown's frontier change that view? The confrontation between slaving and antislaving was from the perspective of people in the Sherbro and Gallinas a much more contested and nuanced process. British colonial officials relied upon Africans for support as often as they dictated policies to them. While southern Sierra Leone merchants and leaders proved more than willing to exploit new opportunities that the British presence provided, they just as often ignored or thwarted European ambitions. British actions were frequently reactive and mitigated by inland realities rather than proactive in their attempt to reform African societies through the expansion of Christianity, European civilization, and legitimate commerce. For most of the first half of the nineteenth century, Freetown was just one source of power and authority, and not always even the most powerful player in the region.

British exposure to internal slavery and slave trafficking also triggered uncertain and often ineffective responses. The expansion of the groundnut industry in the 1830s and 40s was fueled by an equally explosive growth in the domestic slave trade from the Gallinas and Sherbro to Portuguese Guinea. Muslim merchants openly flouted British suppression efforts; at times they even circulated slaves into and around the borders of Freetown itself. While the colonial government ultimately confronted this system, their evolving reactions to it revealed deep uncertainties about their colonial mandate and their limited knowledge of domestic institutions such as slavery. Slaves themselves exploited that uncertainty, fleeing into the colony and triggering debates in Freetown and London about the parameters of radical abolitionism. British colonialism, this analysis makes clear, operated in dialogue with the Mende and Sherbro communities that populated its southern frontier, rather than from a position of commanding authority.

Southern Sierra Leone's integration into the world of Atlantic commerce in the era of abolition reveals not only the relative limits of British power beyond the colony's borders. It also underscores that Africans had and worked to implement their own ideas about shifts in the economy in this period, with important implications for peoples along the coast and the interior. The evolution of the slave and legitimate trades drive home this reality. Operating from within a hundred miles of Britain's first West African colony, African and Cuban merchants developed a dynamic and clandestine slave system that was organized in the swampy creeks that defined coastal southern Sierra Leone. As elsewhere in Africa, the slave trade in its final "illegal" phase evolved in response to British pressures, distinguishing it from earlier eras. Cuban commodities provided grist for the slaving mill, circulating into the hands of powerful rulers who used the exotic goods to pay mercenaries to wage war. Large-scale conflict took place almost strictly between rival local war towns. Though scholars have recognized how the abolition campaign limited the slave trade in the Americas to fewer regions of disembarkation, the nature of Sherbro and Mende warfare and the origins of slaves leaving southern Sierra Leone during this period suggest a similar degree of concentration among zones of slave supply within Africa itself.

This book makes one last important intervention. Since the publication of Philip Curtin's *Census*, scholars of the slave trade have been debating, often fiercely, the value of quantitative approaches to the study of transatlantic slavery.[3] Disagreement stems from the extent to which quantitative data can effectively capture the lived experiences of captives who were traumatized by the slave system. In this book I have tried to reconcile these two approaches, combining the unrivaled depth of statistical and biographical information on slaves and Liberated Africans to bring to life the complex nature of slavery, the slave trade, and colonialism on the frontier of Britain's first West African colony. Sierra Leone offers a unique opportunity to situate individual experiences and life histories in the larger context of the slave trade and the Atlantic World. Though they are generally framed as antagonistic toward one another, quantitative and qualitative methods and data can be put into productive conversation to unearth the realities of slavery and slave trading.

Notes

1 *Ghosts of Amistad: In the Footsteps of the Rebels* (Alexander Street Press, 2014).
2 Scanlan, *Freedom's Debtors.*
3 Curtin, *The Atlantic Slave Trade.* For a recent review of debates over quantitative approaches to the slave trade, see Daniel B. Domingues da Silva and Philip Misevich, "Atlantic Slavery and the Slave Trade: History and Historiography," *Oxford Research Encyclopedia of African History*, online at https://oxfordre.com/africanhistory/view/10.1093/acrefore/97801 90277734.001.0001/acrefore-9780190277734-e-371?rskey=j5xkOb& result=1.

Appendix: A Note on the Registers of Liberated Africans and the Methods Used to Identify Recaptives

The Registers of Liberated Africans were produced following the abolition of the British slave trade in 1807. To prevent further shipments of slaves from crossing the Atlantic, the British signed treaties with the governments of those nations most active in the trade. One result of the treaties was the establishment of Courts of Mixed Commission.[1] Eventually numbering eight in total, these courts adjudicated cases of vessels that were suspected of taking captives onboard illegally. Each case was presided over by two officials: one British and the other of the nation from which the captured slave-trader originated. In many cases, the vessels that the British anti-slavery squadron detained had full slave cargoes still onboard and in such cases the African captives were liberated and subsequently absorbed into the colony where the court was located. The court lacked the authority to punish captains of condemned slavers.

Prior to their liberation, Africans were asked to provide information about themselves, which court officials recorded in large ledger books.[2] Each page of the book was divided into seven columns and each recaptive was given one line on the page. The details that the officials documented included a unique identity number, name, sex (man, woman, girl, boy), age, height, and a description of distinct body markings. The Sierra Leone and Havana officials, who processed the large majority of vessels,[3] added an additional column labeled 'County of Origin,' although Sierra Leone officials eventually discontinued that practice. The Registers clearly indicate that this information was given through an African translator who was previously freed by the courts, and who came from the same region as the slaves onboard the vessel under adjudication, which at least partially mitigated the language barriers that divided Europeans and Africans.

Depending on the court that processed the vessel, either Spanish (Havana) or English (Freetown) colonial officials entered details into the Registers. Both had difficulty transcribing recaptives' names. The clerks used Spanish or English spelling conventions to transcribe what they heard. Despite colonial officials' evident inability to spell what must have been exceptionally unfamiliar names, the association of names in the Registers with those found in contemporary Sierra Leone is undeniable. To make connections between past and present African names, I worked backwards. For names that were transcribed according to Spanish spelling conventions, I sought assistance from a native Spanish-speaker from Cuba, who pronounced each name into a tape recorder. For British transcriptions, I worked with linguists in Sierra Leone to estimate appropriate pronunciations. I then played each name to a large group of informants in Sierra Leone that represented the most commonly spoken languages in the country and they indicated whether the name was associated with particular ethnolinguistic groups.[4] When disagreements between the consultants occurred, the group discussed and at times even passionately debated the origins of the name. When they were unable to resolve the dispute, I discarded the name from my analysis. I also checked the names and identifications in the available scholarly literature on African naming practices.[5]

The results of this procedure were encouraging. Of the 8,871 names from the registers, my informants reached an agreement on nearly three quarters of the sample. Some names were not unique to particular groups. Names that are common to all ethnolinguistic groups were discarded from my analysis. Those that are shared by several ethnolinguistic groups were combined. For example, the longstanding incursion of Mende speakers into the coastal Sherbro region has made naming practices between the two groups difficult to distinguish. Given that Mende and Sherbro speakers are concentrated in southern Sierra Leone, combining these groups makes sense. With this and several additional adjustments, my informants reached conclusions about the origins of more than 4,500 names – around half of the total sample.

These data indicate that most captives embarked in the Gallinas and Sherbro came from areas that are today within the borders of Sierra Leone, which is consistent with other evidence on slave origins from the region. Had I been able to do fieldwork in neighboring Liberia and Guinea, I would likely have been able to identify additional names. Since I first began this research, the Liberated Africans registers have been the focus of several important digital projects. The first, www.African-Origins.org, solicits help from the web-using public to further identify the ethnolinguistic origins of African names. More than one-third of the 91,000 individuals listed on the website have names to which the public has contributed. The project is ongoing. A second site, www.liberatedafricans.org, offers a more comprehensive assessment and profile of the individuals whom the courts liberated. These projects and recent research into Liberated Africans offer rare chances to understand the biographies and even at times life histories of captives drawn into the transatlantic slave trade in the final half century of operation.

1   For the operational aspect of the courts, see Leslie Bethell, "The Mixed Commissions for the Suppression of the Transatlantic Slave Trade in the Nineteenth Century," *Journal of African History* 7, no. 1 (1966): 79-93.
2   The earliest Liberated African Registers, maintained by a British Vice Admiralty Court, are held at Fourah Bay College, in the Sierra Leone Government Archives (SLGA). Registers are also found in the FO84 series of The National Archives, in Kew. The Havana Registers are included in TNA, FO313, vols. 56-62.

3   The Courts presided over more than 600 cases. At times ships captured with slaves on board were acquitted. 29 of the 485 vessels under adjudication in Freetown were cleared of charges. In Havana, seven out of 48 were released.

4   The informants included Susu, Yalunka, Kuranko, Mandingo and Temne speakers and a Mende linguist from Fourah Bay College, the University of Sierra Leone. I am extremely fortunate to have had such knowledgeable informants, particularly Taziff Koroma, who for years aided in the development of this project. Sadly, Taziff passed away before this book was published. I would also like to express my debt to Oscar Grandío Moráguez for recording the pronunciation of recaptive names from the Havana Registers.

5   There is an overall paucity of research on naming practices among Africans in Upper Guinea. Numerous short entries appear around the late-1910s in *Sierra Leone Studies,* which record a handful of names common to particular ethnic groups. Such contributions can also be found, with more rigorous analysis, in the *Sierra Leone Language Review.* For one such example, see Gordon Innes, "A Note on Mende and Kono Personal Names," *Sierra Leone Language Review* 5 (1966): 34-38.

BIBLIOGRAPHY

<u>Primary Sources</u>

Unpublished

<u>Amistad Research Center</u>

American Missionary Association Manuscripts, Sierra Leone,
   Microfilm reels 1-11

<u>British Library</u>

Letter Addressed to the Chairman of the Sierra Leone Company
   by the Rev. Mr. Thomas Clarkson, Folio 1, add. mss.
   12131
Mr. Gray's Journal, Folio 81, add. mss. 12131
Mr. Hermitage's Journal, Folio 43, add. mss. 12131
Mr. Parfitt's Diary on Board the *Calypso*, Folio 272, add. mss.
   12131
Mr. Parfitt's Information on Trade between Sierra Leone and
   Cape Lopez, Folio 174, add. mss. 12131
Mr. Strands' Journal, Folio 65, add. mss. 12131
Mr. Watt's Journal, Folio 122, add. mss. 12131

<u>British National Archives</u>

Board of Trade Correspondence:
   BT6/70

Colonial Office Correspondence:
  CO267/1-409 (select materials)
  CO268/1, 5, 10
  CO270/2-6, 8-9, 11-12, 16-17, 19
  CO271/1-2
  CO272/1-47 (select materials)
  CO323/148
  CO325/37
  CO388/28, 43
  CO879/1, 8-9, 14-15, 17-18, 20, 24-25, 49

Company of Royal Adventurers of England Trading with Africa
Records
  T70/1, 5-7, 1465

Foreign Office Correspondence:
  FO2/1, 8, 11, 13, 17, 21, 24, 28, 33, 38-39, 42
  FO47/1, 3, 7-9, 13, 15
  FO63/351, 442, 456, 471
  FO84/7-497 (select materials)
  FO403/6

High Court of Admiralty Records
  HCA16/83/2218

House of Commons, Sessional Papers
  ZHC/1/82

War Office Correspondence
  WO1/352
  WO32/7643

New-York Historical Society
A Book of Trade for the Sloop *Rhode Island*, Dec. 1748-July 1749,
    Misc. MSS., B.V. *Rhode Island*, New-York Historical So-
    ciety

Sierra Leone National Archives
"Orders and Regulations from the Directors of the Sierra Leone
    Company to the Superintendent and Council for the Set-
    tlement," Sierra Leone National Archives

Registers of Escaped Slaves

Published

*Abridgement of the Minutes of the Evidence, Taken before a Committee of
    the Whole House, to Whom it was Referred to Consider of the
    Slave-Trade, 1789* (Great Britain, House of Parliament,
    printed in 1789).
*Abridgement of the Minutes of the Evidence, Taken before a Committee of
    the Whole House, to Whom it was Referred to Consider of the
    Slave-Trade, 1790* (Great Britain, House of Parliament,
    printed in 1790).
Alldridge, T.J. *The Sherbro and its Hinterland.* London: Macmillan,
    1901.
---. *A Transformed Colony: Sierra Leone as It Was, and as It Is; Its
    Progress, Peoples, Native Customs and Undeveloped Wealth.*
    London: Seeley & Co., 1910.
American State Papers, Foreign Relations. Vol. 5. 16th Congress, 2nd
    Session, Publication No. 346, "Suppression of the Slave
    Trade -- Conference of Foreign Governments on the
    Subject. Communicated to the House of Representa-
    tives, February 9, 1821."
Barber, John W. *A History of the Amistad Captives.* New Haven:
    E.L. & J.W. Barber, 1840.
Barbot, Jean. *A Description of the Coasts of North and South Guinea.*
    London: Henry Lintot and John Osborn, 1746.
Bennett, Norman R. and George E. Brooks, Jr. *New England Mer-
    chants in Africa: A History through Documents, 1802-1865.*
    Brookline: Boston University Press, 1965.
British Parliamentary Papers, Colonies: Africa. Shannon: Irish Univer-
    sity Press, 1968.
British Parliamentary Papers, Slave Trade. Shannon: Irish University
    Press, 1968.

Buxton, Thomas Fowell. *The African Slave Trade and its Remedy.* London: John Murray, 1840.

Canot, Theodore. *Captain Canot, or, Twenty Years of an African Slaver.* New York: Appleton and Co., 1854.

Dapper, Olfert. *Naukeurige Beschrijvinge der Afrikaensche Gewesten.* Amsterdam: J. van Meurs, 1668.

Eltis, David et al. *Voyages: The Trans-Atlantic Slave Trade Database.* www.slavevoyages.org

Falconbridge, Alexander. *An Account of the Slave Trade on the Coast of Africa.* London: J. Phillips, 1788.

Flickinger, D.K. *Off Hand Sketches of Men and Things in Western Africa.* Dayton: Published by the Order of the Trustees of the United Brethren Printing Establishment, 1857.

Fyfe, Christopher. *Sierra Leone Inheritance.* London: Oxford University Press, 1964.

Hair, P.E.H., ed. *Polyglotta Africana.* Graz: Akademische Druck-u. Verlagsanstalt, 1963.

Hair, P.E.H., Adam Jones, and Robin Law. eds. *Barbot on Guinea: The Writings of Jean Barbot on West Africa, 1678-1712.* London: The Hakluyt Society, 1992.

Jones, Adam, ed. *Brandenburg Sources for West African History, 1680-1700.* Stuttgart: F. Steiner Verlag Wiesbaden, 1985.

---, *German Sources for West African History, 1599-1669.* Wiesbaden: F. Steiner, 1983.

Kalous, Milan. *Cannibals and Tongo Players of Sierra Leone.* Trentham: Wright & Carman Ltd., 1974.

Knight, H.C. *Africa Redeemed; or, the Means of Her Relief Illustrated by the Growth and Prospects of Liberia.* London: James Nisbet & Co., 1851.

Kup, Peter, ed. *Sierra Leone Journal, 1795-1796.* Uppsala: Studia Ethnographica Upsaliensia, XXVII, 1967.

Laing, Alexander Gordon. *Travels in the Timannee, Kooranko and Soolima Countries in Western Africa.* London: John Murray, 1825.

Macaulay, Kenneth. *The Colony of Sierra Leone Vindicated from the Misrepresentations of Mr. MacQueen of Glasgow.* London: Cass, 1968, first edition, 1827.

Martin, Bernard and Mark Spurrell, eds. *Journal of a Slave Trader (John Newton), 1750-1754.* London: Epworth Press, 1962.

Martin, Eveline, ed. *Journal of a Slave Dealer: A View of Some Remarkable Axcedents in the Life of Nics. Owen on the Coast of Africa and America from the Year 1746 to the Year 1757.* London: G. Routledge, 1930.

Matthews, John. *A Voyage to the River Sierra-Leone.* London: Printed for B. White and Son, 1788.

Monod, Th., A. Teixeira da Mota et. R. Mauny, eds. *Description de la Côte Occidentale d'Afrique. Sénégal du Cap de Monte, Archipels.* Bissau, 1951.

Morgan, Kenneth, ed. *The British Transatlantic Slave Trade.* 4 Volumes. London: Pickering & Chatto, 2003.

Mouser, Bruce L., ed. *Journal of James Watt: Expedition to Timbo, Capital of the Fula Empire in 1794.* Madison: African Studies Program, University of Wisconsin, 1994.

Newbury, C.W., ed. *British Policy Towards West Africa; Select Documents, 1786-1874.* Oxford: Clarendon Press, 1965.

Rankin, F. Harrison. *The White Man's Grave: A Visit to Sierra Leone in 1834.* 2 Vols. London: R. Bentley, 1836.

[Review of] the Trials of the Slave Traders, Samuel Samo, Joseph Peters, and William Tufft: Tried in April and June 1812, before the Hon. Robert Thorpe, L.L.D…: with two letters on the slave trade/from a gentleman resident at Sierra Leone, to an advocate for the abolition in London. London: Longmans, Green & Co., 1813.

Rules and Regulations of the African Institution. London: Printed by William Phillips, 1807.

Schwarz, Suzanne. ed. *Zachary Macaulay and the Development of the Sierra Leone Company, 1793-1794.* Leipzig: Institut für Afrikanistik, Universität Leipzig, 2000. Part I.

Sixth Annual Report of the Directors of the African Institution, Read on 25 March 1812. London: Printed by Ellerton and Henderson, 1812.

Substance of the Report of the Court of Directors of the Sierra Leone Company to the General Court, held at London on Wednesday the

19th of October, 1791. London: Printed by James Phillips, 1791.

Substance of the Report, Delivered, by the Court of Directors of the Sierra Leone Company, to the General Court of Proprietors, on Thursday the 29th March, 1798. London: Printed by James Phillips & Son, 1798.

Substance of the Report Delivered by the Court of Directors of the Sierra Leone Company, to the General Court of Proprietors, on Thursday, March 27th, 1794. Philadelphia: Printed by Thomas Dorson, 1795.

Thompson, George. *An Account of the Missionary Labors, Sufferings, Travels, and Observations, of George Thompson, in Western Africa, At the Mendi Mission.* New York: Second Edition, 1852.

---. *The Palm Land; or, West Africa Illustrated: Being A History of Missionary Labors and Travels, with Descriptions of Men and Things in Western Africa; Also, a Synopsis of all the Missionary Work on that Continent.* London: Dawsons, 1969, first printed in 1858.

Valdez, Francisco Travassos. *Six Years of a Traveller's Life in Western Africa.* London: Hurst and Blackett, 1861.

Wadstrom, C.B. *An Essay on Colonization.* London: Darton and Harvey, 1794.

West African Sketches: Compiled from the Reports of Sir G.R. Collier, Sir Charles MacCarthy, and other Official Sources. London: Printed for L.B. Seeley and Son, 1824.

Secondary Sources

Unpublished

Anderson, Richard. "Recaptives: Community and Identity in Colonial Sierra Leone, 1808-1863." PhD diss., Yale University, 2015.

Davidson, John. "Trade and Politics in the Sherbro Hinterland, 1849-1890." PhD diss., University of Wisconsin, 1969.

Day, Lynda R. "Historical Patterns in a Stateless Society: Sherbro Land, 1750-1898." MA Thesis, University of Wisconsin, 1980.

Hall, Trevor P. "The Role of Cape Verde Islanders in Organizing and Operating Maritime Trade between West Africa and Iberian Territories, 1441-1616." PhD diss., Johns Hopkins University, 1992.

Holsoe, Svend E. "The Cassava-Leaf People: An Ethnohistorical Study of the Vai People, with Particular Emphasis on the Tewo Chiefdom." PhD diss., Boston University, 1967.

Ijagbemi, E. A. "A History of the Temne in the Nineteenth Century." PhD diss., University of Edinburgh, 1968.

Morgan, Kenneth. "British Merchants and the Slave Trade from Sierra Leone, 1750-1807." Presented at Hull University's Interdisciplinary Conference, "Empire, Slave Trade and Slavery: Rebuilding Civil Society in Sierra Leone. Past and Present." September 26, 2008.

Wills, Mary. "The Royal Navy and the Suppression of the Atlantic Slave Trade, c. 1807-1867: Anti-Slavery, Empire, and Identity." PhD diss., University of Hull, 2012.

Published

Abraham, Arthur. *An Introduction to the Pre-Colonial History of the Mende of Sierra Leone.* Lewiston: Edwin Mellen Press, 2003.

Afigbo, A.E. *The Abolition of the Slave Trade in Southeastern Nigeria, 1885-1950.* Rochester, NY: University of Rochester Press, 2006.

Akyeampong, Emmanuel. *Drink, Power, and Cultural Change: A Social History of Alcohol in Ghana, c. 1800 to Recent Times.* Portsmouth, NH: Heinemann, 1996.

Alpers, Edward A. *Ivory and Slaves: Changing Pattern of International Trade in East Central Africa to the Later Nineteenth Century.* Berkeley: University of California Press, 1975.

Anderson, David M. and Richard Rathbone, eds. *Africa's Urban Past.* Portsmouth: Heinemann, 2000.

Anderson, Richard. "The Diaspora of Sierra Leone's Liberated Africans: Enlistment, Force Migration, and 'Liberation' at Freetown, 1808-1863." *African Economic History* 41 (2013): 101-38.

Anderson, Richard, Alex Borucki, Daniel Domingues da Silva, David Eltis, Paul Lachance, Philip Misevich, and Olatunji Ojo. "Using African Names to Identify the Origins of Captives in the Transatlantic Slave Trade: Crowd-Sourcing and the Registers of Liberated Africans, 1808-1862." *History in Africa* 40 (2013): 165-91.

Austen, Ralph A. "The Abolition of the Overseas Slave Trade: A Distorted Theme in West African History." *Journal of the Historical Society of Nigeria* 5, no. 2 (1970): 257-74.

Bangura, Joseph J. *The Temne of Sierra Leone: African Agency in the Making of a British Colony.* New York: Cambridge University Press, 2017.

Barcia, Manuel. *The Great African Slave Revolt of 1825: Cuba and the Fight for Freedom in Matanzas.* Baton Rouge: Louisiana State University Press, 2012.

---. *Seeds of Insurrection: Domination and Resistance on Western Cuban Plantations, 1808-1848.* Baton Rouge: Louisiana State University Press, 2008.

---. "West African Islam in Colonial Cuba." *Slavery & Abolition* 35, no. 2 (2014): 292-305.

Barry, Boubacar. *Senegambia and the Atlantic Slave Trade.* Cambridge: Cambridge University Press, 1998.

Behrendt, Stephen D. "Human Capital in the British Slave Trade." In *Liverpool and Transatlantic Slavery,* edited by David Richardson, Suzanne Schwarz, and Anthony Tibbles, 66-97. Liverpool: Liverpool University Press, 2007.

---. "Markets, Transaction Cycles, and Profits: Merchant Decision Making in the British Slave Trade," *The William and Mary Quarterly* 58, no. 1 (January 2001), 171-204.

Bender, Thomas, ed. *The Antislavery Debate: Capitalism and Abolitionism as a Problem in Historical Interpretation.* Berkeley: University of California Press, 1992.

Berlin, Ira. *Many Thousands Gone: The First Two Centuries of Slavery in North America.* Cambridge: Belknap Press of Harvard University Press, 1998.

Bethell, Leslie. "The Mixed Commissions for the Suppression of the Transatlantic Slave Trade in the Nineteenth Century." *Journal of African History* 7, no. 1 (1966): 79-93.

Blackburn, Robin. *The American Crucible: Slavery, Emancipation and Human Rights.* New York: Verso, 2011.

Boone, Sylvia Ardyn. *Radiance from the Waters: Ideals of Feminine Beauty in Mende Art.* New Haven: Yale University Press, 1990.

Borucki, Alex, David Eltis, and David Wheat. "Atlantic History and the Slave Trade to Spanish America." *American Historical Review* 120, no. 2 (2015): 433-61.

Bowman, Joye L. "'Legitimate Commerce' and Peanut Production in Portuguese Guinea, 1840s to 1880s." *Journal of African History* 28, no. 1 (1987): 87-106.

Brooks, George E. *Eurafricans in Western Africa: Commerce, Social Status, Gender, and Religious Observance from the Sixteenth to the Eighteenth Century.* Athens: Ohio University Press, 2003.

---. *Kola Trade and State-Building: Upper Guinea Coast and Senegambia, 15th-17th Centuries.* Brookline: African Studies Center, Boston University, 1980.

---. *Landlords and Strangers: Ecology, Society and Trade in Western Africa, 1000-1630.* Boulder: Westview Press, 1993.

---. "A *Nhara* of the Guinea Bissau Region: Mãe Aurélia Correia." In, *Women and Slavery in Africa,* edited by Claire C. Robertson and Martin A. Klein, 295-319. Portsmouth: Heinemann, 1983.

---. "Peanuts and Colonialism: Consequences of the Commercialization of Peanuts in West Africa, 1830-70." *Journal of African History* 16, no. 1 (1975): 29-54.

---. "Samuel Hodges, Jr., and the Symbiosis of Slave and 'Legitimate' Trades, 1810s-1820s." *International Journal of African Historical Studies* 41, no. 1 (2008): 101-116.

---. "The *Signares* of Saint-Louis and Goree: Women Entrepreneurs in Eighteenth-Century Senegal." In *Women in Africa: Studies in Social and Economic Change*, edited by Nancy J. Hafkin and Edna G. Bay, 19-44. Stanford: Stanford University Press, 1976.

---. *Western Africa and Cabo Verde, 1790s to 1830s: Symbiosis of Slave and Legitimate Trades*. Bloomington: AuthorHouse, 2010.

---. *Yankee Traders, Old Coasters and African Middlemen: A History of American Legitimate Trade with West Africa in the Nineteenth Century*. Brookline: Boston University Press, 1970.

Brown, Christopher Leslie. *Moral Capital: Foundations of British Abolitionism*. Chapel Hill: University of North Carolina Press, 2006.

Brown, Robert T. "Fernando Po and the Anti-Sierra Leone Campaign 1826-1834." *The International Journal of African Historical Studies* 6, no. 2 (1973): 249-64.

Byrd, Alexander X. *Captives and Voyagers: Black Migrants across the Eighteenth-Century British Atlantic World*. Baton Rouge: Louisiana State University Press, 2008.

Campbell, Gwyn, Suzanne Miers, and Joseph C. Miller, eds. *Children in Slavery Through the Ages*. Athens, OH: Ohio University Press, 2009.

---. *Women and Slavery, Volume 1: Africa, The Indian Ocean World, and The Medieval North Atlantic*. Athens: Ohio University Press, 2007.

Candido, Mariana P. *An African Slaving Port and the Atlantic World: Benguela and Its Hinterland*. New York: Cambridge University Press, 2013.

Carney, Judith A. *Black Rice: The African Origins of Rice Cultivation in the Americas*. Cambridge: Harvard University Press, 2001.

Carney, Judith A. and Richard Nicholas Rosomoff. *In the Shadow of Slavery: Africa's Botanical Legacy in the Atlantic World*. Berkeley: University of California Press, 2009.

Caron, Peter. "'Of a Nation Which Others do not Understand': Bambara Slaves and African Ethnicity in Colonial Louisiana, 1718-60." *Slavery and Abolition* 18 (1997): 98-121.

Caulker, Patrick S. "Legitimate Commerce and Statecraft: A Study of the Hinterland Adjacent to Nineteenth-Century Sierra Leone." *Journal of Black Studies* 11, no. 4 (1981): 379-419.

Chopra, Ruma. *Almost Home: Maroons between Slavery and Freedom in Jamaica, Nova Scotia, and Sierra Leone*. New Haven: Yale University Press, 2018.

Clarke, John Innes, ed. *Sierra Leone in Maps*. London: University of London Press, 1966.

Clifford, Mary Louise. *From Slavery to Freetown: Black Loyalists after the American Revolution*. Jefferson: McFarland, 1999.

Cohen, Abner. "Cultural Strategies in the Organization of Trading Diasporas." In *The Development of Indigenous Trade and Markets in West Africa*, edited by Claude Meillassoux, 266-81. London: Oxford University Press, 1971.

Cole, Gibril R. *The Krio of West Africa: Islam, Culture, Creolization, and Colonialism in the Nineteenth Century*. Athens, OH: Ohio University Press, 2013.

Cooper, Frederick and Ann Laura Stoler, eds. *Tensions of Empire: Colonial Cultures in a Bourgeois World*. Berkeley: University of California Press, 1997.

Coughtry, Jay. *The Notorious Triangle: Rhode Island and the African Slave Trade, 1700-1807*. Philadelphia: Temple University Press, 1981.

Cowling, Camillia. *Conceiving Freedom: Women of Color, Gender, and the Abolition of Slavery in Havana and Rio de Janeiro*. Chapel Hill: University of North Carolina Press, 2013.

Crooks, J. J. *A History of the Colony of Sierra Leone, Western Africa; with Maps and Appendices*. London: Cass, 1972. first published in 1903.

Crosby, Alfred W. *The Columbian Exchange: Biological and Cultural Consequences of 1492*. Westport: Greenwood Publication Co., 1972.

Crowder, Michael. *Colonial West Africa*. London: F. Cass, 1978.

Curtin, Philip D. *The Atlantic Slave Trade: A Census*. Madison: University of Wisconsin Press, 1969.

---. *Cross-Cultural Trade in World History.* New York: Cambridge University Press, 1984.

---. *Economic Change in Precolonial Africa: Senegambia in the Era of the Slave Trade.* Madison: University of Wisconsin Press, 1975.

---. "Epidemiology and the Slave Trade." *Political Science Quarterly* 83 (June 1968): 190-216.

---. *The Rise and Fall of the Plantation Complex: Essays in Atlantic History.* Cambridge: Cambridge University Press, 1990.

Curtin, Philip D. and Jan Vansina. "Sources of the Nineteenth Century Atlantic Slave Trade." *Journal of African History* 5, no. 2 (1964): 185-208.

Curto, Jose C. *Enslaving Spirits: The Portuguese-Brazilian Alcohol Trade at Luanda and Its Hinterland, c. 1550-1830.* Leiden: Brill, 2004.

Dalby, David. "The Mel Languages: A Reclassification of Southern 'West-Atlantic.'" *African Language Studies* 6 (1965): 1-17.

Davies, K.G. *The Royal African Company.* London: Longmans, Green and Co., 1957.

Davis, David Brion. *The Problem of Slavery in the Age of Emancipation.* New York: Knopf, 2014.

---. *The Problem of Slavery in the Age of Revolution, 1770-1823.* Ithaca: Cornell University Press, 1975.

Dawe, M.T. and F.J. Martin. "The Oil Palm Industry and its Problems in Sierra Leone." In *Proceedings of the First West African Agricultural Conference.* Unknown Publisher: Lagos (1927): 7-8.

Day, Lynda R. "Afro-British Integration on the Sherbro Coast, 1665-1795." *Africana Research Bulletin* 12, no. 3 (1983): 82-107.

Dike, K. Onwuka. *Trade and Politics in the Niger Delta, 1830-1885.* Oxford: Clarendon Press, 1956.

Diouf, Sylviane A. "Devils or Sorcerers, Muslims or Studs: Manding in the Americas." In *Trans-Atlantic Dimensions of Ethnicity in the African Diaspora,* edited by Paul E. Lovejoy and David V. Trotman, 139-57. New York: Continuum, 2003.

---, ed. *Fighting the Slave Trade: West African Strategies*. Athens: Ohio University Press, 2003.

Diptee, Audra A. "African Children in the British Slave Trade during the Late Eighteenth Century." *Slavery & Abolition* 27, no. 2 (2006): 183-96.

Domingues da Silva, Daniel B. *The Atlantic Slave Trade from West Central Africa, 1780-1867*. New York: Cambridge University Press, 2017.

---. "Winds and Sea Currents of the Atlantic Slave Trade." In *The Rise and Demise of Slavery and the Slave Trade in the Atlantic World*, edited by Philip Misevich and Kristin Mann, 152-67. Rochester: Rochester University Press, 2017.

Domingues da Silva, Daniel B., David Eltis, Nafees Khan, Philip Misevich, and Olatunji Ojo. "The Transatlantic Muslim Diaspora to Latin America in the Nineteenth Century." *Colonial Latin American Review* 26, no. 4 (2017): 528-45.

Domingues da Silva, Daniel B., David Eltis, Philip Misevich, and Olatunji Ojo. "The Diaspora of Africans Liberated from Slave Ships in the Nineteenth Century." *Journal of African History* 55, no. 3 (2014): 347-69.

Domingues da Silva, Daniel B. and Philip Misevich. "Atlantic Slavery and the Slave Trade: History and Historiography." *Oxford Research Encyclopedia of African History*. https://oxfordre.com/africanhistory/view/10.1093/acrefore/9780190277734.001.0001/acrefore-9780190277734-e-371?rskey=j5xkOb&result=1

Dorjahn, V.R. and Christopher Fyfe. "Landlord and Stranger: Change in Tenancy Relations in Sierra Leone." *Journal of African History* 3, no. 3 (1962): 391-97.

Dorsey, Joseph C. *Slave Traffic in the Age of Abolition: Puerto Rico, West Africa, and the Non-Hispanic Caribbean, 1815-1859*. Gainesville: University Press of Florida, 2003.

Drescher, Seymour. *Abolition: A History of Slavery and Antislavery*. New York: Cambridge University Press, 2009.

---. "The Shocking Birth of British Abolitionism." *Slavery & Abolition* 33 (2012): 571-93.

Dumett, Raymond E. "Pressure Groups, Bureaucracy and the Decision-Making Process: The Case of Slavery Abolition and Colonial Expansion in the Gold Coast, 1874." *Journal of Imperial and Commonwealth History* 9 (1981): 193-215.

Dumett, Raymond E. and Marion Johnson. "Britain and the Suppression of Slavery in the Gold Coast Colony, Ashanti, and the Northern Territories." In *The End of Slavery in Africa,* edited by Suzanne Miers and Richard Roberts, 71-116. Madison: University of Wisconsin Press, 1988.

Dwyer, David. "The Mende Problem," In *Studies in African Comparative Linguistics with Special Focus on Bantu and Mande,* edited by Koen Bostoen and Jackmy Maniacky, 29-42. Tervuren: Royal Museum for Central Africa.

Eltis, David. *Economic Growth and the Ending of the Transatlantic Slave Trade.* New York: Oxford University Press, 1987.

--. "The Slave Trade and Commercial Agriculture in an African Context." In *Commercial Agriculture, The Slave Trade & Slavery in Atlantic Africa,* edited by Robin Law, Suzanne Schwarz, and Silke Strickrodt, 28-53. London: James Currey, 2016.

---. "The Volume, Age/Sex Ratios, and African Impact of the Slave Trade: Some Refinements of Paul Lovejoy's Review of the Literature." *The Journal of African History* 31, no. 3 (1990): 485-92.

Eltis, David, Stanley L. Engerman, Seymour Drescher, and David Richardson, eds. *The Cambridge World History of Slavery: Volume 4, AD 1804-AD 2016.* New York: Cambridge University Press, 2017.

Eltis, David and Stanley L. Engerman. "Fluctuations in Sex and Age Ratios in the Transatlantic Slave Trade, 1663-1864." *Economic History* Review 46 (1993): 308-23.

---. "Was the Slave Trade Dominated by Men?" *Journal of Interdisciplinary History* 23 (1992): 237-57.

Eltis, David and Lawrence C. Jennings. "Trade between Western Africa and the Atlantic World in the Pre-Colonial Era." *American Historical Review* 93, no. 4 (1988): 936-59.

Eltis, David, Frank D. Lewis and Kenneth L. Sokoloff, eds. *Slavery in the Development of the Americas.* Cambridge: Cambridge University Press, 2004.

Eltis, David, Philip Morgan and David Richardson. "Agency and Diaspora in Atlantic History: Reassessing the African Contribution to Rice Cultivation in the Americas." *American Historical Review* 112, no. 5 (2007): 1329-58.

Eltis, David and David Richardson. *Atlas of the Transatlantic Slave Trade.* New Haven: Yale University Press, 2010.

---, eds. *Extending the Frontiers: Essays on the New Transatlantic Slave Trade Database.* New Haven: Yale University Press, 2008.

---. "Productivity in the Transatlantic Slave Trade." *Explorations in Economic History* 32 (1995): 465-84.

Everill, Bronwen. *Abolition and Empire in Sierra Leone and Liberia.* New York: Palgrave Macmillan, 2013.

Fage, J.D. "African Societies and the Atlantic Slave Trade." *Past and Present* 125 (1989): 97-115.

---. "Slaves and Society in Western Africa, c. 1445-c. 1700." *Journal of African History* 21 (1980): 289-310.

Faulkner, O.T. and C.J. Lewin. "Native Methods of Preparing Palm Oil, II." In *Second Annual Bulletin of the Agricultural Department, Nigeria* (1923): 3-22.

Ferme, Mariane C. *The Underneath of Things: Violence, History, and the Everyday in Sierra Leone.* Berkeley: University of California Press, 2001.

Ferreira, Roquinaldo. *Cross-Cultural Exchange in the Atlantic World: Angola and Brazil during the Era of the Slave Trade.* New York: Cambridge University Press, 2012.

Ferrer, Ada. *Freedom's Mirror: Cuba and Haiti in the Age of Revolution.* New York: Cambridge University Press, 2014.

Fields-Black, Edda L. *Deep Roots: Rice Farmers in West Africa and the African Diaspora.* Bloomington: Indiana University Press, 2008.

Finch, Aisha K. *Rethinking Slave Rebellion in Cuba: La Escalera and the Insurgencies of 1841-1844*. Chapel Hill: University of North Carolina Press, 2015.

Franklin, Sarah L. *Women and Slavery in Nineteenth-Century Colonial Cuba*. Rochester: University of Rochester Press, 2012.

Fyfe, Christopher. *A History of Sierra Leone*. London: Oxford University Press, 1962.

Fyle, C. Magbaily. *The Solima Yalunka Kingdom: Pre-Colonial Politics, Economics and Society*. Freetown: Nyakon Publishers, 1979.

Geggus, David. "Sex Ratio, Age and Ethnicity in the Atlantic Slave Trade: Data from French Shipping and Plantation Records." *Journal of African History* 30, no. 1 (1989): 23-44.

Genovese, Eugene D. *Roll, Jordan, Roll: The World the Slaves Made*. New York: Vintage, 1976.

Getz, Trevor R. *Slavery and Reform in West Africa: Toward Emancipation in Nineteenth-Century Senegal and Gold Coast*. Athens, OH: Ohio University Press, 2004.

Gomez, Michael A. *African Dominion: A New History of Empire in Early and Medieval West Africa*. Princeton: Princeton University Press, 2018.

Grace, John. *Domestic Slavery in West Africa with Particular Reference to the Sierra Leone Protectorate, 1896-1927*. New York: Barnes and Noble Books, 1975.

Green, Toby. *The Rise of the Trans-Atlantic Slave Trade in Western Africa, 1300-1589*. New York: Cambridge University Press, 2012.

Greenberg, Joseph H. *The Languages of Africa*. Bloomington: Indiana University Press, 2nd Edition, 1966.

Guyer, Jane I. and Samuel M. Eno Belinga. "Wealth in People as Wealth in Knowledge: Accumulation and Composition in Equatorial Africa." *Journal of African History* 36, no. 1 (1995): 91-120.

Hair, P.E.H. "An Account of the Liberian Hinterland, c. 1780." *Sierra Leone Studies* 16 n.s. (1962): 218-26.

---. "The Enslavement of Koelle's Informants." *Journal of African History* 6 (1965): 193-203.

---. "Ethnolinguistic Continuity on the Guinea Coast." *Journal of African History* 8 (1967): 247-68.

---. "Sources on Early Sierra Leone: (9) Barreira's' 'Account of the Coast of Guinea,' 1606." *Africana Research Bulletin* 7, no. 1 (1976): 34-60.

Hall, Gwendolyn Midlo. *Slavery and African Ethnicities in the Americas: Restoring the Links.* Chapel Hill: University of North Carolina Press, 2005.

Hall, H.U. *The Sherbro of Sierra Leone.* Philadelphia: The University Press, University of Pennsylvania, 1938.

Hancock, David. *Citizens of the World: London Merchants and the Integration of the British Atlantic Community, 1735-1785.* Cambridge: Cambridge University Press, 1995.

Harms, Robert. *The Diligent: A Voyage through the Worlds of the Slave Trade.* New York: Basic Books, 2002.

---. *River of Wealth, River of Sorrow: The Central Zaire Basin in the Era of the Slave and Ivory Trade, 1500-1891.* New Haven: Yale University Press, 1981.

Harrell-Bond, Barbara E., Allen M. Howard, and David E. Skinner. *Community Leadership and the Transformation of Freetown (1801-1976).* The Hague: Mouton, 1978.

Havik, Philip J. *Silences and Soundbites: The Gendered Dynamics of Trade and Brokerage in the Pre-Colonial Guinea Bissau Region.* Münster: Lit, 2004.

Hawthorne, Walter. *From Africa to Brazil: Culture, Identity, and an Atlantic Slave Trade, 1600-1830.* New York: Cambridge University Press, 2010.

---. *Planting Rice and Harvesting Slaves: Transformations along the Guinea-Bissau Coast, 1400-1900.* Portsmouth: Heinemann, 2003.

Heywood, Linda M. "Portuguese into African: The Eighteenth-Century Central African Background to Atlantic Creole Cultures." In *Central Africans and Cultural Transformations in the American Diaspora,* edited by Linda M. Heywood, 91-115. New York: Cambridge University Press, 2002.

Heywood, Linda M. and John K. Thornton. *Central Africans, Atlantic Creoles, and the Foundation of the Americas, 1585-1680.* New York: Cambridge University Press, 2007.

Higman, B. W. *Slave Populations of the British Caribbean, 1807-1834.* Baltimore: Johns Hopkins University Press, 1984.

Holsey, Bayo. *Routes of Remembrance: Refashioning the Slave Trade in Ghana.* Chicago: University of Chicago Press, 2008.

Holsoe, Svend E. "Slavery and Economic Response among the Vai (Liberia and Sierra Leone)," In *Slavery in Africa: Historical and Anthropological Perspectives,* edited by Suzanne Miers and Igor Kopytoff, 287-303. Madison: University of Wisconsin Press, 1970.

---. "Theodore Canot at Cape Mount, 1841-47." *Liberian Studies Journal* 4 (1971-2): 163-83.

Hooper, Jane. *Feeding Globalization: Madagascar and the Provisioning Trade, 1600-1800.* Athens, OH: Ohio University Press, 2017.

Hopkins, A.G. "Economic Imperialism in West Africa: Lagos, 1880-92." *Economic History Review* 21 (1968): 580-606.

Howard, Allen M. "Mande and Fulbe Interaction and Identity in Northwestern Sierra Leone, Late Eighteenth through Early Twentieth Centuries." *Mande Studies* 1 (1999): 13-39.

---. "Nineteenth-Century Coastal Slave Trading and the British Abolition Campaign in Sierra Leone." *Slavery and Abolition* 27, no. 1 (2006): 23-49.

---. "The Relevance of Spatial Analysis for African Economic History: The Sierra Leone-Guinea System." *Journal of African History* 17, no. 3 (1976): 365-88.

---. "The Role of Freetown in the Commercial Life of Sierra Leone," In *Freetown: A Symposium,* edited by Christopher Fyfe and Eldred Jones, 38-64. Freetown: University of Sierra Leone Press, 1968.

---. "Trade and Islam in Sierra Leone, 18th - 20th Centuries." In *Islam and Trade in Sierra Leone,* edited by Alusine Jalloh and David E. Skinner, 21-63. Trenton: Africa World Press, 1997.

Ijagbemi, E.A. "The Freetown Colony and the Development of Legitimate Commerce in the Adjoining Territories." *Journal of the Historical Society of Nigeria* 5, no. 2 (1970): 243-56.

Inikori, J.E., ed. *Forced Migration: The Impact of the Export Slave Trade on African Societies.* New York: Africana Pub. Co., 1982.

---. "The Import of Firearms into West Africa, 1750-1807: A Quantitative Analysis." *Journal of African History* 18, no. 3 (1977): 339-68.

Inikori, Joseph E. and Stanley L. Engerman, eds. *The Atlantic Slave Trade: Effects on Economies, Societies, and Peoples in Africa, the Americas, and Europe.* Durham: Duke University Press, 1992.

Innes, Gordon. "A Note on Mende and Kono Personal Names." *Sierra Leone Language Review* 5 (1966): 34-38.

Jalloh, Alusine and David E. Skinner, eds. *Islam and Trade in Sierra Leone* (Trenton, N. J.: Africa World Press, 1997).

Jenkinson, Hilary. "The Records of the English African Companies." *Transactions of the Royal Historical Society* 6 (1912): 185-220.

Johnson, Walter. "On Agency." *Journal of Social History* 37, no. 1 (2003): 113-24.

Jones, Adam. "The Kquoja Kingdom: A Forest State in Seventeenth Century West Africa." *Paideuma* 29 (1983): 23-43.

---. *From Slaves to Palm Kernels: A History of the Galinhas Country (West Africa), 1730-1890.* Wiesbaden: F. Steiner, 1983.

---. "Theophile Conneau at Galinhas and New Sestos, 1836-1841: A Comparison of the Sources." *History in Africa* 8 (1981): 89-106.

---. "White Roots: Written and Oral Testimony on the 'First' Mr Rogers." *History in Africa* 10 (1983): 151-62.

---. "Who were the Vai?" *Journal of African History* 22, no. 2 (1981): 159-78.

Jones, Adam and Marion Johnson. "Slaves from the Windward Coast." *The Journal of African History* 21, no. 1 (1980): 17-34.

Jones, Denise. "Robert Bostock of Liverpool and the British Slave Trade on the Upper Guinea Coast, 1769-93." In *Slavery, Abolition and the Transition to Colonialism in Sierra Leone*, edited by Paul E. Lovejoy and Suzanne Schwarz, 69-88. Trenton, N. J.: Africa World Press, 2015.

Jones, Hilary. *The Métis of Senegal: Urban Life and Politics in French West Africa*. Bloomington: Indiana University Press, 2013.

Keefer, Katrina H.B. "Group Identity, Scarification, and Poro among Liberated Africans in Sierra Leone, 1808-1819." *Journal of West African History* 3, no. 1 (2017): 1-25.

---. "Scarification and Identity in the Liberated Africans Department Register, 1814-1815." *Canadian Journal of African Studies* 47, no. 3 (2013): 537-53.

Kelley, Sean M. *The Voyage of the Slave Ship Hare: A Journey into Captivity from Sierra Leone to South Carolina*. Chapel Hill: University of North Carolina Press, 2016.

Klein, Herbert S. and Francisco Vidal Luna. *Slavery in Brazil*. New York: Cambridge University Press, 2010.

Klein, Martin A. *Islam and Imperialism in Senegal: Sine-Saloum, 1847-1914*. Edinburgh: Edinburgh University Press, 1968.

---. *Slavery and Colonial Rule in French West Africa*. Cambridge: Cambridge University Press, 1998.

---. "Social and Economic Factors in the Muslim Revolution in Senegambia." *Journal of African History* 13 (1972): 419-41.

Knight, Franklin W. *Slave Society in Cuba during the Nineteenth Century*. Madison: University of Wisconsin Press, 1970.

Kopytoff, Igor, ed. *The African Frontier: The Reproduction of Traditional African Societies*. Bloomington: Indiana University Press, 1987.

Kopytoff, Jean Herskovits. *A Preface to Modern Nigeria: The "Sierra Leoneans" in Yoruba, 1830-1890*. Madison: University of Wisconsin Press, 1965.

Kuczynski, Robert. *Demographic Survey of the British Colonial Empire.* Vol. 1. West Africa. London: Oxford University Press, 1948.

Law, Robin. "The Historiography of the Commercial Transition in Nineteenth-Century West Africa." In *African Historiography: Essays in Honour of Jacob Ade Ajayi,* edited by Toyin Falola, 91-115. Harlow: Longman, 1993.

---. *The Slave Coast of West Africa, 1550-1750: The Impact of the Atlantic Slave Trade on an African Society.* Oxford: Clarendon Press, 1991.

---. *Ouidah: The Social History of a West African Slaving 'Port,' 1727-1892.* Athens: Ohio University Press, 2004.

---, ed. *From Slave Trade to "Legitimate" Commerce: the Commercial Transition in Nineteenth-Century West Africa.* Cambridge: Cambridge University Press, 1995.

Law, Robin, Suzanne Schwarz, and Silke Strickrodt, eds. *Commercial Agriculture, the Slave Trade and Slavery in Atlantic Africa.* London: James Currey, 2013.

Law, Robin and Silke Strickrodt, eds. *Ports of the Slave Trade (Bights of Benin and Biafra): Papers from a Conference of the Centre of Commonwealth Studies, University of Stirling, June 1998.* Stirling: Centre for Commonwealth Studies, 1999.

Lawrance, Benjamin N. *Amistad's Orphans: An Atlantic Story of Children, Slavery, and Smuggling.* New Haven: Yale University Press, 2015.

Little, Kenneth. "The Mende Farming Household." *The Sociological Review* 40, no. 4 (1948): 37-56.

---. *The Mende of Sierra Leone: A West African People in Transition.* London: Routledge & Kegan Paul Limited, 1951.

---. "The Political Function of the Poro: Part I." *Africa: Journal of the International African Institute* 35, no. 4 (1965): 349-65.

---. "The Political Function of the Poro: Part II." *Africa: Journal of the International African Institute* 36, no. 1 (1966): 62-72.

Lloyd, Christopher. *The Navy and the Slave Trade: The Suppression of the African Slave Trade in the Nineteenth Century.* London: Longmans, Green, 1949.

Lovejoy, Henry B. "The Registers of Liberated Africans of the Havana Slave Trade Commission: Implementation and Policy, 1824-1841." *Slavery & Abolition* 37, no. 1 (2016): 23-44.

Lovejoy, Paul E. *Caravans of Kola: The Hausa Kola Trade, 1700-1900.* Zaria: Ahmadu Bello University Press Ltd., 1980.

---. "Forgotten Colony in Africa: The British Province of Senegambia (1765-83)." In *Slavery, Abolition and the Transition to Colonialism in Sierra Leone*, edited by Paul E. Lovejoy and Suzanne Schwarz, 109-26. Trenton, N. J.: Africa World Press, 2015.

---. "The Impact of the Atlantic Slave Trade on Africa: A Review of the Literature." *Journal of African History* 30 (1989): 365-94.

---. "Internal Markets or an Atlantic-Sahara Divide? How Women Fit into the Slave Trade of West Africa." In *Women and Slavery*, Volume 1, edited by Gwyn Campbell, Suzanne Miers, and Joseph C. Miller, 259-79. Athens: Ohio University Press, 2007.

---. *Jihad in West Africa during the Age of Revolutions.* Athens, OH: Ohio University Press, 2016.

---. *Transformations in Slavery: A History of Slavery in Africa.* Cambridge: Cambridge University Press, 3rd Edition, 2011.

---. "The Upper Guinea Coast and the Trans-Atlantic Slave Trade Database." *African Economic History* 38 (2010): 1-27.

---. "The Volume of the Atlantic Slave Trade: A Synthesis." *Journal of African History* 23, no. 4 (1982): 473-501.

Lovejoy, Paul E. and Jan S. Hogendorn. *Slow Death for Slavery: The Course of Abolition in Northern Nigeria, 1897-1936.* New York: Cambridge University Press, 1993.

Lovejoy, Paul E. and David Richardson. "British Abolition and its Impact on Slave Prices Along the Atlantic Coast of Africa, 1783-1850." *Journal of Economic History* 55, no. 1 (1995): 98-119.

Lovejoy, Paul E. and Suzanne Schwarz, eds. *Slavery, Abolition and the Transition to Colonialism in Sierra Leone.* Trenton: Africa World Press, 2015.

Lowther, Kevin G. *The African American Odyssey of John Kizell: A South Carolina Slave Returns to Fight the Slave Trade in His African Homeland.* Columbia, SC: University of South Carolina Press, 2011.

Lynn, Martin. *Commerce and Economic Change in West Africa: The Palm Oil Trade in the Nineteenth Century.* Cambridge: Cambridge University Press, 1997.

MacCormack, Carol P. "Control of Land, Labor and Capital in Rural Southern Sierra Leone." In *Women and Work in Africa,* edited by Edna G. Bay, 35-53. Boulder: Westview Press, 1982.

---. "Slaves, Slave Owners, and Slave Dealers: Sherbro Coast and Hinterland." In *Women and Slavery in Africa,* edited by Claire C. Robertson and Martin A. Klein, 271-94. Portsmouth: Heinemann, 1997.

Mann, Kristin. "Shifting Paradigms in the Study of the African Diaspora and of Atlantic History and Culture." In *Rethinking the African Diaspora: The Making of a Black Atlantic World in the Bight of Benin and Brazil,* edited by Kristin Mann and Edna G. Bay, 3-21. London: Frank Cass, 2001.

---. *Slavery and the Birth of an African City: Lagos, 1760-1900.* Bloomington and Indianapolis: Indiana University Press, 2007.

Manning, Patrick. "Contours of Slavery and Social Change in Africa." *American Historical Review* 88 (1983): 835-57.

---. "The Enslavement of Africans: A Demographic Model." *Canadian Journal of African Studies* 15, no. 3 (1981): 499-526.

---. *Slavery and African Life: Occidental, Oriental and African Slave Trades.* Cambridge: Cambridge University Press, 1990.

---. *Slavery, Colonialism and Economic Growth in Dahomey, 1640-1960.* Cambridge: Cambridge University Press, 1982.

Martin, Susan M. *Palm Oil and Protest: An Economic History of the Ngwa Region, South-Eastern Nigeria, 1800-1980.* Cambridge: Cambridge University Press, 1988.

McGowan, Winston. "The Establishment of Long-Distance Trade between Sierra Leone and Its Hinterland, 1787-1821." *Journal of African History* 31, no. 1 (1990): 25-41.

McSheffrey, Gerald M. "Slavery, Indentured Servitude, Legitimate Trade, and the Impact of Abolition on the Gold Coast, 1874-1901: A Reappraisal." *Journal of African History* 24 (1983): 349-68.

Meillassoux, Claude. *The Anthropology of Slavery: The Womb of Iron and Gold.* Chicago, University of Chicago Press, 1991.

Mendes, António de Almeida. "The Foundations of the System: A Reassessment of the Slave Trade to the Spanish Americas in the Sixteenth and Seventeenth Centuries." In *Extending the Frontiers: Essays on the New Transatlantic Slave Trade Database*, edited by David Eltis and David Richardson, 63-94. New Haven: Yale University Press, 2008.

Miers, Suzanne and Martin A. Klein, eds. *Slavery and Colonial Rule in Africa.* London: Frank Cass, 1999.

Miers, Suzanne and Igor Kopytoff, eds. *Slavery in Africa: Historical and Anthropological Perspectives.* Madison: University of Wisconsin Press, 1977.

Miers, Suzanne and Richard Roberts, eds. *The End of Slavery in Africa.* Madison: University of Wisconsin Press, 1988.

Miller, Joseph C. *Way of Death: Merchant Capitalism and the Angolan Slave Trade, 1730-1830.* Madison: University of Wisconsin Press, 1988.

---. "West Central Africa." In *The Atlantic Slave Trade*, edited by David Northrup. 3rd ed. Boston: Cengage Learning, 2011.

Misevich, Philip. "The Origins of Slaves Leaving Sierra Leone in the Nineteenth Century." In *Extending the Frontiers: Essays on the New Transatlantic Slave Trade Database*, edited by David Eltis and David Richardson, 155-75. New Haven: Yale University Press, 2008.

---. "In Pursuit of Human Cargo: Philip Livingston and the Voyage of the Sloop *Rhode Island*." *New York History* 86, no. 3 (2005): 185-204.

Misevich, Philip and Kristin Mann, eds. *The Rise and Demise of Slavery and the Slave Trade in the Atlantic World.* Rochester: Rochester University Press, 2017.

Morgan, Philip. "Caribbean Slavery." In *The Rise and Demise of Slavery and the Slave Trade in the Atlantic World*, edited by Philip Misevich and Kristin Mann, 64-99. Rochester: Rochester University Press, 2017.

---. "The Cultural Implications of the Atlantic Slave Trade: African Regional Origins, American Destinations and New World Developments." *Slavery & Abolition* 18 (1997): 122-45.

Mouser, Bruce L. *American Colony on the Rio Pongo: The War of 1812, The Slave Trade, and the Proposed Settlement of African Americans, 1810-1830*. Trenton, NJ: Africa World Press, 2013.

---. "Iles de Los as Bulking Center in the Slave Trade, 1750-1800." *Revue Française d'Histoire d'Outre-mer* 83 (1996): 77-90.

---. "Rebellion, Marronage and Jihad: Strategies of Resistance to Slavery on the Sierra Leone Coast, c. 1783-1796." *Journal of African History* 48, no. 1 (2007): 27-44.

---. "Theophilus Conneau: The Saga of a Tale." *History in Africa* 6 (1979): 97-107.

---. "Trade, Coasters and Conflict in the Rio Pongo from 1790 to 1808." *Journal of African History* 14, no. 1 (1973): 45-64.

---. "Women Slavers of Guinea-Conakry." In *Women and Slavery in Africa*, edited by Claire C. Robertson and Martin A. Klein, 320-39. Portsmouth: Heinemann, 1983.

Northrup, David. "African Mortality in the Suppression of the Slave Trade: The Case of the Bight of Biafra." *Journal of Interdisciplinary History* 9, no. 1 (1978): 47-64.

---. "Becoming African: Identity Formation among Liberated Slaves in Nineteenth-Century Sierra Leone." *Slavery & Abolition* 27, no. 1 (2006): 1-21.

---. "The Compatibility of the Slave and Palm Oil Trades in the Bight of Biafra." *Journal of African History* 17, no. 3 (1976): 353-64.

---. "Igbo and Myth Igbo: Culture and Ethnicity in the Atlantic World, 1600-1850." *Slavery & Abolition* 21 (2000): 1-20.

273

---. *Trade without Rulers: Pre-Colonial Economic Development in South-Eastern Nigeria.* Oxford: Clarendon Press, 1978.

Nowak, Bronislaw. "The Slave Rebellion in Sierra Leone in 1785-1796." *Hemispheres* 3, no. 3 (1986): 151-69.

Nwokeji, G. Ugo. "African Conceptions of Gender and the Slave Traffic." *William and Mary Quarterly* 58, no. 1 (2001): 47-68.

---. "The Atlantic Slave Trade and Population Density: A Historical Demography of the Biafran Hinterland." *Canadian Journal of African Studies* 34, no. 3 (2000): 616-55.

---. *The Slave Trade and Culture in the Bight of Biafra: An African Society in the Atlantic World.* New York: Cambridge University Press, 2010.

Nwokeji, G. Ugo and David Eltis. "Characteristics of Captives Leaving the Cameroons for the Americas, 1822-1837." *Journal of African History* 43 (2002): 191-210.

---. "The Roots of the African Diaspora: Methodological Considerations in the Analysis of Names in the Liberated African Registers of Sierra Leone and Havana." *History in Africa* 29 (2002): 365-79.

Opare-Akurang, Kwabena. "The Administration of the Abolition Laws, African Responses and Post-Proclamation Slavery in the Gold Coast, 1874-1940." In *Slavery and Colonial Rule in Africa,* edited by Suzanne Miers and Martin A. Klein, 149-66. London: Frank Cass, 1999.

Osagie, Iyunolu Folayan. *The Amistad Revolt: Memory, Slavery, and the Politics of Identity in the United States and Sierra Leone.* Athens: University of Georgia Press, 2003.

Parker, John. *Making the Town: Ga State and Society in Early Colonial Accra.* Portsmouth: Heinemann, 2000.

Person, Yves. "Ethnic Movements and Acculturation in Upper Guinea since the Fifteenth Century." *African Historical Studies* 4, no. 3 (1971): 669-89.

Peterson, John. *Province of Freedom: A History of Sierra Leone, 1787-1870.* London: Faber and Faber, 1969.

Pettigrew, William A. *Freedom's Debt: The Royal African Company and the Politics of the Atlantic Slave Trade, 1672-1752.* Chapel Hill: University of North Carolina Press, 2013.

Rashid, Ismail. "'Do Dady nor Lef me Make dem Carry me': Slave Resistance and Emancipation in Sierra Leone, 1894-1928." In *Slavery and Colonial Rule in Africa,* edited by Suzanne Miers and Martin A. Klein, 208-31. London: Frank Cass, 1999.

---. "Escape, Revolt and Marronage in Eighteenth and Nineteenth Century Sierra Leone Hinterland." *Canadian Journal of African Studies* 34, no. 3 (2000): 656-83.

Rediker, Marcus. *The Amistad Rebellion: An Atlantic Odyssey of Slavery and Freedom.* Updated Edition. New York: Penguin Books, 2013.

Richards, W.A. "The Import of Firearms into West Africa in the Eighteenth Century." *Journal of African History* 21, no. 1 (1980): 43-59.

Richardson, David. "Consuming Goods, Consuming People: Reflections on the Transatlantic Slave Trade." In *The Rise and Demise of Slavery and the Slave Trade in the Atlantic World,* edited by Philip Misevich and Kristin Mann, 31-63. Rochester: Rochester University Press, 2017.

Roberts, Richard L. *Warriors, Merchants, and Slaves: The State and the Economy in the Middle Niger Valley, 1700-1914.* Stanford: Stanford University Press, 1987.

Robertson, Claire C. and Martin A. Klein, eds. *Women and Slavery in Africa.* Madison: University of Wisconsin Press, 1983.

Roddan, G.M. "Cultivation of Swamp Rice in Sierra Leone." *Tropical Agriculture* 19 (1942): 84-86.

Rodney, Walter. "African Slavery and Other Forms of Social Oppression on the Upper Guinea Coast in the Context of the Atlantic Slave-Trade." *Journal of African History* 7 (1966): 431-43.

---. "The Guinea Coast." In *Cambridge History of Africa.* Vol. 4., 223-324. Cambridge: Cambridge University Press, 1975-1985.

---. *A History of the Upper Guinea Coast, 1545-1800*. Oxford: Clarendon Press, 1970.

---. *How Europe Underdeveloped Africa*. Washington D.C.: Howard University Press, 1981.

---. "Jihad and Social Revolution in Futa Djalon in the Eighteenth Century." *Journal of the Historical Society of Nigeria* 4, no. 2 (1968): 269-84.

---. "A Reconsideration of the Mane Invasions of Sierra Leone." *Journal of African History* 8, no. 2 (1967): 219-46.

Salau, Mohammed Bashir. *Plantation Slavery in the Sokoto Caliphate: A Historical and Comparative Study*. Rochester: University of Rochester Press, 2018.

Scanlan, Padraic X. *Freedom's Debtors: British Antislavery in Sierra Leone in the Age of Revolution*. New Haven: Yale University Press, 2017.

Schaffer, Matt. "Bound to Africa: The Mandinka Legacy in the New World." *History in Africa* 32 (2005): 321-69.

Schwarz, Suzanne. "Commerce, Civilization and Christianity: The Development of the Sierra Leone Company." In *Liverpool and Transatlantic Slavery*, edited by David Richardson, Suzanne Schwarz, and Anthony Tibbles, 252-276. Liverpool: Liverpool University Press, 2007.

---. "Extending the African Names Database: New Evidence from Sierra Leone." *African Economic History* 38 (2010): 137-63.

---. "Reconstructing the Life Histories of Liberated Africans: Sierra Leone in the Early Nineteenth Century." *History in Africa* 39 (2012): 175-207.

Searing, James F. *West African Slavery and Atlantic Commerce: The Senegal River Valley, 1700-1860*. New York: Cambridge University Press, 1993.

Seton, Vivian, Konrad Tuchscherer, and Arthur Abraham, eds. *The Autobiography of an African Princess: Fatima Massaquoi*. New York: Palgrave Macmillan, 2013.

Shaw, Rosalind. *Memories of the Slave Trade: Ritual and the Historical Imagination in Sierra Leone*. Chicago: University of Chicago Press, 2002.

Shumway, Rebecca. *The Fante and the Transatlantic Slave Trade.* Rochester: University of Rochester Press, 2011.

Sherwood, Marika. *After Abolition: Britain and the Slave Trade Since 1807.* New York: Palgrave Macmillan, 2007.

Sibthorpe, A.B.C. *The History of Sierra Leone.* New York: Humanities Press, 1971, first published in 1868.

Siddle, D.J. "War Towns in Sierra Leone: A Study in Social Change." *Africa* 38, no. 1 (1968): 47-56.

Sinha, Manisha. *The Slave's Cause: A History of Abolition.* New Haven: Yale University Press, 2016.

Skinner, David E. "Islam and Education in the Colony and Hinterland of Sierra Leone (1750-1914)." *Canadian Journal of African Studies* 10 (1976): 499-520.

---. "Mande Settlement and the Development of Islamic Institutions in Sierra Leone." *The International Journal of African Historical Studies* 11 (1978): 32-62.

Smallwood, Stephanie E. *Saltwater Slavery: A Middle Passage from Africa to American Diaspora.* Cambridge: Harvard University Press, 2007.

Socolow, Susan M. "Buenos Aires: Atlantic Port and Hinterland in the Eighteenth Century." In *Atlantic Port Cities: Economy, Culture, and Society in the Atlantic World, 1650-1850,* edited by Franklin W. Knight and Peggy K. Liss, 240-61. Knoxville: University of Tennessee Press, 1991.

Stilwell, Sean. *Slavery and Slaving in African History.* New York: Cambridge University Press, 2014.

Strickrodt, Silke. *Afro-European Trade in the Atlantic World: The Western Slave Coast, c. 1550-c. 1885.* Suffolk: James Currey, 2015.

Swindell, Ken. "Family Farms and Migrant Labour: The Strange Farmers of the Gambia." *Canadian Journal of African Studies* 12, no. 1 (1978): 3-17.

---. "Serawoollies, Tilibunkas and Strange Farmers: The Development of Migrant Groundnut Farming along the Gambia River, 1848-95." *Journal of African History* 21, no. 1 (1980): 93-104.

Temperley, Howard. *British Antislavery, 1833-1870*. London: Longman, 1972.

Thomson, Steven. "Revisiting 'Mandingization' in Coastal Gambia and Casamance (Senegal): Four Approaches to Ethnic Change." *African Studies Review* 54, no. 2 (2011): 95-121.

Thornton, John K. *Africa and Africans in the Making of the Atlantic World, 1400-1800*, 2nd Edition. Cambridge: Cambridge University Press, 1998.

---. "The Slave Trade in Eighteenth Century Angola: Effects on Demographic Structures." *Canadian Journal of African Studies* 14, no. 3 (1980): 417-27.

---. *Warfare in Atlantic Africa, 1500-1800*. London: University College London Press, 1999.

Vasconcellos, Colleen A. *Slavery, Childhood, and Abolition in Jamaica, 1788-1838*. Athens, GA: University of Georgia Press, 2015.

Verger, Pierre. *Trade Relations between the Bight of Benin and Bahia from the 17th to 19th Century*. Ibadan: Ibadan University Press, 1976.

Walker, James W. St. G. *The Black Loyalists: The Search for a Promised Land in Nova Scotia and Sierra Leone, 1783-1870*. Longman: Longman, 1976.

Wheat, David. *Atlantic Africa and the Spanish Caribbean, 1570-1640*. Chapel Hill: Published by the Omohundro Institute of Early American History and Culture and the University of North Carolina Press, 2016.

White, E. Frances. "Creole Women Traders in the Nineteenth Century." *International Journal of African Historical Studies* 14, no. 4 (1981): 626-42.

---. *Sierra Leone's Settler Women Traders: Women on the Afro-European Frontier*. Ann Arbor: University of Michigan Press, 1987.

Williams, Eric. *Capitalism and Slavery*. Chapel Hill: University of North Carolina Press, 1944.

Wondji, C. "The States and Cultures of the Upper Guinea Coast" In *General History of Africa: Africa from the Sixteenth*

Century to the Eighteenth Century, edited by B.A. Ogot, 368-98. London: Heinemann Press, 1992.

Wright, Donald R. *The World and a Very Small Place in Africa.* Armonk: M.E. Sharpe, 1997.

Wylie, Kenneth C. *The Political Kingdoms of the Temne: Temne Government in Sierra Leone, 1825-1910.* New York: Africana Pub. Co., 1977.

Wyse, Akintola. *The Krio of Sierra Leone: An Interpretive History.* London: Hurst, in Association with the International African Institute, 1989.

Yannielli, Joseph. "George Thompson among the Africans: Empathy, Authority, and Insanity in the Age of Abolition." *Journal of American History* 96 (2010): 979-1000.

---. "Mo Tappan: Transnational Abolitionism and the Making of a Mende-American Town." *Journal of the Civil War Era* 8 (2018): 190-214.

Zeuske, Michael. *Amistad: A Hidden Network of Slavers and Merchants.* Princeton: Markus Wiener, 2015.

---. "Rethinking the Case of the Schooner *Amistad*: Contraband and Complicity after 1808/1820." *Slavery & Abolition* 35 (2014): 156–64.

INDEX

D

E

F

285